THE NEW TESTAMENT WORLD

THE NEW TESTAMENT WORLD
Insights from Cultural Anthropology

Third Edition, Revised and Expanded

Bruce J. Malina

Westminster John Knox Press
Louisville, Kentucky

Book design by Sharon Adams
Cover design by Mark Abrams
Cover photo: Christian Sarcophagus, *3rd c. Rome, Museo Laterano. Courtesy of Alinari/Art Resource, New York.*

Published by Westminster John Knox Press
Louisville, Kentucky

This book is printed on acid-free paper that meets the American National Standards Institute Z39.48 standard. ∞

PRINTED IN THE UNITED STATES OF AMERICA

01 02 03 04 05 06 07 08 09 10 — 10 9 8 7 6 5 4 3 2 1

Library of Congress Cataloging-in-Publication Data is on file at the Library of Congress, Washington, D.C.

ISBN 0-664-22295-1

For all my Franciscan teachers, notably Sylvester Makarewicz
and Ernest Latko in the United States,
Julian Arent and Neal Kaminski in the Philippines,
and the Faculty of Biblical Studies in Jerusalem (1966–67).

With gratitude for your encouragement, wisdom, and insight.

Contents

viii   Contents

Figures and Tables

Preface

This book was written with the beginning student of the New Testament in mind. Its purpose is to present, from the area of cultural anthropology, some useful models that might aid in fathoming the social-system context of the behavior of the people presented in the New Testament. Most New Testament study takes place in terms of verbal and literary analysis, historical description of persons and events, as well as some geographical and archeological information, all of which serve to clarify some features of these documents. Such information is certainly of great value for making the New Testament intelligible. However, most of the time Bible students take all such information and conceive it as operating in much the same way as it would operate in our own society. Such unconscious shuffling of cultural contexts might make the Bible immediately relevant to the student, but at what cost to the meaning intended by the original authors, the meaning most Christians would hold to be intended by God?

The purpose for using anthropological models in New Testament study is precisely to hear the meaning of the documents in terms of the social systems in which they were originally proclaimed. The models chosen for this book are mid-range models in the sense that they serve to explain segments of behavior rather than the whole cultural picture of the eastern Mediterranean in the first century A.D. Choosing models is based on presuppositions, and in the Introduction I set out the presuppositions behind model building in general and in cultural anthropology in particular. Models from cultural anthropology do not offer an alternative explanation of the Bible, nor do they do away with literary critical, historical, and theological study. Rather, they add a dimension not available from other approaches, along with a way to check on the hunches of interpreters when it comes to questions of what any given author said and meant to say.

The choice of models presented in this book derives from a judgment of usefulness for students of the Bible as they come to grips with the data presented in introductory level New Testament courses. Chapter 1 deals with honor and shame, the pivotal values of Mediterranean culture in antiquity and in the present. Chapter 2 looks to the social psychology of the persons described in the documents; chapter 3 to their implicit perception of all goods as limited; chapter 4 to their pervading concerns about envy and the evil eye; chapter 5 to what they meant by kinship and marriage; and chapter 6 to their purity rules. The final chapter, chapter 7, presents a model of small group development to help interpreters understand how the story of Jesus unfolded as well as to illustrate how this story was appropriated by post-Jesus groups. Throughout the book I have attempted to point out U.S. implicit cultural assumptions in the areas under consideration, thus allowing for a comparative perspective.

The work is premised, then, on the presumption that to understand what people say and mean to say one must know their social system. And the social system undergirding the New Testament is that of the Eastern Mediterranean of the first century A.D. The models presented in this book derive for the most part from contemporary Mediterranean anthropologists. Is there any continuity between the Mediterranean world of today and that of the first-century A.D.? The anthropologist Francis L. K. Hsu, who has done much to demonstrate the validity of cultural continuity, notes,

> Cultures borrow much from each other in role matters such as foods, artifacts, etiquette, theories of nature, and tools for control of human beings and things. But there is little evidence that people change in any fundamental way, and as a whole, their patterns of feeling about themselves, about each other, and about the rest of the world. (*Rugged Individualism: Essays in Psychological Anthropology.* Knoxville: University of Tennessee Press, 1983, 174)

In order for the models to generate the understanding they were designed to, the student must read the New Testament, for the way this book is written, it makes little sense apart from constant recourse to the New Testament writings themselves. Specifically, the reader must go through the passages listed at the end of the book, where we deal with testing the models for each chapter. The reader must also look up the biblical passages cited in the course of the chapter. Beginning Bible students should note that, as a rule, sentences in the New Testament that are in the passive voice imply that God is the doer of the action. Passive voice means that the grammatical subject of the sentence is acted on. For example, "John kicks the horse" is active voice because John, the grammatical subject, does the acting. In "John is kicked," the subject of the sentence, John, is acted on, and we are not told who is doing the acting. This is passive voice. *Passive voice sentences in the New Testament mean God is the actor or doer.* So, for example, "many are called, few are chosen" means that God calls many (in Israel), but does not choose all; "to whom much is given" means those to whom God gives much; "all power in heaven and on earth has been given to me" means God has given me all power everywhere; and "your sins are forgiven" means God forgives you your sins.

The first edition of this revised and expanded work was written in the summer of 1979. At that time there was little to suggest by way of preparatory or supportive reading. Now, as the chapter bibliographies indicate, there is quite a bit of information available. For some who are launching on the task of a scholarly interpretation of the New Testament, this book may seem too perplexing. Should this be the case, especially for the student doing a New Testament introduction in a self-study way, I would strongly recommend the work I have prepared for just such a situation: *Windows on the World of Jesus* (Louisville, Ky.: Westminster/John Knox Press, 1993).

Finally, for those who might find it difficult to imagine exactly what a book like this is intended to do, I might suggest that the easiest way to empathize with its purpose is to view some films. Basic to the task is the film *Kypseli: Women and Men Apart—A Divided Reality*, by Susannah M. Hoffman, Richard Cowan, and Paul Aratow, available from the Lifelong Learning Center, University of California Extension Media Center, Berkeley, California 94720. Kypseli, the village presented in the film, is a contemporary Greek community in which Jesus, Paul, and the first several generations of Jesus followers would be readily at home, apart from recent technology.

There are, moreover, a number of feature films that can only be understood with the perspectives presented in this book. First of all, for example, is the popular *Godfather* series, which, like *Prizzi's Honor*, illustrates many of the basic themes of Mediterranean life, even if in U.S. garb. Less popular but quite appropriate are *Eleni*, the true story of the plight of a Greek woman and her family during the Greek Communist uprising of the 1950s; *Wedding in Galilee*, describing a Palestinian family's attempt to lead a normal (Mediterranean) life in face of continued Israeli (Central European) oppression (rated R); and the recent Spanish film (with subtitles) of great poignancy and visual beauty *The Grandfather*, premised on the themes of kinship, kinship status, honor and shame, and patron client. Finally, the film *Lawrence of Arabia* offers a number of scenes highlighting honor and shame, challenge and response, and especially, in-group and out-group interactions.

Good models are meant to explain, guide, reveal, and aid discovery. The New Testament passages listed in the exercises as well as in the text are by no means exhaustive examples. And not all the suggestions generated by the models have been followed through in the text. The attentive student will find much to add to what is stated in the book and much to uncover that has not been explicitly pointed to at all. Good models at the introductory level are meant to bring creative insights to the beginner. Perhaps the models presented here will continue to serve that end as they have for growing numbers of Creighton University undergraduates who found this material stimulating and useful in their introduction to New Testament studies. I am grateful to them for their shared insights.

Bruce J. Malina
Creighton University

Acknowledgments

Some of the material in chapters 2 and 3 has appeared in different form in two articles: "Limited Good and the Social World of Early Christianity," *Biblical Theology Bulletin*, vol. 8, no. 4 (1978), pp. 162–176, and "The Individual and the Community—Personality in the Social World of Early Christianity," *Biblical Theology Bulletin*, vol. 9, no. 3 (1979), pp. 126–138, and is used here with the permission of the publisher.

The two Venn diagrams in chapter 6 from Mary Douglas' "Deciphering a Meal," are reprinted by permission of *Daedalus*, Journal of the American Academy of Arts and Sciences, Cambridge, Massachusetts. Winter 1972, "Myth, Symbol, and Culture."

Introduction

Bible Study and Cultural Anthropology

The objective of this book is to sketch out some of the dimensions involved in studying the writings of the Bible for the purpose of gaining some understanding of them on their own terms. What does such a study entail? Suppose you found yourself passing through Syria toward the end of the first century A.D. As you made your way through some Syrian Hellenistic city, you heard the following words being read aloud as you walked by a somewhat crowded private dwelling:

> εἰσὶν γὰρ εὐνοῦχοι οἵτινες ἐκ κοιλίας
> μητρὸς ἐγεννήθησαν οὕτως,
> καὶ εἰσὶν εὐνοῦχοι οἵτινες εὐνουχίσθησαν
> ὑπὸ τῶν ἀνθρώπων,
> καὶ εἰσὶν εὐνοῦχοι οἵτινες εὐνούχισαν
> ἑαυτοὺς διὰ τὴν βασιλείαν τῶν οὐρανῶν. (Matt. 19:12)

You might pray to God to give you some insight into the meaning of that scripture verse, but chances are nothing will happen unless you know Greek. Yet if you insist on eavesdropping on that first-century group of people because, for some reason or other, you believe that what they listen to in their first-century world is of some importance to you, then your first requirement would be to find a translator so that you might find out what is being said. Bible translations serve this purpose.

But what do such Bible translations offer you? At most they let you, a foreigner, get to know what those first-century Greek-speaking folks were saying. But what persons say and what they mean to say are often quite distinct. Should a young man tell his girlfriend that he loves the gold of her hair, does he mean that her hair would make an excellent hedge against inflation? And why would he want a hedge against inflation rather than a fence, a wall, or a stand of trees? The words we use do in fact embody meaning, but the meaning does not come from the words. Meaning inevitably derives from the general social system of the speakers of a language. What one says and what one

1

means to say can thus often be quite different, especially for persons not sharing the same social system. By translating the Gospel of Matthew into English, what we do is transplant our first-century Syrian Hellenists into our modes of speaking, and all too often we presuppose that what they say embodies our modes of meaning as well. An English translation of Matthew 19:12 yields the following:

> For there are eunuchs who have been so from birth,
> and there are eunuchs who have been made eunuchs by other people,
> and there are eunuchs who have made themselves eunuchs
>   for the sake of the kingdom of heaven.

This is the English equivalent of what you would have heard as you eavesdropped on the post-Jesus group reading Matthew in the scene above. When you heard it in Greek in first-century Syria, you were the foreigner observing and overhearing a group of natives. But when you read your Bible translation in America at the beginning of the twenty-first century, you transfer the coherent words of first-century non-Americans into your own social setting. In effect, you are listening to the words of a transplanted group of foreigners from another time and place, with you, the native, wondering what in the world these people are talking about. Why the mention of eunuchs at all? Eunuchs are hardly the topic of our dinnertime conversations, much less the object of prolonged sermonizing in our churches. And why the peculiar listing of three types of eunuchs? While we employ all sorts of verbal listings, do we have any such three-type listings that we habitually use in our conversations?

Perhaps the first and largest step that a contemporary American can take toward understanding the Bible is to realize that in reading the Bible in English (or even Greek), we are in fact listening to the words of a transplanted group of foreigners. It takes only the ability to read to find out what these foreigners are saying, but it takes far more to find out what they mean. If meaning derives from a social system, while wording (e.g., speaking or writing) simply embodies meaning from the social system, then any adequate understanding of the Bible requires some understanding of the social system embodied in the words that make up our sacred scripture. That the author of Matthew's Gospel speaks of eunuchs, for example, can be easily verified. That the word "eunuch" refers to a castrated male can also be easily verified. But why the reference to a castrated male? What does being called a eunuch mean to a first-century Palestinian man? What does it mean in terms of male social roles and values? How can a person in contemporary America find out such information relative to the first-century Mediterranean world? The purpose of this book is to explain how we might retrieve such information as well as to set out some examples of such information and its use for understanding the Bible.

Questions about the social norms and values that made up the world of first-century Palestine, as well as methods for answering such questions, are rather new in biblical studies. Such questions and methods are the contemporary product of a whole series of useful approaches to understanding the Bible. They have developed largely because they are the logical outcome of attempts to understand the word of God in our own day and age.

At bottom, biblical scholarship from antiquity to the present (e.g., read St. Augustine, *On Christian Doctrine*) presupposes that studying the Bible for the purpose of gaining some understanding is much like eavesdropping on a transplanted group of foreigners in order to understand them. Hence scholars have provided reliable translations to help people find out what those foreigners are saying. If the Bible is important to us, we would want to know where these foreigners come from so that we might relate what they are saying to concrete objects found in their world. We would want to know about the persons they make reference to, about when they lived, about what they did and built. Scholars have produced biblical encyclopedias to provide this sort of information. We might also want to situate the country of origin of these foreigners in terms of geographical space and environment. The various biblical atlases help us do this.

If we look through our Bible translations, encyclopedias, and atlases, we will find information about who our foreigners are, what they say, and where they come from—but all from the viewpoint of our contemporary American existence. All this information makes it more than apparent that they are indeed foreigners, not from our country and not from our society. Is this amount of information sufficient for you to understand what they say and mean to say as you read their words in the Bible? Or is it just enough to help you situate them relative to yourself and to place them relative to other foreign groups?

Chances are that if other people knew only your name, your social rank, some of your statements, and some geographical information about you, you would say that they really cannot understand you yet. What more would they have to know? What more would you have to know to understand a foreigner? Just as you get to know yourself by comparison with others—by comparing how you are similar to and different from others, how you are just like others and unique relative to others—so you might ask the same questions about our hypothetical group of foreigners. How are they similar to others in their area of the world and period of history; how are they different? How are they just like other people in their time and place; how are they unique relative to others? How did they dissociate themselves from other larger groups to form distinct, separate groups with somewhat shared yet unique histories? Scholarly histories of the Bible present this sort of information. Now, is this information sufficient for you to understand our group of foreigners? Would you think others might understand you sufficiently if they knew about what moved your ancestors to come to the United States and how they got here; how they settled where they did; how they variously intermarried in terms of your family tree; how your parents decided to marry; how you grew up from childhood to adolescence? While these *how* questions take us a few steps beyond the what, who, when, and where questions that we began with, do they suffice to generate any sort of full understanding? If our information is still insufficient, let us try another tack.

Suppose I listen carefully to everything you say. I could then catalog your speech patterns and relate them to various contexts of your life. I could come to know the patterns you use to tell a joke, to threaten your friends and acquaintances, to flatter your parents, to cajole a person of the opposite sex, to pray to God or your friends or the IRS, to greet a teacher or an equal. My catalog would consist of the different forms of speech that you use for different purposes in different social contexts. When such forms of speech get written down, we can call them literary forms or patterns. Normally there is a relationship between the literary and speech form you might use and the social context in which you find yourself. You can find hundreds of such patterns of writing—which you know very well though you may not know you know them so well—in newspapers. You know that a food ad is different from a movie ad, so you won't look up the food ads to find out what is playing at the local cinema. You know how the society-page wedding announcements and social event descriptions differ from the social questions submitted to "personal advice" columnists, and how these differ from questions answered by medical columnists. You also know how all of the above differ from the literary form of obituaries, editorials, letters to the editor, local and national news stories, and articles on that most important of pages, the sports page, with its endless literary forms for football, soccer, baseball, basketball, hockey, track and field, and the like.

Now, suppose I can also catalog the speech and writing forms of our hypothetical group of foreigners. Will that help me understand them sufficiently? From such literary study, I can tell you what they are saying, the English equivalents of their words, and how they put their sentences together to express threat, fear, greeting, birth announcements, arguments, teaching, jokes, consolation, law, encouragement, and the like. I can likewise tell you how they construct their extemporaneous or prepared paragraphs into prose and poetry, into history and legend, into letters and speeches. For example, consider the eunuch passage previously cited from Matthew 19:12. I can tell you quite a bit about the way it is written by comparing it with other similar literary forms in the Bible. It has the basic pattern of a numbered parable such as we find in the book of Proverbs (the Hebrew word for proverb and parable is identical, *mashal*). For starters, look at Proverbs 30:33:

> For pressing milk produces curds,
>   pressing the nose produces blood,
>   and pressing anger produces strife.

The way such literary patterns work is that the first and second (or more) elements are concrete, imaginable pictures, while the last item of the series is abstract and moral, dealing with some hidden dimension of human behavior. The first two (or more) elements set the stage for understanding the final element. In the above parable, how does churning milk and hitting a person in the nose set the stage for understanding the final element?

This pattern is clear in the explicitly numbered parables, for example, Proverbs 30: 18–19:

> Three things are too wonderful for me;
>   four I do not understand:
> the way of an eagle in the sky,
>   the way of a serpent on a rock,
> the way of a ship on the high seas,
>   and the way of a man with a maiden.

The question to ask here is how do the common features of the concrete pictures—a flying eagle, a slithering serpent on a rock, and a ship on the sea—set the stage for the final point? What do the eagle, the serpent, and the ship in question have in common? You might note that none of them leaves a trace once they have gone by. How does this insight set the stage for understanding the final point, which is abstract and moral, dealing with a hidden dimension of human behavior?

In a parable, something other and something more is pointed to by the concrete picture, and it is up to the hearer to figure out the something other and something more. This is typical of "devious" Oriental wisdom, and such wisdom abounds in the parables of Jesus. There are other such numbered parables attributed to Jesus in Matthew. For example, in Matthew 8:20, Jesus says to a scribe, "Foxes have holes, and birds of the air have nests; but the Son of man has nowhere to lay his head."

In Matthew 10:41–42, he tells the twelve disciples,

> "He who receives a prophet because he is a prophet shall receive a
> prophet's reward, and he who receives a righteous man because he is

a righteous man shall receive a righteous man's reward. And whoever gives to one of these little ones even a cup of cold water because he is a disciple, truly, I say to you, he shall not lose his reward."

And in Matthew 11:7–9, Jesus speaks to the crowds about John:

"What did you go out into the wilderness to behold? A reed shaken by the wind? Why then did you go out? To see a man clothed in soft raiment? . . . Why then did you go out? To see a prophet? Yes, I tell you, and more than a prophet."

Thus the literary pattern of our eunuch passage is that of a numbered parable in which the first two (or more) elements offer concrete pictures that set the stage for understanding the final element, which is the main point.

Relative to the Bible, modern biblical commentaries will furnish you with this sort of literary analysis along with the *what, when, where,* and historical *how* mentioned above. This sort of literary analysis, the study of writing patterns or literary forms, is another dimension of the what and how question we might put to the people in our documents in order to understand them. Again, if you had all the information singled out so far, would you have enough to understand our hypothetical group of foreigners sufficiently? If people had this sort of information about you, would that be enough for them to say that they know you as well as they can?

So far one sort of question has been left out of the picture, although it constantly lurks behind all of the who, what, when, where, and how questions we might put to our hypothetical foreigners. This question, of course, is the why question. In the eunuch passage, why precisely is there the mention of eunuchs? What meaning does the value embodied in the social role of eunuch bear, and why does it bear that meaning in that particular social system? The specific details needed to answer these questions will be spelled out in chapter 1. But to set out those details in a meaningful way and to evaluate them adequately, a number of presuppositions of a rather abstract sort have to be set out so that you might better understand the perspectives of this book. These presuppositions deal with the meaning and dimensions of cross-cultural knowledge, of why questions and their answers, with regard both to ourselves and to those who people the pages of the Bible. You can very well skip the remainder of this chapter and move on to the rest of the book without appreciable damage to the book's contents. But if in the subsequent chapters you begin to wonder how any author can make the claims set forth relative to people so much removed from us in time and place, you would do well to study the rest of this chapter.

Presuppositions behind This Book

Knowledge about others as well as ourselves might be conveniently divided into three types: (1) awareness knowledge or "that" knowledge: information about something or someone—that something or someone does or does not exist (what/who) or its/his/her location in space (where) or time (when); (2) usable knowledge, or "how-to" and "how" knowledge: information necessary to use something or interact with someone properly or to understand how uses and interactions are generated; (3) principle knowledge or "why" knowledge: information about cultural scripts and cues, about the cultural models behind the applicable facts, along with the required faith in or commitment to the presuppositions and assumptions that make the cultural scripts, cues, and models evident. If all this sounds a bit abstract, consider what sort of knowledge is needed to invent, develop, maintain, and operate a television set. "Why" knowledge, the knowledge of principles, is about the big picture, about the meaning of it all, about the implied values and meanings that ultimately explain behavior. For example, if someone were to attempt to understand you sufficiently, along with the who, what, when, where, and how of your life, that someone would need to understand the why of your life, your standpoint toward or horizon on life. That person would have to know your experiences; how you imagined those experiences; what insights helped you make sense of those experiences in terms of social expectations; how you learned to think about those insights in terms of socially available models of meaning; what effect those models of meaning had on you and those important to you; and, finally, how you acted, what you did about it, and how such action led to new experiences, images, insights, models, criticism, actions, and so on.

Nature, Culture, Person

If you examine your life, you will see that you have occupied a number of standpoints and lived life from a number of horizons. A succession of standpoints and horizons make up your personal story thus far. If someone had the information that went into the making of your story, that person would be able to grasp the meaning of it all, the why of your life so far. On what basis would that person come to understand you? I suggest that the sort of understanding I am speaking of is based on a presupposition in our own culture that might be articulated as follows: *All human beings are entirely the same, entirely different, and somewhat the same and somewhat different at the same time* (see Figure 1).

Figure 1. *The Basic Presupposition—Nature, Culture, Person*

ALL PEOPLE ARE

↓

100% THE SAME   =   Nature—the area of the "objective,"
of physical "sensations," of Its

↓

50% THE SAME
50% DIFFERENT   =   Culture—the area of the "social,"
of group-shared "conceptions," of We

↓

100% DIFFERENT   =   Person—the area of the "subjective,"
of unique "perceptions," of I

↓

AT THE SAME TIME, SIMULTANEOUSLY, CONCURRENTLY

From this point of view, human beings are individualized or personalized representatives of human nature immersed in particular cultures. That also means that all human knowing is simultaneously objective, subjective, and social.

The first part of the presupposition, *all human beings are entirely the same*, focuses our attention on similarities. Who posed for the picture of the human heart in an anatomy textbook? Does it matter? A focus on recurrent similarity produces the area we in our culture call "nature," that is, all that exists apart from purposeful, willful human influence. We also call this area "the objective," and ascribe it to the "sciences." Nature is said to subsist in regular, patterned forms that make up our physical environments. Within this perspective, scientists are said to "discover" patterns of similarity called "laws," and so long as they prescind from willful, human influence, their enterprise is said to be "objective."

The second part of the presupposition, *all human beings are entirely different*, focuses our attention on the uniqueness of individuals. Of whom can you use the word "I" with meaning? A focus on uniqueness produces what we call "personhood"—the area of personal story, of incommunicable biography. Persons are said to develop and live out their stories in unique fashion, a fashion said to be "subjective."

The third part of the presupposition, *all human beings are somewhat the same and somewhat different*, focuses our attention on the interplay of similarities and differences within human communities. To what does the word "we" refer? If you and I are truly unique and therefore incommunicable in our uniqueness, how do we communicate at all? We communicate on a "we" basis. The focus on this interplay of partial similarity and difference produces the area called "culture." Culture is an organized system of symbols by which persons, things, and events are endowed with rather specific and socially shared meanings, feelings, and values. Cultures are said to "create" patterns of shared meaning and feeling that combine to shape the social experiences of a given group. Humanists, as opposed to scientists, attempt to "articulate" such patterns of shared symbolic meaning, and, more often than not, the outcomes of their enterprise are said to be "creative interpretations," or "learned opinions." Their enterprise is said to be "social."

I should like to insist that the presupposition under scrutiny concludes with the phrase *at the same time*. Scientists study human sensations; cultures create human conceptions; individuals generate personal perceptions. Yet human knowing is, in fact, simultaneously objective, subjective, and social. Nature, culture, and person tend to kaleidoscope, with all three simultaneously present, yet with emphasis on the one or the other, depending on various factors. To understand your story adequately, I need to know not only the who, what, when, where, and how of your physical and psychological human nature and unique personhood, but also the whys and wherefores of our commonly shared cultural story that fill the who, what, when, where, and how with mutually appreciable meaning and value.

To return to our transplanted group of foreigners, in our case the New Testament writings, our eavesdropping can generate understanding only if we pay careful attention to the cultural system that "created" them and which they embodied. In terms of nature, the persons described in the New Testament would be just like us and everyone else in the world. In terms of personhood and uniqueness, they would be as unfathomable as we are to each other. On the other hand, in terms of cultural story, cultural cues, cultural script, they would be somewhat like us, yet somewhat unlike us: like us in terms of human nature; unlike us in terms of the cultural interpretation of human nature.

Consider what we have so far relative to understanding such New Testament writings like the Synoptic Gospels or Paul. What we have is a group of first-century A.D. (when) Hellenistic writings, written in Greek, for the most part by persons from "the house of Israel," deriving from the northeastern and eastern shores of the Mediterranean (what, who, where), in an area where Greek and Semitic dialects were the usual languages. Yet the area was part of the Roman Empire, throughout which the common language was Common Greek. Bible translations offer English equivalents of what the authors of the writings have to say. To aid our imagination, atlases and encyclopedias offer information about the concrete environment, about artifacts, and about significant individuals and groups mentioned directly or indirectly in the documents. Histories explain how events prior to the New Testament period came to influence the situation in which the Jesus movement group began, how the post-Jesus movement organization got under way and initially developed, and the like. Commentaries on the individual New Testament writings point out the meanings of words and the literary forms of individual books (Gospels, history, letters, tracts, "apocalypse") as well as the meanings of specific passages within given writings (parables, proverbs, genealogies, birth announcements, psalms, conflict discussions, wonder stories, recommendations, travel plans, and the like). Biblical commentators often focus on the meaning of a literary form or the meaning of words in that culture, while historians talk about the political and religious significance of behavior. However, the question of meaning is a why question. On what basis can a why question be adequately answered? On what basis can a why question in your life, in your group's behavior, be adequately answered? I submit that such why questions can only be answered in terms of cultural story. If commentators, historians, and ordinary Bible readers derive meaning from the New Testament, the question we might put to them is whether such meaning comes from *their* cultural story or the cultural story of the people who produced the documents. Were I to interpret all your actions in terms of my own behavior, I am afraid you might end up wishing to hit me in the mouth. After all, where I come from, all who "carry out" groceries from a supermarket pride themselves on their shoplifting abilities, and I would presume the same for you and everyone else. You might find this very offensive. Yet when it comes to deriving meaning from the Bible, there is no one to give you pause, to urge you to reconsider, to hit you in the mouth in case of misinterpretation.

The misinterpretation I am referring to comes from identifying your cultural story with human nature: "Since we do it this way, all people of all times must have done it this way." Children, of course, normally judge everyone and everything in terms of their own circumscribed, limited experience. When I was a child I thought all older women certainly spoke some Slavic language, while some might know how to speak heavily accented English as well. In point of fact, this was my experience with all the older women in my neighborhood. To use that experience as a norm for human behavior would be rather egocentric and short-sighted. In learned circles such a judgment is labeled *ethnocentrism*. It entails imposing your own cultural interpretations of persons, things, and events on other people. When applied to history, such ethnocentrism is called *anachronism*—imposing the cultural artifacts, meanings, and behavior of your own period on people of the past. Ethnocentric anachronisms are cute on the lips of children, readily discernible when it comes to concrete things, for example, Jesus' family taking an airline flight for their flight to Egypt; Paul buying a King James Version of the Bible to quote in the original English when he preached; or Jesus traveling from Nazareth to Jerusalem in a jeep. But such ethnocentric anachronisms are insidiously irretrievable when it comes to the meanings of behavior. For example, Jesus condemned divorce, and people in our society get divorced, so Jesus must be condemning that sort of behavior in our society. However, the fundamental question is, do marriage and divorce mean the same thing when Jesus speaks of them and when we speak of them?

Understanding Culture

The only way to avoid such misinterpretations, such ethnocentric anachronisms, is to understand the culture from which our foreign writings come. And since we learn best in terms of how things are similar and different to what we experience, we would also do well to understand our own cultural story and realize that, in most instances, the cultural stories of other peoples are very different from our own. This, of course, includes the cultural stories of those persons depicted in biblical documents. In this way we might come to understand those foreigners we have eavesdropped on as we attempt to imagine the behavior they allude to.

What then does culture mean, and how do we come to understand a culture? *Culture*, in this book, refers to what cultural anthropologists mean when they use the term. For example, Kroeber and Kluckhohn define *culture* as follows:

> Culture consists of patterns, explicit and implicit, of and for behavior acquired and transmitted by symbols, constituting the distinctive achievement of human groups, including their embodiments in artifacts: the essential core of culture consists of traditional (i.e., historically derived and selected) ideas and especially their attached values; culture systems may, on the one hand, be considered as products of action, on the other as conditioning influences upon further action. (*Culture: A Critical Review of Concepts and Definitions*, Cambridge: Peabody Museum, 1952, 181)

What this definition suggests is that culture is a system of symbols relating to and embracing people, things, and events that are socially symboled. Symboling means filling people, things, and events with meaning and value (feeling), making them meaningful in such a way that all the members of a given group mutually share, appreciate, and live out of that meaning and value in some way. For example, on the level of nature, human beings mate and reproduce because males of the species fertilize the ova of females of the species. When the fertilized ovum comes to term, the female drops the off-spring. What culture does is take this process and the agents in the process and fill them with meaning and value. The sperm contributor is interpreted as "father," the ovum bearer as "mother," and the offspring as "child." I am sure you do not celebrate Ovum Bearer's Day, even if you are terribly scientifically minded. Nor do you view the sperm contributor who hangs around the ovum bearer of your existence as the family sperm bank. Rather, you relate to these beings as parents (a cultural interpretation of their role and activity). Together with them, you form a family (a cultural interpretation of the naturing and nurturing group). You learn to interpret their relationship to each other and to you as affection and loyalty (a cultural interpretation of this inner group relation or event).

What culture does is take what is available in the physical and human environment and interpret it socially and fill it with socially shared meaning and feeling. The world of human beings is a culturally interpreted social world. In this perspective we are somewhat like and somewhat unlike the rest of humankind. We are like others, naturally, insofar as all peoples (as far as we know) mate, reproduce, live in some variation of a cave (house), get around (transportation), and the like. We differ from others culturally insofar as different groups of people assign different meanings and values to being a father or mother, a man or a woman, to having children, and to types of housing, modes of transportation, and so on. A child may be viewed as an economic asset or an economic liability. All houses are not constructed equally; there are high-class and low-class houses. Transportation for an Eskimo is not the same as transportation for a typical U.S. suburbanite, and a twenty-year-old, "pre-used" car does not mean the same thing as the latest-model luxury automobile. Culture is all about the distinctive, shared meanings and feelings characteristic of a given group at a certain time and place.

Language is a most important aspect and perhaps the best example of the meaning of culture. As a natural phenomenon, language is sounds produced by humans in terms of airwaves that are patterned in a socially appreciable way as the air passes from the lungs through the vocal chords over tongue and teeth and through the mouth cavity. You can sense such human sounds when these airwaves hit the tympanum of your ear and register some impression in your brain. Culture fills these naturally and personally produced air waves with meaning and feeling by patterning them in socially appreciable ways. Thus more than one person shares the same patterns, allowing for communication on a "we" level—the "we" being all of us who share the same patterns of meaning and feeling. When you do not share speech patterns, you simply do not understand a language. When you do not share behavior patterns, you simply do not understand what another person is doing. Should you identify your language (culture) with human being (nature), you would tend to think that all people should speak Human (English), just as you do. And if they do not, they are either subhuman or nonhuman. This is ethnocentrism again. The same holds for behavior (and language is a form of behavior). Should you identify your forms and patterns of behavior (culture) with human being (nature), you would tend to think that all human beings should behave according to the patterns or norms of your group. If they do not, they are either subhuman or nonhuman.

The Bigger Picture—Cultural Cues

To avoid the pitfalls to understanding posed by ethnocentrism, it is useful to try to get the bigger picture into which any given thought, utterance, or action normally fits. This larger frame is the overall system of the culture, the so-called cultural matrix or cultural script. What I mean might be illustrated as follows. When we claim to understand a person's hostile behavior on a given occasion, we mean that we consider it in terms of a more complete pattern of behavior, a larger frame, which characterizes the range of behaviors typical of this person or people in general in a given culture. On the other hand, when a particular mode of behavior does not seem to follow a pattern that we know, and we cannot place it in a larger frame comprehensible to us, we usually claim not to understand the behavior. When we understand a word, we mean that we know how it can be used in context with other words, a larger frame. We understand what bone, leg, finger, or head signify in their relation to the larger structure of which they are parts. In our culture, the fall of an apple is understood only in the larger frame of gravity. These examples (can you add others?) indicate that human understanding is *relative*, that is, each item we understand derives its culturally adequate meaning from something else, the larger frame, to which it is related and in which it seems to fit.

You might ask, "Where does it stop?" It stops when we cannot find a frame or larger pattern for the idea, person, or event that we wish to understand. This, in fact, is the normal experience of a person in a new and unrelated culture, observing strange and unusual (in the sense of not usual) behavior for the first time. In such a situation a person finds no frame for the behavior he or she wishes to understand. *Culture shock* is an accumulation of such experiences that overwhelms a person. A similar sort of culture shock is the normal experience of a person faced with new real-life information or problems that no longer fit the ultimate larger frame previously used to understand and cope with such information or problems in the past. Take, for example, the larger frame symboled with the word "God." Many question the existence of God simply because they outgrow their symbol of the ultimate "really Real" that served them so well in childhood and early adolescence. Their symbol for the ultimate larger frame is no longer adequate for the new realities they wish to understand. Moving on to more adequate, larger frames, both in cross-cultural understanding and in religious experience within one's culture, is a sort of "conversion" experience. But conversion from what to what? Where did you begin to learn and be grabbed by the meanings and values that you personify?

Was your first difficult decision in life choosing what language to speak as you emerged from your mother's womb? Did you have to take time out of your busy play schedule as an infant to decide whether you would behave as a boy or a girl? How did you ultimately decide that "nanee, nanee, poopoo" was a terrible thing to say to a fellow three-year-old? All these aspects of culture are assimilated by a process called *enculturation*. They usually "come without saying." And as adults, we like to observe about them, "That goes without saying." These aspects are assimilated in such a way that most people do not even realize the extent to which their culture's values and meanings, its ideas and feelings, determine what is really real for them. The patterns of culture become a sort of second nature helping all in our group to make sense of experience and to interact with each other and our environment with meaning and satisfaction. They also give us the certainty that particular persons, things, and events make no sense, lack meaning, and are thoroughly dissatisfying.

In short, we assimilate the meanings and values of our culture much as we have assimilated our shared language. All cultural symbols, from simple ones like offering a poor person a handout to complex ones like marriage and kinship, are patterned. They follow socially shared rules and norms just as our common language does. And just as many people speak English quite well without formal knowledge of grammar (the patterns or rules of the language), so countless people carry on quite well in our culture without any formal knowledge of the patterns and norms underlying their behavior. But whether explicit or implicit, there certainly are patterns and rules underlying behavior. For example, even without formal and explicit knowledge of phonetics, you know a foreigner when you hear one; so also without formal and explicit knowledge of cultural norms, you know male and female behavior when you see it.

Just what sort of cultural norms go to make up the essential core of a given culture? In other words, what sort of cultural cues did we assimilate from those significant others who reared us to live in a meaningful way in our society? We might conveniently differentiate six classes of such cultural cues:

1. *Perception*: those cues defining how a person, thing, or event is to be perceived; the meaning it is said to bear relative to me and others. These cues of

perception make up the central, large frames of reference in the culture, a culture's consensus reality. They include the cognitive orientation of the culture, such as the pivotal perceptions that all goods in life are limitless, that every effect has an adequate cause, that morally good persons win out in the end, that lawful competition leads to achievement. To see how these work, consider what you would do if your car broke down or if the light in your room went out. First of all, do you ascribe the breakdown to some person (the people on the GM assembly line who made you a lemon), or to some thing (faulty sparkplug)? Do you try to remedy the situation by recourse to significant people (by praying to them), or do you check the immediate adequate cause (e.g., the light bulb, switch, fuse box, etc.)? Your behavior would flow from implicit norms of perception shared by all of us in this culture. If it did not, you would be judged as really odd, not all there, harmless but crazy, and the like.

2. *Feeling*: those cues telling us what and how we must feel in a given situation. For example, should you see a young man doing 60 in a 25-mile-per-hour zone on a motorcycle, then watch him proceed to slam into a pole, should you laugh or look serious? If you move over toward him, are you to sit back and feel superior or move in and offer help? Who is to behave how, with what feeling, at a funeral? Do males and females alike cry, or are males to look stoically impassive, while females give free vent to their feelings in tears and wailing? How is one to feel at a football game, the wedding of a friend, or the purchase of a new car? We had to learn how to feel in specific situations.

3. *Acting*: those cues telling us what we must do or avoid doing both in general and on specific occasions. For example, who is supposed to invite whom on a date, the male or the female? How should a male walk and hold his hands and head? How should a female walk and hold her hands and head? What are male gestures, female gestures? What is the proper behavior in an embarrassing situation, fight or flight? What should you do to someone picking on you unfairly, be it a bully or the IRS? And what if they pick on you fairly? Again, we all learned such sorts of cues for acting.

4. *Believing*: those cues telling us what we must believe in and profess. We believe in those persons, things, and events about which we think we should and can be unashamedly intolerant should they be called into question, mocked, or ridiculed. To identity what you believe in, think of what you would rather fearlessly stand up for: your parents, brothers, and sisters; the American flag when mocked by a foreigner; going to college to get ahead in the world or just because learning is good in itself; being treated as an individual number or as an individual person; holding good ideals or holding no ideals; having practical know-how or just book knowledge; being good in

sports or in dating, or just knowing about sports and dating. We, too, learned our "beliefs-in."

5. *Admiring*: those cues telling us what and whom we must hold in awe, what and whom we ought to admire and respect. For example, what sorts of persons do your parents tell you they wish you were like? What sorts of persons do you want to be like? Who do college women think they should be dating—men outstanding in sports or men rather committed to their studies? What is your preference in a "good-looking" man or woman? Who do you think embodies what you stand for: some public figure such as an actor or actress, a politician, a national or world celebrity? Your learned cues for admiring will tell you.

6. *Striving*: those cues telling us what are worthwhile goals in life, with significant others legitimating our selection. For example, how do you know that your career choice, your marriage choice, or your choice of where to live are worthwhile? Do parents, peers, and friends support your choices? What sort of success do you look for in life: money, sex, service, devotedness, family, power over others, publicity? The cues for striving that we have learned set out the culturally available goals.

Now, just as we learned and assimilated language in the process of being enculturated, so too we have learned and assimilated sets of cultural cues that lead us to perceive, feel, act, believe, admire, and strive in ways that make sense to us as well as others in our society. What these cues do is produce meaningful behavior, behavior that is patterned and endowed with feeling, with emotion. The cues generate valuable behavior, behavior that is valued and makes sense within a range of meanings and feelings. The reason for my going over the meaning of culture and cultural cues in this context is to call your attention to the fact that it is extremely likely that the group of foreigners presented in our New Testament writings were people who were likewise enculturated into cues of perception, feeling, acting, believing, admiring, and striving. Jesus, the Gospel authors and the persons referred to in their writings, Paul, the Pharisees, Sadducees, the early post-Jesus group members— all these persons derived from and lived according to the patterns of their societies. Their behavior made sense; their interactions took place according to the patterns of their culture; their values were judged noble or ignoble in line with the cues shared in the groups of the time. When they got angry at each other, they knew why. For the modern believing Christian, the incarnation of the word of God means the enculturation of God's word. And the only way the word of God, both in the New Testament writings and in the person of Jesus, can make sense to us today is by studying it within the larger frame of first-century A.D. Palestinian and Mediterranean culture. For along with learning the who, what, when, where, and how of the New Testament, the study of the culture of the period and region will offer insight into the whys of the behavior pictured in our documents.

Why the Bigger Picture—Humans as Model Makers

How then do we come to understand another culture? How do we understand anything? Understanding seems to lie in the genetic ability of most human beings (after puberty) to think abstractly. *Abstract thinking*, often called generalization or generalized reasoning, is the ability to think in terms of ideas or concepts instead of concrete images. Ideas and concepts are abstract representations of the essences of things; they are the result of the ability to "chunk" common qualities from a large number of concretely different items, and then to express these chunks in terms of nonconcrete signs and symbols. For example, instead of imagining (or talking about) an individual Jonathan apple or Bartlett pear or cooking banana or Melba peach or Italian plum or navel orange or Hawaiian pineapple, we can form the idea or concept of fruit. Now, what the word *fruit* refers to is an idea of what all in the previous list have in common, their similarities. And this common or similar element of "fruitness" really has no concrete, physical existence at all; it is really not concrete at all. Obviously, what concretely exists are actual and specific apples, pears, bananas, and the like. This is a sort of first-level abstraction or chunk, for we can go further. We can take such abstractions as fruit, meat, vegetables, bread, and the like and produce a still higher abstraction, in this case "food." Every higher abstraction is a sort of bigger picture. Moreover, along with generating such abstractions, we also have the ability to make relationships among or between abstractions. We can say, for example, food is necessary for human life. And even beyond this, we can take statements of relationships and put them in sequences called *syllogistic reasoning*; we can make deductions from general abstract principles to concrete cases, and inductions from concrete cases to general abstract principles. We can analyze by taking abstractions apart into lower-level abstractions to the concrete level; and we can synthesize by putting chunks together to ever higher levels of abstraction.

Why do human beings think abstractly? Perhaps the main reason, as the experimental psychologists tell us, is that human beings are unable to keep any more than seven (plus or minus two) disparate elements in mental focus at one time. What abstraction enables us to do is to represent and make some order among the countless experiences we undergo in the course of our interacting with our multiple environments. In short, our ability to think abstractly enables us to generate some orderly or patterned understanding of our complex experiences. The word *culture* that we have described previously is such an abstraction.

Patterns of abstract thought, or patterns of relationships among abstractions, are called *models* (sometimes *theories*, or when very high-level abstractions, *paradigms*). Models are abstract, simplified representations of more complex, real-world objects and interactions. Like abstract thought, the purpose of models is to enable and facilitate understanding. Of course, such understanding can then be applied to predict and to control, but understanding comes first. Understanding, then, is the result of the process of abstraction in terms of patterns that order, classify, and give shape to human experiences. What is adequate understanding? As I just mentioned, models are generalizations or abstract descriptions of real-world experiences; they are approximate, simple representations of more complex forms, processes, and functions of physical and nonphysical phenomena. Now, because models are simplifications, they are notorious for misrepresenting the real-world experiences they attempt to describe. To reduce the misfit as much as possible, our cultural tradition—both scientific and humanistic—espouses a validation process presently called *the scientific method*. The scientific method consists of the following steps: (1) postulate a model (or theory or paradigm); (2) test the model against the "real-world" experience it relates to; (3) modify the model in terms of the outcome of the test to reduce the misfit by detecting errors of omission or commission. This method serves as a safeguard against the twin pitfalls of human understanding: superficiality and inaccuracy. Models really cannot be proved right or wrong. After all, they are postulated; that is, they derive from a sort of insight that seems to hold experiences together in such a way as to make sense. Models can only be validated. What validation means is that the generalizations or abstract statements deriving from the model have been checked out according to the steps of the scientific method and have been found adequate, given the experiences or data the model is meant to chunk. In other words, all data readily fit the postulated model, and anyone can check it out.

Understanding cultures is possible because of our ability to think abstractly, to make models of experience, and to compare the various models we come up with. Model making or abstract thinking explains how we can understand a culture other than our own as well as understand our own culture. But how can we even attempt to understand an alien culture like that of those who people the New Testament? Our own culture outfits us with two important cues of perception that work to this end. The first is the awareness of the possibility that we ourselves can change, that there are many roles open to us, and that people in history and in our own milieu have taken on roles other than the ones we have. The second cue is the ability to take on the role of another empathically, to move into someone else's shoes, to perceive from someone else's horizon or standpoint. (Sympathy is sharing or commiserating with someone else's feelings or experience, like when you feel sympathy for a dog that hurts its paw.) Empathy leads to an awareness of the actual differences and potential similarities between another and yourself, between another group and your own group.

Models in Cultural Anthropology

So what we need in order to understand our hypothetical group of foreigners—the New Testament writings and the behavior of the people portrayed in them—are some adequate models that would enable us to understand cross-culturally, that would force us to keep our meanings and values out of their behavior, so that we might understand them on their own terms. If you will recall, the purpose of models is to generate understanding. Models formulate relationships among the persons, things, and events that we want to study. These relationships between various persons and groups, or persons and things, as well as the interactions and activities such persons and groups undertake—all these have to be named and described. For example, the ovum bearer of your existence gets named "mother"; mothers do not exist except in terms of children, so mother presupposes child, and child presupposes mother. What is the normal behavior of mother toward child? This interaction might be called "nurturing," and we might generalize by saying that in our society mothers nurture their children. So big deal! But why the mother-child interaction? What does it mean relative to the social group in general? What does it mean relative to social roles, role playing, role taking, and role making within a given culture?

Models in anthropology at a rather high level of abstraction derive from certain presuppositions, much like models in chemistry, physics, and biology. The presuppositions that underlie the models revolve around the nature of groups or social systems. The question posed about the mother-child interaction (What does it mean relative to the social group in general?) presupposes that a social system entails a collectivity of interacting persons whose interaction is structured or patterned and oriented around common concerns or purposes. In other words, meaningful human behavior is behavior according to socially shared patterns (*structure;* remember the cultural cues above) performed for socially meaningful purposes (*functions*). If we were to take a still photograph of our entire society, freeze all activity for a moment, so to say, and then analyze what is going on in terms of what relationships and for what purposes, we would end up with a general image of the main outline of the structures of the society along with their functions. This sort of still picture, when verbalized as social theory or model, is called *structural functionalism.* The still picture that we see is one of a society that is cohesive and integrated by consensus on meanings, values, and norms. The various smaller social systems, such as family, government, economics, education, and religion, are bound together by common values and norms, and these smaller systems (called *social institutions*) interact with each other in a cooperative and harmonious way. Thus society is in equilibrium, in good balance, and the social system tends to persist with minor amounts of adaptive change. Changes in one institution lead to changes in others, so if you wanted to start a revolution, you could do so by changing any one of the lesser social systems.

The structural functionalist model presupposes that every society is a relatively persistent, stable, well-integrated structure of elements. Every element in a society has a function that helps maintain society as a whole system. Every functioning social structure is based on a consensus of values among its members. In this static, still-photo model, any social change is deviance.

Now, still-life photographs, much like those taken by reconnaissance planes or satellites, are very useful in helping to understand what was going on when the picture was taken. So one good way to understand our group of foreigners is to find out what sort of structures or patterns of behavior were typical in their society, what norms expressed the "oughts" for this sort of behavior, and how such behavior supported and fulfilled a useful social function.

Structural functionalism pictures social systems as the result of consensual obligation, with people freely choosing to oblige themselves in a certain way. But this is obviously not the whole picture. As with human behavior in general, so too social systems reveal freedom as well as constraints. You are free to leave your classroom, but you are not free to walk through the walls except by using a door or window. Socially, you are free to date and marry anyone in the whole world. But you are constrained, held back, from actually doing so by your own limited physical, psychological, and social existence. You cannot meet everyone in the world in a lifetime; you cannot be everywhere at once; you do not have access to all social groups and classes, and so on. I mention *freedom* and *constraint* because, while the structural functionalist model emphasizes consensus or freedom in the formation and endurance of social systems (the still-life photo approach), the flip-side theory would emphasize the constraints human groups put on each other. This flip side theory is called *conflict theory* (also known as coercion, power, or interest model or theory).

The conflict theory is more like a slow-motion film. It would have us imagine social systems as consisting of various groups (e.g., groups instancing the institutions of family, government, economics, education, religion) that have differing goals and interests and therefore use coercive tactics on each other to realize their own goals. Each group protects the distinctive interests of its members. Furthermore, relations between various groups include disagreement, strain, conflict, and force—as well as consensus and cooperation. If dissent and conflict are part of the normal social process, then any social system must also protect and assert its members' interests in relation to other systems, even by challenging the established order. No system can survive if it fails to maintain a creditable balance between its members' personal needs and the demands of the broader society. Thus the mother-father-child set of norms (the family) must function to protect and develop its members so that they may achieve their goals and assert their interests within a societal context of conflict.

The conflict model presupposes that all units of social organization, that is, all persons and groups in a society, are continuously changing unless some force intervenes. Change is all around us, ubiquitous. Wherever there is social life, there is conflict. What holds social systems and their subsystems together is not consensus, but constraint, the coercion of some by others, not universal agreement. While value systems can generate change, constraint generates conflict. Conflict is all around us because constraint is all around us wherever human beings set up social organizations.

From this perspective and in terms of this sort of model, a good way to understand our group of foreigners is to find out what elements or factors interfere in the normal process of change. Absence of conflict would be surprising and abnormal. What sorts of conflict typify the behavior depicted in the New Testament? In this slow-motion-film model, there is an unending process of change in society—as in the individual human being. Social change, deviance, is normal. Social pressures toward obligatory consent (as happens in U.S. peer groups) lead to reactions that result in changes of various sorts.

As I mentioned previously, human beings create models in order to understand their experiences. No model that we know of is useful for every conceivable purpose. There is no model to help understand all models, just as there is no language that would enable a person to understand all languages. The still-photo structural functionalist model, as well as the slow-motion-film conflict model, is useful for understanding relationships and activities within social systems and between social groups. (They would help explain my question, What does the mother-child interaction of nurturing mean relative to the social group in general?) But a further question remains. What about the individual in the group? How and why do mothers come to know they are mothers and then act accordingly? How and why do fathers, children, bankers, physicians, hoboes, the sick, the well, the rich, the poor take on their social roles and play them out the way they do within social systems?

If you recall, according to the structural functionalist model and its flip side, the conflict model, a social system is a group of persons whose interaction is structured and oriented around common concerns or purposes. This definition describes, at a high level of abstraction, what the previous models see and describe and how they explain behavior. Now, another definition of *social system* is a system of symbols that acts to establish powerful, pervasive, and long-lasting moods and motivations in people, formulating conceptions of value-objects, and clothing these conceptions with such an aura of factuality that the moods and motivations are perceived to be uniquely realistic (adapted from Clifford Geertz). In this definition the social system is a system of symbols that people hold and that hold people. These symbols include meanings and values, as well as feelings about these meanings and values, that are attached to and embodied in and by persons, things, and events. The social system, as a system of symbols, consists of persons (self and others), things (nature, time, space), and events (activities of persons and things) that constitute the consensus reality of a culture. Even situations that confront people are not simply a backdrop for their behavior. These situations, too, are interpreted in terms of symbolic meaningfulness. People do not simply respond to situations; rather they respond to the way they read and define the situation in terms of their symbolic expections. The range of meanings within a situation (say, exiting from a supermarket) is interpreted symbolically by those who are defining the situation. (For example, the person exiting from a supermarket just shoplifted, just purchased groceries, just quit her job in the supermarket, just made out in the back room with the manager, etc.). However, no symbol can mean just anything. (The person exiting from the supermarket cannot be said to be leaving his house, building a garage, operating on a cancer victim, etc., ad infinitum—it is always easier to be infallibly wrong than approximately correct.) The symbol gets its range of meanings from the available shared social expectations, that is, from the available shared social symbol system, much as words get their meaning from the available shared social speech system. This sort of model, which analyzes social systems in terms of the symbols that comprise them, is called the *symbolic model* (also called interpretative model, symbolic theory; and, to some extent, symbolic interactionist theory).

The symbolic model presupposes that human individual and group behavior is organized around the symbolic meanings and expectations that are attached to objects that are socially valued. Such socially valued objects include the self, others, nature, time, space, and the All (God). Any existing person or group is a complex of symbolic patterns that at least temporarily maintains both personal and social equilibrium (like the structural functionalist model), but that requires continual readjustment in new and shifting situations (like the conflict model). These readjustments include slight to great alterations of ideas, values, moods, attitudes, roles, and social organization.

Thus the symbolic model presupposes that for the most part, human interactions are symbolic interactions. People are always wrapped in social roles, sets of social rights and obligations relative to others. These symbolic roles situate people in relation to others and give them social status, for example, the status of mother, father, son, daughter, rich, poor, and the like. The social system then turns out to be a patterned arrangement of role sets, status sets, and status sequences, consciously recognized and regularly at work in a given society. Social structures thus keep people apart, bring them together, define differences, point up similarities, and constrain and facilitate action.

From the standpoint of the symbolic model, a good way to understand our group of foreigners is to find out what roles, significant symbols, gestures, and definitions of situations our documents express or imply. What symbols embody the cultural cues of perception? What sorts of interaction take place between elites and the low-born, and how do people define themselves in their various statuses?

In what follows, I use models from various anthropologists who have studied Mediterranean society or societies similar to the ones we find, explicitly or implicitly, in our documents. Some of these anthropologists use structural functionalist models; others use conflict models; and still others use symbolic models. I will pick and choose among them in order to try to understand various broad areas of behavior. By laying out models of various areas of life, by showing how these models are implied or expressed in our documents, I would hope to have you add to the examples I present. Our common purpose is to understand this spuriously familiar group of foreigners represented by the New Testament documents. Our understanding will be in terms of the whys of their behavior, in terms of behavior typical of their culture. The adequacy of our understanding will depend on the adequacy of our models. I would invite you to validate the models, to see if they do indeed explain, and to realize the spread of cultural difference that separates us from first-century post-Jesus groups. The various areas I have chosen to consider might serve as a set of eyeglasses you can put on when you read the documents. You should find that you can see what was going on in that world much better. You should discover how and why people behaved the way they did and what they considered significant and important in life. When you take those eyeglasses off and return to our twenty-first-century United States, you will be faced with another world, a world with a different set of hows and whys of human behavior, a different set of what people consider significant and important in life.

If the differences between their world and ours prove too great, the variance between their moral judgments and ours too disturbing, the focus between their religious concerns and ours too distant, the chances are good that our interpretation has a higher probability of being accurate. After all, from the perspective of our time and place, our foreigners are foreigners, alien human beings, from a distant place and a distant time.

Summary

Trying to understand the writings of the New Testament in an adult, scholarly way is much like trying to understand a group of foreigners somehow dropped in our midst. Nearly all scholarly aids to understanding the Bible offer information about the who, what, when, where, and how of these foreign writings. Such information is valuable and highly necessary. However, most of us need a why sort of answer to feel satisfied that we do in fact understand.

To answer a why question in relation to human social behavior, our own culture provides us with a truism as a starting point: All human beings are entirely the same, entirely different, and somewhat the same and somewhat different at the same time. The area of sameness asks why questions about the physical environment and about human beings as part of that physical environment: this is nature. The area of difference asks why questions about unique individuals and their unique personal stories: this is person. The area of partial similarity and partial difference asks why questions about the human environment people have developed as the framework or model of their social behavior: this is culture.

Cultures symbol people, things, and events in such a way that all persons in the group share the patterns of meaningfulness that derive from this symboling process. These patterns are assimilated and learned in the enculturation process, much as we all learn and assimilate the patterns of speech common to our group. For purposes of understanding, cultural stories might be broken down into the cultural cues that people assimilate. Such cues include those of perception, feeling, acting, believing, admiring, and striving.

The process of breaking down complex human activity for the purpose of understanding it, like breaking down a cultural story into its constituent cues, is called modeling. Models are generated because human beings, after puberty, can think abstractly. Models in human thought are simple, abstract representations of human experiences and interactions that are often highly complex. Models are made for purposes of understanding and thus controlling and predicting. Cultural anthropology attempts, as its main focus, to understand cultures other than our own by means of formulating adequate models, models that are neither superficial nor inaccurate. The so-called scientific method serves as a check on models. In cultural anthropology, three main types of models are used: the structural functionalist, the conflict type, and the symbolic.

In the remainder of the book, a number of specific models will be presented, mostly of the symbolic sort. At the end of the book, some examples will be given for each chapter with the hope that you yourself will check out the adequacy of the model on the basis of information provided in the New Testament documents.

References and Suggested Readings

Useful Social Science Encyclopedias and Dictionaries

Ashley, David, and David Michael Orenstein. *Sociological Theory: Classical Statements.* 3d ed. Boston: Allyn & Bacon, 1995.

Barnard, Alan, and Jonathan Spencer. *Encyclopedia of Social and Cultural Anthropology.* London: Routledge & Kegan Paul, 1996.

Culturegrams: The Nations Around Us. 2 vols. Provo, Utah: The David M. Kennedy Center for International Studies, Brigham Young University, 1995.

Encyclopedia of World Cultures. 9 vols. Boston: G. K. Hall, 1995.

Honigmann, J., ed. *Handbook of Social and Cultural Anthropology.* Chicago, Ill.: Rand McNally, 1973.

Kuper, Adam, and J. Kuper, eds. *The Social Science Encyclopedia.* 2d ed. London: Routledge & Kegan Paul, 1995.

Levinson, David, and Melvin Ember, eds. *Encyclopedia of Cultural Anthropology.* 4 vols. New York: Henry Holt, 1996. [Sponsored by Human Relations Area Files at Yale University]

Mitchell, G. Duncan. *A New Dictionary of the Social Sciences.* New York: Aldine, 1979.

O'Sullivan, Tim, John Hartley, Danny Saunders, Martin Montgomery, and John Fiske. *Key Concepts in Communication and Cultural Studies.* 2d ed. London and New York: Routledge & Kegan Paul, 1994.

Readings and Resources Relevant to This Chapter

Carney, Thomas F. *The Shape of the Past: Models and Antiquity.* Lawrence, Kans.: Coronado Press, 1975.

Elliott, John H. "Social Scientific Criticism of the New Testament: More on Methods and Models." *Semeia* 35 (1986):1–33.

———. *What Is Social-Scientific Criticism?* Guides to Biblical Scholarship. Minneapolis: Fortress Press, 1993.

Esler, Philip F. "Reading the Mediterranean Social Script." In *The First Christians in Their Social Worlds: Social-Scientific Approaches to New Testament Interpretation*, ed. Philip F. Esler, 19–36. London: Routledge & Kegan Paul, 1994.

———. "Social Worlds, Social Sciences and the New Testament." In *The First Christians in Their Social Worlds: Social-Scientific Approaches to New Testament Interpretation*, ed. Philip F. Esler, 1–18. London: Routledge & Kegan Paul, 1994.

Fernea, Elizabeth Warnock. *Guests of the Sheik: An Ethnography of an Iraqi Village.* New York: Doubleday, 1965.

Halliday, M. A. K. *Language as a Social Semiotic: The Social Interpretation of Language and Meaning.* Baltimore: University Park Press, 1978.

Hanson, K. C., and Douglas E. Oakman. *Palestine in the Time of Jesus: Social Structures and Social Conflicts.* Minneapolis: Fortress Press, 1998.

Kroeber, A. L., and Clyde Kluckhohn, with Wayne Unterreiner. *Culture: A Critical Review of Concepts and Definitions.* Papers of the Peabody Museum of American Archaeology and Ethnology, Harvard University, 47/1. Cambridge: Peabody Museum, 1952.

Malina, Bruce J. "What Are the Humanities: A Perspective for the Scientific American." In *The Humanities and Public Life*, ed. William L. Blizek, 37–47. Lincoln: Pied Piper Press, 1978.

_____. "The Social Sciences and Biblical Interpretation." *Interpretation* 37, no. 3 (1982):229–242.

_____. "Why Interpret the Bible with the Social Sciences." *American Baptist Quarterly* 2 (1983):119–133.

_____. "Mark 7: A Conflict Approach." *Forum* 4, no. 3 (1988):3–30.

_____. *Windows on the World of Jesus: Time Travel to Ancient Judea.* Louisville, Ky.: Westminster/John Knox, 1993.

_____. "Reading Theory Perspectives." In *The Social World of Jesus and the Gospels*, 3–31. London: Routledge & Kegan Paul, 1996.

_____. "The Received View and What It Cannot Do." In *The Social World of Jesus and the Gospels*, 217–41. London: Routledge & Kegan Paul, 1996.

Malina, Bruce J., and Richard L. Rohrbaugh. *A Social-Scientific Commentary on the Synoptic Gospels.* Minneapolis: Fortress Press, 1993.

_____. *A Social-Scientific Commentary on the Gospel of John.* Minneapolis: Fortress Press, 1998.

May, David M. "'Drawn from Nature or Common Life': Social and Cultural Reading Strategies for the Parables." *Review and Expositor* 94 (1997):199–214.

Neyrey, Jerome H. "A Symbolic Approach to Mark 7." *Forum* 4, no. 3 (1988):63–92.

Neyrey, Jerome H., ed. *The Social World of Luke-Acts: Models for Interpretation.* Peabody, Mass.: Hendrickson, 1991.

Pilch, John J. "A Structural Functional Analysis of Mark 7." *Forum* 4, no. 3 (1988): 31–62.

_____. *Introducing the Context of the New Testament: Hear the Word.* Vol. 2. Mahwah, N.J.: Paulist Press, 1991.

Rohrbaugh, Richard L., ed. *The Social Sciences and New Testament Interpretation.* Peabody, Mass.: Hendrickson, 1996.

Rubinstein, Moshe F. *Patterns of Problem Solving.* Englewood Cliffs, N.J.: Prentice-Hall, 1975.

Stegemann, Ekkehard W., and Wolfgang Stegemann. *The Jesus Movement: A Social History of Its First Century.* Trans. O. C. Dean, Jr. Minneapolis: Fortress Press, 1999.

Turner, Jonathan H., with P. R. Turner *et al. The Structure of Sociological Theory.* 6th ed. Belmont, Calif.: Wadsworth, 1998.

Van Staden, P., and A. G. Van Aarde. "Social Description or Social-Scientific Interpretation? A Survey of Modern Scholarship." *Hervormde Teologiese Studies* 47 (1991):55–87.

1

Honor and Shame

Pivotal Values
of the First-Century Mediterranean World

To form some idea concerning what it means to study cultural patterns, you might try to imagine the earth as empty and void, without distinguishing features like rivers and mountains, rocks and trees—just one big smooth and even place. Think of it all like the trackless, vast land of a boundless desert. Now imagine a group of people coming on the scene. With their hands in the supple sand, they start making lines to indicate to each other that this side is "my side," that side is "your side." Another group comes along, makes a line, and declares that this side is "our side," that side is "your side." The wind comes and covers over the explicit lines, yet all continue to act as though they were still there, implicit in the sand. What happens in such line drawing? Etymologically, the words "define" and "delimit" refer to the process of drawing lines, setting up boundaries between inside and outside, hence between insiders and outsiders.

Meaning building is like contriving lines in the shapeless stuff of the human environment, thus producing definition or socially shared meaning. Such lines obviously are drawn through and around time (hence the social times of childhood, adolescence, adulthood, middle age, retirement, old age) and space (hence the social spaces often implicitly marked by the "boundaries" between the United States and Canada, your house and your neighbor's). What is not so obvious is that socially contrived lines are likewise drawn within and around individual people (the social lines that mark off self from others, that mark off roles and statuses); groups of people (the social lines marking my family off from others, my relatives on my mother's side from those on my father's side, insiders from outsiders); nature (the socially contrived lines that mark off all the stuff that people study in the sciences and in economics, and that people experience in our physical environment); and God or gods (the socially contrived lines marking off who or what people believe is ultimately in control and thus holds it all together).

We are all born into systems of lines that mark off nearly all of our experiences. Such lines define the self, others, nature, time, space, and God/gods.

It is probable that people continue to bother to make such lines because human beings have an overpowering drive to know where they are. Line drawing enables us to define our various experiences so as to situate ourselves and everything and everyone that we might come into contact with. Our ancestors passed down to us the set of lines they inherited, and thus we find ourselves in a cultural continuum that reaches back to the sources of our cultural heritage.

If you think about it, such line drawing is rather arbitrary and can be highly ambiguous in significance, charged with conflicting meaning. When I draw a line between me and you, what does that mean? Does it mean you can never come to my side without fear of conflict? Does it mean your side is of less value than my side? Does it mean we can never change the lines once they are drawn? Since the lines are socially contrived and can be highly ambiguous, such boundary markers are often a source of anxiety and conflict as well as satisfaction and fulfillment. For example, think of the time line marking retirement age. Does it mark satisfaction and fulfillment of a life of work, or rejection and uselessness? Does it lead to a period of reward or a period of punishment? The set of social lines we assimilate in the enculturation process provides all of us with a sort of socially shared map that helps and urges us to situate persons, things, and events with special emphasis on the boundaries. It shows us that there is a place for everyone and everything, and it teaches us that persons and things out of place are abnormal. For example, take good old country farm dirt. Dirt in the field is in its proper place, but when the same dirt gets into your house, the house is considered "dirty" and unclean (more synonyms: *impure, profaned, polluted*). Dirt is matter out of place. Return it to where it belongs and your house is clean (more synonyms: *pure, purified, unpolluted*) once again. People out of place in a negative way are called "deviants." They too are considered unclean, impure, profaned. We often lock up deviants in a sort of social garbage can so as to keep our community clean, pure, sacred, unpolluted, and hence safe. On the other hand, there are people out of place in a positive way. Such people are called "prominent people." While they are abnormal, they are not unclean, impure, or polluted. Rather they are super-clean or super-pure, so to say. They fall outside the normal limits of the prevailing purity system, much like diamonds and gold found buried in the "dirt." In a later chapter we shall deal with clean and unclean, sacred and profane, at greater length.

At this point I would like to consider three sets of person-lines that come together and are perceived to flow together quite consistently in the Mediterranean world. These three boundary markers are called *authority, gender status,* and *respect.* Where these three come together, they mark off something called *honor.*

In order to understand honor, we have to begin with a larger frame. In the United States, the social institution on which most Americans focus their attention, interests, and concerns is economics. When the average U.S. family is in difficulty, it is invariably due to the fact that the U.S. provisioning system—the system of jobs, goods and services, production, and consumption—is in trouble. Thus we can fairly say, given our U.S. experience, that the focal institution of American society is economics. Within this framework, the organizing principle of American life is instrumental mastery—the individual's ability to control his or her environment, personal and impersonal, in order to attain quantity-oriented success: wealth, ownership, "good looks," proper grades, and all other measurable indications of success. Now, in the Mediterranean, currently and especially in the past, the focal institution of the various societies has been and is kinship. The family is truly everything. While Americans, with their economic concerns, might find it interesting that before the Industrial Revolution of the nineteenth century, the family was both production and consumption unit, such is no longer the case in the United States even for farm families. Given U.S. social arrangements, persons enculturated here would find it hard to realize what it might mean for the family to be the central institution in a social system.

When the family is the highlighted institution of concern, then the organizing principle of life is belongingness. Success consists in having and making the right interpersonal connections, in being related to the right people. In other words, given belongingness as the organizing principle, success in life means maintaining ties to other persons within sets of significant groups. The central group in this set is one's kinship group. A person's identity depends on belonging to and being accepted by the family. Such belonging and acceptance, however, depend on a person's adhering to the traditional rules of order by which Mediterranean families are organized and maintained. And those traditional rules of order are rooted in the complementary codes surrounding the basic values of honor and shame.

Honor, as we shall see, is basically a claim to worth that is socially acknowledged. It surfaces especially where the three defining features of authority, gender status, and respect come together. Let me define *authority*, *gender status*, and *respect*. *Authority* means the ability to control the behavior of others. Authority is a symbolic reality. It should not be confused with physical force. Often rather old and weak persons such as generals or mob bosses can personally exert little physical force. Yet they have much authority and readily control the behavior of others. On the other hand, the U.S. military establishment has unbelievable physical force at its disposal, but in most of the world it has little authority!

Gender status (or roles) refers to the sets of obligations and entitlements—

what you ought to do and what others ought to do to or for you—that derive from symboling biological gender differentiation. Are male "oughts" the same as female "oughts"? Is the way people ought to treat a man the same as they ought to treat a woman? Gender status refers to the male and female "oughts" recognized in a social group.

Finally, by *respect* I mean the attitude one must have and the behavior one is expected to follow relative to those who control one's existence. This attitude and subsequent behavior was traditionally called "religion" by people in the Mediterranean world well into the sixteenth century. Bible translations call this attitude "piety," and sometimes "fear." For example, "The fear of the Lord is the beginning of wisdom" (Ps. 111:10) actually refers to respect for the Lord. Respect is due to those who control our existence. When you were a child, who had immediate control of your existence? Parents. Who had control of their existence? Grandparents. Who presently controls both you and your parents and grandparents? Various local, state, and national government officials; various employers; and the wealthy in the halls of power. And who controls all these? Who is at the top of the ladder? The one who holds it all together, our God or gods. Now, the proper attitudes of respect and homage, along with the behavior you are expected to follow in relation to those who controlled and control your existence, is what this respect is about. It is also what "religion" was about in the first-century New Testament world.

Understanding Honor

Honor might be described as socially proper attitudes and behavior in the area where the three lines of authority, gender status, and respect intersect. If this all sounds a bit too abstract (which it is—remember, we are working on a model), then try this approach. Honor is the value of a person in his or her own eyes (that is, one's claim to worth) *plus* that person's value in the eyes of his or her social group. Honor is a claim to worth along with the social acknowledgment of worth. Members of a society share the sets of meanings and feelings bound up in the symbols of authority, gender status, and respect. The range of persons that owe you respect is bound up with your male and female roles, which are also bound up with where you stand on the status ladder of your group. When you lay claim to a certain status as embodied by your authority and in your gender role, you are claiming honor. For example, a father in a family (gender role, status on the ladder of society) commands his children to do something, and they obey (authority), as God (the gods) intended: they treat him honorably. Other people seeing this would acknowledge that he is an honorable father. But should this father command

and his children disobey, the children would dishonor him, and the father's peers would ridicule him, thereby acknowledging his lack of honor as a father. Try another example. Say a teacher (in the first century all public teachers were male [= gender status]; the role of teacher likewise presupposes standing in the community of men [= status on the social ladder]) sets out a teaching that his disciples do not agree with; they do not acknowledge his teaching authority and thus show disrespect. To bystanders, this would be an occasion of dishonoring him, since even his disciples do not believe him. Should his disciples believe him, see the truth of his teaching, accept what he says on his authority, then the bystanders of the community would acknowledge that he is in fact a teacher, hence worthy of honor. One more example: Say a young man elopes with the daughter of an honorable father. What would the daughter's behavior mean? The father as father (gender role) has the right and duty to decide on the marriage of his daughter (authority); she is embedded in his family, as it were. The daughter must acknowledge her father's status relative to her, since this is his divinely attributed rank (authority) on the status ladder. By eloping, the daughter acts out the symbol of disregarding her father's authority over her; she dismisses and disregards his authority and his God-given duty. What will the community say about the father's claim to social standing, his honor? Of course his daughter dishonors him by eloping, and the community would deny his claim to honor, since he could not even control his daughter as fathers should.

Honor, then, is a claim to worth *and* the social acknowledgement of that worth. For a person in a society concerned with honor, there is a constant dialectic, a thinking back and forth, between the norms of society and how the person is to reproduce those norms in specific behavior. A person constantly thinks about what he or she ought to do, about what is ideally acknowledged in the society as meaningful and valuable, and then examines his or her actions in the light of those societal norms and oughts. When a person perceives that his or her actions do in fact reproduce the ideals of society, he or she expects others in the group to acknowledge this fact, and what results is a grant of honor, a grant of reputation. To honor a person is to acknowledge publicly that his or her actions conform with social oughts. Honor as pivotal value in a society implies a chosen way of conduct undertaken with a view to and because of entitlement to certain social treatment in return. Other people not only say that a person is honorable; they also treat that person in the way that honorable persons are treated. It is something like our credit rating. A good credit rating makes money available, allows a person to incur debt and acquire goods for immediate use, and reflects on a person's social standing in our society. What the first-century persons were interested in was their honor rating. The entitlement to worth is the entitlement to status, and status (one's set of entitlements and obligations) derives from the recognition of one's social identity. Consequently, who persons are in society depends on their honor rating, which situates persons on the status ladder of the community.

Thus a person's claim to honor requires a grant of reputation by others before it becomes honor in fact. If a person's claim to honor because of some action results in no social grant of reputation, then the person's action (and frequently the person him/herself) is labeled ridiculous, contemptuous, or foolish, and is treated accordingly. (Note the use of the words "fool" and "foolish" in Proverbs, Ecclesiastes, and the New Testament.) So the problem of honor for the person claiming it depends on how, by whom, and on what grounds others will judge and evaluate a person's actions as worthy of repute.

How Does a Person Get a Grant of Honor?

Honor, like wealth, can be ascribed or acquired. *Ascribed honor*, like ascribed wealth, is honor that you get simply for being you, not because of anything you do to acquire it. For example, if you should inherit a a large sum of money, that would be ascribed wealth. Should you be born into a very wealthy family, that too would be ascribed wealth. Should someone you never met before give you a million dollars, that would be ascribed wealth. Ascribed honor is similar. Ascribed honor is the socially recognized claim to worth that befalls a person, that happens passively, so to say. In this category, honor derives from the fact of birth ("Like mother, like daughter," Ezek. 16:44; "like father, like son," Matt. 11:27; see also Deut. 23:2; 2 Kings 9:22; Isa. 57:3; Hos. 1:2; Sir. 23:25–26; 30:7). Being born into an honorable family makes one honorable since the family is the repository of the honor of past illustrious ancestors and their accumulated acquired honor. One of the major purposes of genealogies in the Bible is to set out a person's honor lines and thus socially situate the person on the ladder of statuses. Genealogy points to one's ascribed honor (thus Matt. 1:2–16; Luke 3:23–38; questions about Jesus' family and origin look to the same thing in Mark 6:3; Matt. 13:54–57; Luke 4:22; John 7:40–42; for Paul read Rom. 11:1; Phil. 3:5).

Honor can also be ascribed to someone by a notable person of authority. It can be ascribed by God, the king, aristocrats—in sum, by persons who can claim honor for others and can force acknowledgment of that honor because they have the power and rank to do so. Thus Jesus, as an utterly shamed and disgraced crucified person, is ascribed honor by God because God raised him, thus indicating God's good pleasure in Jesus. John's Gospel articulates this view most clearly, since for John, Jesus' death is an exaltation, a glorification.

The statement that Jesus "sits at the right hand of God" is the same sort of assessment. For Paul, members of his churches can also expect such ascribed honor (Rom. 8:17–30).

Acquired honor, on the other hand, is the socially recognized claim to worth that a person acquires by excelling over others in the social interaction that we shall call *challenge and response*. Challenge and response is a sort of social pattern, a social game, if you will, in which persons hassle each other according to socially defined rules in order to gain the honor of another. Honor, like all other goods in first-century Mediterranean society, is a limited good (see chapters 4 and 5 below). There is only so much to go around, or at least that is what people learn to perceive. Now, because honor is the pivotal value (much like wealth in our society), nearly every interaction with nonfamily members has undertones of a challenge to honor.

How Honor Is Acquired

Challenge and response is a sort of constant social tug of war, a game of social push and shove. You might look at it as a type of social communication, for any social interaction is a form of communication in which messages are transferred from a source to a receiver. Some person (source) sends a message by means of certain culturally recognized channels to the receiving individual, and this produces some sort of effect. The source here is the challenger, while the message is a symboled thing (a word, a gift, an invitation) or event (some action) or both. The channels are always public, and the publicity of the message guarantees that the receiving individual will react in some way, since even his nonaction is publicly interpreted as a response. Consequently, challenge-response within the context of honor is a sort of interaction in at least three phases: (1) the challenge in terms of some action (word, deed, or both) on the part of the challenger; (2) the perception of the message by both the individual to whom it is directed and the public at large; and (3) the reaction of the receiving individual and the evaluation of the reaction on the part of the public (see Figure 2 and the explanation that follows).

The challenge is a claim to enter the social space of another. This claim may be positive or negative. A positive reason for entering another's social space would be to gain some share in that space or to gain a cooperative, mutually beneficial foothold. A negative reason would be to dislodge another from that person's social space, either temporarily or permanently. Thus the source sending the message—always interpreted as a challenge—puts out some behavior, either positive (like a word of praise, a gift, a sincere request for help, a promise of help plus the actual help) or negative (a word of insult,

Figure 2. *Challenge and Response*

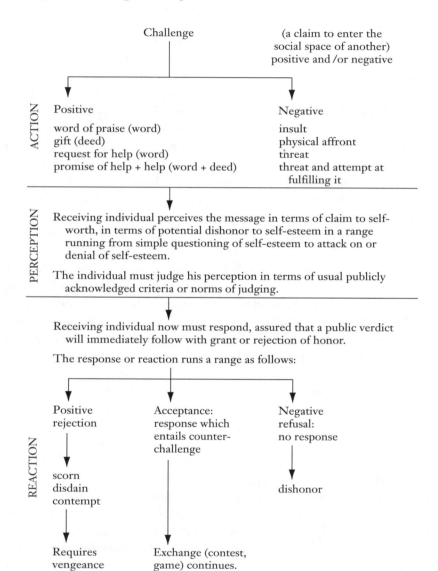

a physical affront of various degrees, a threat along with the attempt to fulfill it). All such actions constitute the message that has to be perceived and interpreted by the receiving individual as well as the public at large.

As a rule, challenger and receiver are men, although elite women could and did challenge men (e.g., the queen of Sheba and Solomon in 1 Kings). Similarly, women among themselves compete in challenge-riposte interactions. Moreover, men may be challenged by actions directed to the women or other men for whom they are responsible. Receivers of a challenge look on the action from the viewpoint of its potential to dishonor their self-esteem, their self-worth. They have to judge whether and how the challenge falls within the socially acknowledged range of such actions, from a simple questioning of self-esteem to an outright attack on self-esteem to a total denial of self-esteem. Perception of the message is a sort of second step. It is very important to note that the interaction over honor, the challenge-response game, *can take place only between social equals.* Hence receivers must judge whether they are equal to the challenger, whether the challenger honors them by regarding them as an equal as is implicit in the challenge, or whether the challenger dishonors them by implying equality when there is none, either because the receiver is of a higher or lower status. Thus in the Gospels, the various Pharisaical and scribal groups that challenge Jesus imply that he is their equal. On the other hand, the high priests and Pilate do not regard Jesus' activity as a challenge but rather an annoyance by an inferior who can be swept aside.

The third step in the interaction would be the reaction to the message. This involves the receiver's behavior that enables the public to pass a verdict: a grant of honor taken from the receiver of a challenge and awarded to the successful challenger, or a loss of honor by the challenger in favor of the successful recipient of the challenge. Any reaction on the part of the receiver of a challenge comprises his response. Such responses cover a range of reactions, from a "positive" refusal to act, through acceptance of the message, to a "negative" refusal to react. By this I mean that a person receiving the challenge message can refuse the challenge positively by a display of scorn, disdain, or contempt. If he is inferior or equal to the challenger, that would require the challenger to take steps to obliterate the insulting response, since such a response locates the challenger as an inferior. On the other hand, the receiver can accept the challenge message and offer a counterchallenge, and the exchange between them will continue. Or finally, the receiver can react by offering nothing by way of response; he can fail or neglect to respond, and this would imply dishonor for the receiver.

The challenge, then, is a threat to usurp the reputation of another, to deprive another of his reputation. When the person challenged cannot or does not respond to the challenge posed by his equal, he loses his reputation in the eyes of the public. People will say he cannot or does not know how to defend his honor. He thus loses his honor to the challenger, who correspondingly gains in honor.

Given Mediterranean culture's consensus reality, the appropriate honor-based cultural cues of perception, action, and belief are symboled in the behavior of conquering kings who take on the titles of the ones they vanquish. These cues are likewise symboled in the behavior of the early post-Jesus group members, who applied to the resurrected Jesus all the titles of those whose task it was to overcome evil and death: Messiah, Lord, son of David, Son of God, and the like.

Now, in the first-century Mediterranean world, every social interaction that takes place outside one's family or outside one's circle of friends is perceived as a challenge to honor, a mutual attempt to acquire honor from one's social equal. Thus gift-giving; invitations to dinner; debates over issues of law; buying and selling; arranging marriages; arranging what we might call cooperative ventures for farming, business, fishing, mutual help, and the like—all these sorts of interaction take place according to the patterns of honor called challenge-response. Because of these constant and steady cues in Mediterranean culture, anthropologists call it an *agonistic* culture. The word *agon* is Greek for an athletic contest or a contest between equals of any sort. What this means, then, is that the society we are considering is a society that looks on all social interactions outside the family or substitute family (circle of friends, in-group) as a contest for honor. Since honor and reputation, like all goods in life, are limited, then every social interaction of this type comes to be perceived as an affair of honor, a contest or game of honor, in which players are faced with wins, ties, and losses.

Honor Symboled by Blood

Honor is always presumed to exist within one's own family of blood, that is, among all those one has as blood relatives. A person can always trust his blood relatives. Outside that circle, all people are presumed to be dishonorable—untrustworthy, if you will—unless proved otherwise. It is with all these others that one must play the game, engage in the contest, put one's own honor and one's family honor on the line. Thus no one outside the family of blood can be trusted until and unless that trust can be validated and verified. So men of the same village or town who are not blood relatives relate to each other with an implied deep distrust that in practice prevents any effective form of cooperation. Strangers to the village, that is, people of the same cultural group but not resident in the same place, are looked on as potential enemies, while foreigners, that is, those of other cultural groups just passing through, are considered as certain enemies. Consequently, any interaction or conversation between two unrelated men or two unrelated women (the genders don't mix) are engagements in which both sides probe for the least hint of the other's intentions or activities. Such interactions are not concerned with sociability but rather are expressions of opposition and distance.

Honor Symboled by Name

Such sentiments of opposition, distance, and exclusiveness among fellow villagers and their families find a more extended expression in competition for a good name. Again, one's good name, that is, one's reputation, holds the central concern of people in every context of public action and gives purpose and meaning to their lives, again like money does in our society. From another point of view, good name and family reputation are also central, because families in the first-century world were not entirely self-sufficient and independent economically. Social life requires some degree of interdependence, cooperation, and shared enterprise. In Mediterranean society, such extrafamilial cooperation takes the form of a free association of a contractual kind. In biblical terms, people made implicit or explicit "covenants" with each other. Now, with whom would you enter into any sort of cooperative covenant or contract? In the United States, an auto dealer won't sell you a new car unless your credit rating is good. In the Mediterranean world, no one would freely associate with you in covenant relationship unless your honor rating were good, so good name and family reputation are the most valuable of assets (see chapter 3).

By and large, then, competition for reputation and honor takes the form of an ongoing contest or rivalry—an ongoing win, tie, or lose game in which *both* how one plays and whether one wins or not are equally important. Attempts to damage reputations are constantly made, yet great stress is laid on face-to-face courtesy in terms of formalities. The prestige level of the members of the community is a matter of continual comment. Every quarrel normally leads to imputations of acts and intentions that are dishonorable— and that have nothing to do with the quarrel. Prestige derives from the domination of persons rather than things. Hence any concern people show for the acquisition of goods derives from the purpose of gaining honor through generously disposing of what one has acquired among equals or socially useful lower-status clients. In other words, honor is acquired through beneficence, not through the fact of possession and/or the keeping of what one has acquired. Thus money, goods, and any sort of wealth are really a means to honor, and any other use of wealth is considered foolish. The acquisitive and grasping rich are greedy fools!

Consequently, the honorable person is one who knows how to and can maintain his or her social boundaries in the intersection of authority, gender, and social respect, including God. The shameless person is one who does not observe social boundaries. The fool is one who takes a shameless person seriously. Specifically, then, how is honor displayed and recognized?

How Honor Is Displayed and Recognized

You will recall that the set of social boundaries that we assimilate through enculturation defines our culture's consensus reality for us. It provides us with a sort of socially shared map that enables and urges us to situate persons, things, and events within proper boundaries. Now, this social road map is most often condensed and expressed in somewhat compact symbolic form in one's physical person. What I mean—and I shall return to this point later—is that your physical person, your body, works as a sort of personalized road map of the social values of our society. For example, as our social road map marks off my house from your house, giving free access to your house to those who are and can be intimate with you, similarly, the ones who have free access to touching, kissing, and caressing you (your physical person) will generally be those who have free access to your house. Your physical person replicates your general social space, your house. By "replication" I mean the use of similar and often identical patterns of behavior in different domains.

Back to our example. Just as you can let service personnel into your house for specific purposes, so you can let service personnel have limited access to your physical person for specific purposes: the plumber or electrician for the house; the physician or dentist for your physical person. The rules for interaction with service personnel are generally very similar. In each case you must allow intimacies in areas that are normally private; in each case the personnel are duly licensed (and in the economy-focused United States, bonded); in each case the personnel are paid for their services in money to signify that the transaction is over, complete, with no lingering debt of interpersonal obligation—even if you feel grateful to the person who stopped the flooding in your basement or helped you walk again. This sort of replication—the presence of identical rules in different domains—is rather common in cultures.

To return to the discussion of honor, the physical person (one's body) is normally a symboled replication of the social value of honor. The head and front of the head (face) play prominent roles. To be seated at the head of the table, to be at the head of the line, to head an organization, are replications of crowning the head, of others taking off their hats to you, of others bowing their heads in your presence. Honor and dishonor are displayed when the head is crowned, anointed, touched, covered, uncovered, made bare by shaving, cut off, struck, or slapped. The symbolic nature of the face, a part for the whole, is much like that of the head, with the added dimension of the spatial *front*, the focus of awareness. To *affront* someone is to challenge another in such a way that the person is, and cannot avoid being, aware of it. In an affront challenged persons are obliged to witness the challenge to their face. In return, the recognition of the challenge takes place on the face. In Semitic culture, this focus of recognition is the center of the face, the nose: a Hebrew word for anger refers metaphorically to flared nostrils, and a reference to flared nostrils is most often translated "wrath."

To put it mildly, a physical affront is a challenge to one's honor. Unanswered it becomes a dishonor in the judgment of persons witnessing the affront. Physical affronts symbol the breaking of required social and personal boundaries, thus causing resentment. Resentment means the psychological state of feeling distressed and anxious because the expectations and demands of the ego are not acknowledged by the actual treatment a person receives at the hands of others. It is a sense of moral indignation at the perceived injustice in the behavior of others towards me—not in keeping with my power, gender status, and social role. In brief, others refuse to recognize my honor and prestige, and their physical effrontery symbols that refusal. They have crossed into the social space that is me.

To bring things back to normal, what is required is a response, a sort of pushing challengers to their own side of the line, along with a fence-mending operation. This process of restoring the situation after the deprivation of honor is usually called satisfaction or getting satisfaction. To allow one's honor to be impugned, hence taken, is to leave one's honor in a state of *desecration*—vitiated, profaned, debased—and this would leave a person socially dishonored and dishonorable. On the other hand, to attempt to restore one's honor, even if the attempt is unsuccessful, is to return one's honor to the state of the sacred, to resanctify and reconsecrate it, leaving one socially honored and honorable (hence making one a person of valor, of standing).

Again, it is very important to note that according to the social patterns of the honor contest, not everyone can engage in the game. According to the unwritten rules or implicit code, *only equals can play*. Only an equal can actually challenge another in such a way that all perceive the interaction as a challenge. Only an equal—who must be recognized as such—can impugn a person's honor or affront another. The reason for this is that the rules of the honor contest require that challengers stand on equal social terms. Thus an inferior on the ladder of social standing, authority, and gender status does not have enough honor to resent the affront of a superior. On the other side, a superior's honor is simply not committed, not engaged, by an inferior's affront, although the superior has the power to punish impudence. Thus a man can physically affront his children or wife; a high-status person can strike a lower-status person; free men can buffet slaves; the occupying Roman army can make sport of most low-status locals. These interactions do not imply an honor contest in themselves. (They may imply the honor of another, e.g. patrons who are to protect the interests of their clients. But this complicates things at this point; I will refer to it later.) In other words, in the social game of honor, persons are answerable for their honor only to their social equals, to those with whom, in the perceptions of the society, they can compete.

To get back to physical affronts, any physical boundary-crossing on the part of another presumes and implies the intention to dishonor. In honor societies, actions are more important than words, and how one speaks is more important than what one says. In physical effrontery, the challenge to honor is presumed to exist unless it is clearly and totally apparent that no challenge is intended (e.g., a child striking an adult). Yet to claim that one did not intend dishonor (e.g., by saying "I didn't mean it" or "Excuse me") is to require a certain indulgence on the part of the one affronted, and this indulgence may or may not be granted. Much would depend on the degree of dishonor involved (e.g., how, in what circumstance, where a person struck or touched another); the status of the person challenging (who did the striking); and the degree of publicity (what audience witnessed the event).

Again, publicity, witnesses, are crucial for the acquisition and bestowal of honor. Representatives of public opinion must be present, since honor is all about the tribunal or court of public opinion and the reputation that court bestows. Literally, public praise can give life and public ridicule can kill.

Honor and the Interpretation of a Challenge

It should be obvious by now that two levels of interpretation are involved in the challenge and riposte of honor: (1) that of the individual challenged—his or her estimation of the intention and status of the challenger; (2) that of the public witnessing the challenge—a witnessing group's interpretation of the intention and status of the challenger and the challenge in the public forum. Given these two necessary elements, there will be various styles of challenging, running from a direct affront through indirect challenges of rather ambiguous actions.

To deal with the last first, the style called an ambiguous affront is a challenging word or deed put forth "accidentally on purpose." For example, I may "accidentally" bump into you and knock you down, or I may tell some man that someone else said that his daughter is a fine whore. This sort of challenge puts the one challenged in a dilemma. The person must decide what the community will judge the challenge to be, for the victim of an affront or challenge is dishonored only when and where that person is forced by the public to recognize that one has been challenged and did not respond. This is where swearing or nonlegal oath making comes into play. The purpose of such swearing (e.g., in business: "I swear to God this is a healthy jackass") is to eliminate ambiguity and make explicit one's true intentions. An oath activates a type of implicit curse (e.g., if the jackass is sick and dies, God will punish me for calling the Deity to witness to an untruth, hence dishonoring God). And public opinion judges a person dishonored if he or she does not submit to an oath. (Read the law regarding a wife suspected of adultery in Num. 5:11–31; see also Luke 1:73; Acts 2:30; 23:12, 14–21; Heb. 7:20–28; the antithesis in Matt. 5:33–37 looks to oath making in business.) If one makes an oath to another, then only the oath maker, not the other person, can be dishonored after the oath; but the oath, like the word of honor, must be freely made to engage the game of challenge and response.

What then is a word of honor? A person can commit his honor in the contest of life only by sincere intention. To demonstrate this sincerity of intention, this steadfastness of purpose, a person can give a word of honor, which functions like making an oath or swearing. But such oath making or swearing only engages the individual him/herself, not God or others. Such a word of honor is only necessary for those who find what a person says or does ambiguous or incredible. Jesus' characteristic "truly, I say to you" functions like a word of honor (cf. Matt. 5:18, 26; 6:2, 5, 16; 8:10; 10:15, 23, 42; 11:11; 13:17; 16:28; 17:20; 18:3, 13, 18, 19; 19:23, 28; 21:21, 31; 23:36; 24:2, 34, 47; 25:12, 40, 45; 26:13, 21, 34; Mark 3:28; 8:12; 9:1, 41; 10:15, 29; 11:23; 12:43; 13:30; 14:9, 18, 25, 30; Luke 4:24; 12:37; 18:17, 29; 21:32; 23:43; John 1:51; 3:3, 5, 11; 5:19, 24, 25; 6:26, 32, 47, 53; 8:34, 51, 58; 10:1, 7; 12:24; 13:16, 20, 21, 38; 14:12; 16:20, 23; 21:18).

The reason for giving a word of honor is that moral commitment in telling the truth unambiguously in such honor cultures derives from the social commitment or loyalty to persons to whom such commitment is due. In first-century limited-good society, there was no such thing as universal, social commitment (e.g., the perception of all humans as equally persons, or even of all males in some brotherhood of all men). Rather, the right to the truth and the right to withhold the truth belong to the "person of honor" and to contest these rights is to place a person's honor in jeopardy, to challenge that person. Lying and deception are or can be honorable and legitimate. To lie in order to deceive an outsider, one who has no right to the truth, is honorable. In the Israelite tradition, Ben Zakaiists believed that "men may vow to murderers, robbers, or tax-gatherers that what they have is heave-offering even though it is not heave-offering; or that they belong to the king's household even though they do not belong to the king's household" (Mishnah, *Nedarim* 3.4).

On the other hand, to be called a liar by anyone is a great public dishonor. The reason for this is that truth belongs only to one who has a right to it. To lie really means to deny the truth to one who has a right to it, and the right to the truth only exists where respect is due (in the family, to superiors, and not necessarily to equals with whom I compete or to inferiors). Thus to deceive by making something ambiguous or to lie to an out-group person is to deprive the other of respect, to refuse to show honor, to humiliate another. And one may lie to a person one is prepared to challenge and affront. It is not dishonoring for a person to affront another who is an equal or an inferior.

The boundary lines marking off a person in some way likewise include all that the person holds worthwhile and worthy. What this means is that along with personal honor, an individual shares in a sort of collective or corporate honor. Included within the bounds of personal honor are all those worthies who control a person's existence, that is, parents, patrons, king, and God—all whom one holds vertically sacred. Also included are one's other family members—the horizontally sacred. The reason for this is that like individuals, social groups possess a collective honor.

And just as honor is personal or individual as well as collective or corporate (e.g., family honor, ethnic group honor, and the like), so another way to challenge a person is by means of what might be called a corporate affront. Instead of affronting you, I affront someone intertwined with your honor. Reaction to a challenge and the consequent deprivation of honor of someone other than the person in question can only happen when that person's honor is involved in some way. This can happen by dishonoring another's wife (who is perceived as embedded in her husband), dishonoring his extended family (like his father or blood cousin in his presence), or even dishonoring those socially judged to be unable to defend their honor personally. The Bible often refers to these socially defenseless persons—orphans, widows, and, before Deuteronomy, resident aliens—as people incapable of defending their own honor. The aged and infirm who are males are marginal cases. Then there are those who are socially barred from responding to challenges to their honor because of their unequal, superior, exalted status, for example, one's highly placed patron, the king, or God (gods). Thus a person may take up the challenge to one's patron, king, or God because they are intertwined in one's own honor.

As mentioned earlier, a dishonored person must attempt to restore honor. It is the attempt that counts, not the actual restoration of the status previously held. We might call this attempt "satisfaction," and satisfaction is not the same as triumph. There are a number of movie plots in which the hero or heroine gets a sort of satisfaction in the end, although he or she loses a contest against overwhelming odds in a bloody way. What is required and suffices for satisfaction in our honor society is (1) that the one dishonored has the opportunity to achieve satisfaction, and (2) that this person follows the rules of the game in doing so. Satisfaction then has the nature of an ordeal, implying a judgment of destiny or fate, of God's sanction. If the dishonored person or that person's family do not follow the socially approved rules, then the challenge-response game is over, and feud or war results.

Honor and Going to Court

Furthermore, it is considered highly dishonorable and against the rules of honor to go to court and seek legal justice from one's equal. This too reduces the challenge-response code to a feud or war. First of all, the one challenged and taking some action in court only aggravates the dishonor (what some challenger did to the person) by publicizing it. Further, satisfaction in court, legal satisfaction, does not restore one's honor because (1) to go to court is to demonstrate inequality and vulnerability, and puts one's own honor in jeopardy; (2) court procedure allows those who deprived you of honor to gloat over your predicament; and (3) to have the court obtain recompense or ask for an apology from another is dishonoring in itself, implying that one cannot deal with one's equals. Honor demands restoration or satisfaction by oneself or one's extended self. To appreciate this, note how in our society—or in movies depicting segments of our society—those above or outside the law— like the very wealthy, street gangs, organized criminals, the Mafia—are a sort of law to themselves and avoid being dishonored by recourse to normal legal procedures. In the first-century world, normal legal procedures were used to dishonor someone or some group perceived to be of higher, more powerful status, and recourse to such procedures was an admission of inequality. This inequality, of course, can be highly ambiguous, and again, it is up to public opinion to dole out the honor.

Dimensions of Collective Honor

Since first-century Mediterranean societies did not consider individualism a pivotal value as we do (cf. chapter 2), collective or corporate honor was one of their major focuses. Social groups, like the family, neighborhood, village, or region, possessed a collective honor in which the members participated (note John 1:46: "Can anything good come out of Nazareth?"; Titus 1:12:

"Cretans are always liars, evil beasts, lazy gluttons."). This perception might be expressed as "I am who I am and with whom I associate." Depending on the dimensions of the group, which can run a replicating range from the single nuclear family to kingdom or region, the *head* of the group is responsible for the honor of the group with reference to outsiders and symbolizes the group's honor as well. Hence members of the group owe loyalty, respect, and obedience of a kind that commits their individual honor without limit and without compromise. There are two types of groupings: natural and optional.

Natural groupings depend on circumstances over which the individual has no control, for example, birth, residence, nationality, social standing. In natural groupings, a person's intentions to belong to the group are of no importance at all. One is born physically and symbolically into the group, and there is nothing one can do about it. The grouping is not the result of any choice, competition, or contract. What this means is that one belongs naturally, by blood, so to say, to the group. And this very fact obliges the person to respect, observe, and maintain the boundary lines, the definitions, the order within the group.

In order to understand the assessments of honor within natural groupings, recall what I said previously about the varying range of challenge messages. Challenges are not all of the same degree or quality but move along a spectrum from a simple invitation to share a cup of wine to an extreme like murder. Just as there are varying degrees of challenge, so too the response reaction ought to be at least of the same quality as the challenge for the persons involved to maintain their honor.

I would like to distinguish, for clarity's sake, three hypothetical degrees. These degrees of challenge would depend on whether the challenge to honor is revocable or not, whether the boundaries can be readily repaired or not, and whether the implied or actual deprivation of honor is light, significant, or extreme and total. Thus challenges or transgressions of the boundaries marking off the person run within three degrees. The first degree involves extreme and total dishonor of another with no revocation possible. This is outrage and would include murder, adultery, kidnapping, bearing false witness, and total social degradation of a person by depriving one of all that is necessary for one's social status. These, in sum, include all the things listed in the second half of the Ten Commandments aside from theft, for this in fact is what is listed there: outrages against one's fellow Israelite that are simply not revocable but require vengeance. The second degree would be a significant deprivation of honor with revocation possible, for example, by restoring stolen items, by making monetary restitution for seducing one's unbetrothed, unmarried daughter, and the like. The third and lowest degree of challenge to honor would be the regular and ordinary interactions that require normal social responses, for example, repaying a gift with one of equal of better value, or allowing others to marry my children if they let my children marry theirs. In other words, any implicit or explicit dishonor must allow for satisfaction commensurate with the degree of dishonor present.

Now, to return to our natural groupings, note that any sort of first-degree dishonor done within the group is considered sacrilegious and comprises a category of transgression quite out of the ordinary. Those controlling our existence in natural groups are sacred, religious persons. Thus, murdering a parent is not simply homicide, it is parricide, parent-killing. The same with murdering a king (regicide) and, in the Middle Ages, murdering a pope (papacide). Such crimes against members of one's natural groupings, against those who share in one's natural honor, are always felt to be extremely grievous and socially disorienting. On the other hand, homicide committed on outsiders is not sacrilegious and might even be meritorious, as in defense of the group's honor in war—and often in peace. Outsiders are not sacred. The Romans called the crime of first-degree transgression in natural groupings *nefas*, and branded the perpetrator *sacer* (literally, "sacred"), meaning the gods would certainly get him for what he did. Likewise aristocracies and the patronage relations between wealthy landowners and resident tenants resemble the natural groupings of family, village, region and social status in each of these.

Optional groupings, on the other hand, depend on a person's choices and result from contracts, quasi-contracts, or competition. Such choices, however, are almost invariably made due to social compulsion and necessity. At times such grouping are called "voluntary" groupings, even "voluntary associations." Yet Mediterraneans as a rule do not volunteer for anything outside of their natural grouping. If they had their "druthers," Mediterraneans would confine everything to natural groupings. Yet given the press of social circumstances and the vagaries of life, at times persons find themselves under compulsion to join groupings outside of their natural in-groups.

In optional groupings, the persons involved have no sacred qualities as persons because of who they are in relationship to others. Rather, it is the posts, positions, or offices in such groupings that bear the qualities otherwise embodied by persons in natural groupings. While in-group opinion and general public opinion are at work in natural groupings, in optional groupings public opinion is sovereign. Some such optional groupings in the first century would be trade guilds, municipalities (systems of villages), cities with republican forms of government, elective burial organizations, and Palestinian parties such as the Pharisees, Sadducees, Essenes, and the like. Perhaps after Jesus' death and resurrection, those who believed in Jesus likewise looked on their groups as optional associations much like the Palestinian parties after whom they often modeled themselves.

From the viewpoint of collective honor, depending on the quality of the grouping, the sacred persons or elective posts have power over all the dimensions of honor in their respective groups. They arbitrate questions of value; they delimit what can be done or maintained without sacrilege; they define the unconditional allegiance of the members. This is what Jesus and Paul did for the optional groupings that formed around them; this is what scribal leaders did for the optional groupings that adhered to them; and this is what the emperor in Rome or the high priest in Jerusalem did for the natural groupings under their authority. Thus these sacred persons or prominent post holders themselves symbol both social honor—they have precedence relative to others in their groups—and ethical honor—they are perceived to be implicitly good and noble. The reason for this is that social honor or eminence (being head of something or someone) is normally readily convertible into ethical honor or implicit goodness, just as capital or collateral assures credit in our money system. Honor (social precedence) guarantees against dishonor (immoral or ignoble ethical bearing). Thus the king of the nation (or the father of the family) simply cannot be dishonored within the group; he is above criticism. What he is guarantees the evaluation of his actions. Any offense against him only stains the offender.

Further, the king in his kingdom (like the father in his family) can do no wrong because he is the arbiter of right and wrong. Any criticism apart from the conventional, usual protests (e.g., taxes are too high) is rated an act of disloyalty, a lack of commitment. No one has a right to question what the king decides to do, just as no individual in the kingdom has any right to follow what he or she might personally think is right or wrong. The king (father) must be followed and obeyed; he is sufficient conscience for all concerned. This proper attitude is symboled in rituals of honor, and one must pay honor (worship originally meant worthiness, a recognition of worth) even if one does not feel inclined to. On the other hand, when persons feel another is worthy of honor, they pay honor, and when they pay honor, they underscore what they believe they ought to feel. In sum, honor causes a society to derive what ought to be done from what in fact is done. That is, the social order as it should be is derived from the social order as it actually is. Paying honor to those to whom it is owed legitimates established authority and further integrates societal members in their system of obligatory consent.

Honor and the Moral Division of Labor: The Double Standard

As mentioned previously, honor refers to the intersection of the societal boundaries of authority, respect for those in statuses above us, and gender roles. What I have said to this point, for the most part, looks to authority, respect, and both males and females. But by and large, the honor of the natural group is divided up into what may be called a gender or moral division of labor. This gender division of labor looks mainly to the family or kinship group but can be replicated in other dimensions of life.

To understand this point, let us begin with the significant gender symbols of these societies. First of all, male honor is symboled by the testicles, which stand for manliness, courage, authority over family, willingness to defend one's reputation, and refusal to submit to humiliation. (How does this relate to the eunuch parable in Matt. 19:12? See Lev. 21:20; Deut. 23:1; 25:11; Jer. 5:8; Ezek. 23:20; cf. also Amos 5:2–6.) Female honor, on the other hand, is symboled by the maidenhead (hymen) and stands for female sexual exclusiveness, discretion, shyness, restraint, and timidity. A man clearly lacks both the physiological basis for sexual exclusiveness or sexual "purity" (he cannot symbolize invasion into his space as a woman can, except for homosexual anal intercourse!), and his masculinity is in doubt if he maintains sexual purity, that is, if he does not challenge the boundaries of others through their women. Women, for their part, symbol their purity by warding off even the remotest advances to their symbolic space, yet it is the responsible man's duty to protect, defend, and look after the purity of his women (wife, sister, daughter), since their dishonor directly implies his own.

The division of honor into male and female corresponds to the division of roles in the family of husband, wife, and children. This aspect of family is called the family of procreation, to distinguish it from the family from which the individuals came—called the family of orientation. In the family of procreation, honor delegates implicit goodness or virtue as expressed in sexual exclusiveness to females, and social precedence with the duty of defending female sexual exclusiveness to the males. This sort of division of honor gets replicated in arrangements of space. (Remember: replication means the same patterns or rules in different domains.)

Female space or female things—the places where females are allowed, the things that females deal with exclusively, such as the kitchen and kitchen utensils, the (public) well and drawing water, spinning and sewing, the (public) oven and bread baking, sweeping out the house, etc.—all these female spaces and things are centripetal to the family dwelling or village of residence. That means they face toward the inside, with a sort of invisible magnet of social pressure turning females inward, toward their space in the house or the village. All things taken from the inside to the outside are male; all things remaining on the inside are female. The places of contact between the inside and outside (the family courtyard, the village square, or the area by the city gate) are male when males are present, although females may sometimes enter either when no males are present or when properly chaperoned or when their males are present. In this arrangement, the wife normally becomes financial administrator with the key to the family chest when and because the husband must go out—to fields, to other villages, on pilgrimage. However, men who must go out for protracted periods of time without their women, such as traders, traveling merchants, certain types of shepherds, wandering preachers, and the like, necessarily leave their honor in doubt, since their wives are left alone for rather long periods.

Consequently, a man's honor is involved in the sexual purity of his mother (although his father has the main obligation in this regard), wife, daughters, and sisters—but not in his own sexual purity. According to this pattern, then, *the sexual purity or exclusiveness of the female is embedded within the honor of some male.* The man is responsible for the maintenance of this sexual exclusiveness; it is delegated to the man, so to say. Hence the woman remains with her own responsibility alleviated, unless she courts disaster by stepping out of socially acceptable boundaries. Thus the honorable woman, born with the proper sentiments of positive shame (i.e., concern for her honor) which she inherits from her mother ("Like mother, like daughter." Ezek. 16:44), strives to avoid the human contacts that might expose her to dishonor. She cannot be expected to succeed in this endeavor unsupported by male authority and control. This perception underlies public opinion, which makes the deceived husband or father the object of ridicule and dishonor and entitles him to avenge any outrage committed against him in this way. Furthermore, women not under the tutelage of a man—notably childless widows and divorced women without family ties—are viewed as stripped of female honor, hence more like males then females, therefore sexually predatory, aggressive, "hot to trot," hence dangerous. Only remarriage would restore their true gender roles, but often this is not socially possible. Hence the precarious position of the widow and divorcee (and the importance of a bill of divorce enabling and entitling the woman to a new marriage if this can be arranged for her). This cultural attitude toward widows is clearly articulated in 1 Timothy 5:3–16.

Toward Defining Honor and Shame

As mentioned previously, honor means a person's (or group's) feeling of self-worth and the public, social acknowledgment of that worth. Honor in this sense applies to both genders. It is the basis of one's reputation, of one's social standing, regardless of gender. In this common context, where honor is both male and female, the word "shame" is a positive symbol. It refers to a sense of shame. Positive shame, a sense of shame, means sensitivity about one's own reputation, sensitivity to the opinion of others. To have shame in this sense is an eminently positive value. Any human being worthy of the title "human," any human group worthy of belonging to humankind, needs to have shame, to be sensitive to its honor rating, to be perceptive to the opinion of others. A sense of shame makes the contest of living possible, dignified, and human, since it implies acceptance of and respect for the rules of human interaction. On the other hand, a shameless person or group is one who does not recognize the rules of human interaction, who does not recognize social boundaries. The shameless person is a person with a dishonorable reputation beyond all social doubt, one outside the boundaries of acceptable moral life, hence a person who must be denied the normal social courtesies. To show courtesy to a shameless person makes one a fool, since it is foolish to show respect for boundaries when a person acknowledges no boundaries, just as it would be foolish to continue to speak English to a person who does not know the language at all.

One can speak of honor and shame of both males and females specifically as they pertain to those areas of social life covering common humanity, notably, natural groupings in which males and females share a common collective honor: the family, village, city, and their collective reputation. However, actual, everyday, concrete conduct that establishes one's reputation and redounds on one's group is never independent of the gender or moral division of labor. Actual conduct, daily concrete behavior, always depends on one's gender status. At this level of perception, when honor is viewed as an exclusive prerogative of one of the genders, then honor is always male, and shame is always female. Thus in the area of individual, concrete behavior (and apart from considerations of the group), honor and shame are gender specific. This is a sort of lower level of abstraction at which individual males symbol honor and individual females symbol shame (see Figure 3).

At this level of abstraction, male honor is symboled in the testicles and covers typically male behavior, running from the ethically neutral to the ethically valued: manliness, courage (the willingness to challenge and affront another male), authority, defense of the family's honor, concern for prestige, and social eminence—all this is honorable behavior for the male. Female shame, on the other hand, is symboled in the maidenhead and likewise covers a range running from the ethically neutral to the ethically valued: feelings of sensitivity or "shame" to reveal nakedness, modesty, shyness, blushing, timidity, restraint, sexual exclusiveness—all this is positive shame for the female and makes her honorable.

To move up once again to a higher level of assessment in which honor and

Figure 3. *Honor and Shame: Moral Division of Labor*

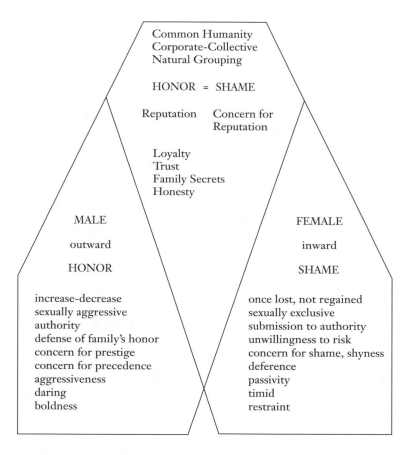

Common Humanity
Corporate-Collective
Natural Grouping

HONOR = SHAME

Reputation   Concern for
              Reputation

Loyalty
Trust
Family Secrets
Honesty

MALE   FEMALE

outward   inward

HONOR   SHAME

increase-decrease   once lost, not regained
sexually aggressive   sexually exclusive
authority   submission to authority
defense of family's honor   unwillingness to risk
concern for prestige   concern for shame, shyness
concern for precedence   deference
aggressiveness   passivity
daring   timid
boldness   restraint

shame refer to both males and females, people acquire honor by personally aspiring to a certain status and having that status socially validated. On the other hand, people *get shamed* or *are shamed* (not *have shame*) when they aspire to a certain status and this status is denied them by public opinion. At the point a person realizes he or she is being denied the status, the person is or gets shamed; he or she is humiliated, disgraced, stripped of honor for aspiring to an honor not socially his or hers. Honor assessments thus move from the inside (a person's claim) to the outside (public validation). Shame assessments move from the outside (public denial) to the inside (a person's recognition of the denial). To be shamed or get shamed, thus, is to be thwarted or obstructed in one's personal claim to worth or status, along with one's recognition of loss of status involved in this rejection.

Again, as a common value, applicable to natural groupings, honor runs a range from internal goodness to social eminence or power. The wicked, powerful king has honor in terms of social eminence, while the good but poor and powerless family has honor in terms of ethical goodness. Assessments of honor along this sort of spectrum take a replicating twist that might help us understand experiencing shame—the "weeping and gnashing teeth" in Matthew, for example. For any fusion of male and female elements in a higher-level symbol can always unravel into its constituent parts. What I mean is that just as a female who loses her shame gets shamed and therefore no longer has shame but is shameless, so also natural groups can lose their shame by getting shamed to such an extent that they no longer have shame but are shameless. Certain families and institutions (e.g., husbands serving as pimps, first-century tavern and inn owners, actors, prostitutes as a group) are considered irretrievably shameless. The reason for this is that they respect no lines of exclusiveness and hence symbol the chaotic. In this sense, honor as goodness (the female aspect) may lead to a judgment according to which once it is lost, it can never be regained—exactly like female sexual exclusiveness. On the other hand, emphasis on honor as social eminence or authority (the male aspect) may lead to a judgment according to which honor can be increased or decreased at the expense of others. Such fluctuating honor will be used as a gauge of social standing.

With the family as repository of natural honor, marriage, as we shall see, is always the fusion of the honor of two families. Honor as positive shame or ethical goodness comes from the mother; she symbols it. Honor as social eminence comes from the father; he symbols it. The fusion of honor in an honorable marriage thus makes up the social inheritance with which the new family of procreation gets set to play the game of life.

A Significant Clarification

In conclusion, I should like to reflect on the wider frame within which honor and shame belong. That frame is the category called values. Honor and shame are values. Values are about the quality and direction of behavior. Since values are essentially qualities that inhere in something else, what that something else might be is always open to dispute within social limits, of course. Or to say this in other words, if honor is about a claim to worth that is socially acknowledged, the question is what, in fact, has a claim to worth. Is taking the last place at table, serving others, forgiving others, or seeking reconciliation with others claim-worthy? Some have stated that Jesus acted without concern for honor because he advocated the worth of serving and forgiveness. In fact he acted quite in line with honor by claiming the worth for such "female" behavior, which he urges on his followers. In other words, honor and shame patterns do not determine what is honorable or shameful.

The determination of what specific behaviors or objects are of worth depends on factors other than these values.

Thus honor and shame serve as socially preferred sanctions or orientation for behavior (other orientations include assurance and anxiety as well as integrity and guilt). Honor and shame are of core concern in societies where approval, especially of parents, kin, or fictive kin, is more important than the actual performance of a deed. In fact the deed often has little if any value in itself except through the approval given a person by those significant in-group others.

Some would say that it is impossible for contemporary Mediterranean values to be found in the ancient societies once localized in that region. The procedure in this book is to have you validate the model. Read the New Testament documents with the lenses of honor and shame and see whether the model serves in fact to clarify or explain all instances of interpersonal behavior narrated in the documents. Francis Hsu, a well-known U.S. anthropologist with psychological interests, has noted that "our most important environment is the social environment." He goes on to note that while similar values exist in various environments, "the basic pattern of affect of each society is likely to persist, in some cases, over thousands of years." In the Mediterranean, honor and shame are the basic patterns of affect, of what is symbolically meaningful.

Summary

From a symbolic point of view, honor stands for a person's rightful place in society, a person's social standing. This honor position is marked off by boundaries consisting of authority, gender status, and location on the social ladder. From a functionalist point of view, honor is the value of a person in his or her own eyes plus the value of that person in the eyes of his or her social group. Honor is a claim to worth along with the social acknowledgment of worth. The purpose of honor is to serve as a sort of social rating that entitles a person to interact in specific ways with his or her equals, superiors, and subordinates, according to the prescribed cultural cues of the society.

Honor can be ascribed or acquired. Ascribed honor befalls or happens to a person passively through birth, family connections, or endowment by notable persons of power. Acquired honor is honor actively sought and garnered most often at the expense of one's equals in the social contest of challenge and response. Figure 2 describes this type of interaction, which is a rather institutionalized conflict model.

Honor, both ascribed and acquired, is often symboled by blood (one's blood relations, group) and name. A good name fundamentally means adequate honor to carry on the social interactions necessary for decent human existence. Honor is frequently symboled in certain behaviors and in the treatment given one's physical person. Physical affronts are always symbolic affronts that require a response. Failure to respond means dishonor, disgrace. Just as the head and features of the head symbol a person's honor, so also does the head of a group symbol the honor of that group. For honor has both individual and corporate or collective dimensions. Whenever the honor of another is bound up with an individual's own honor, that individual is required to defend and represent the honor of all bound up with him and at times, her. This sort of collective honor is to be found in natural and optional groupings. Natural groupings, like ascribed honor, befall a person and depend on circumstances beyond the person's control. Relations within the natural grouping are sacred, blood, or pure relationships that tie persons directly together. Optional groupings, like acquired honor, result from calculated choices usually made under social duress. Relationships within optional groupings are focused on posts and functions, and these posts and functions are considered sacred and pure, although many different people can hold them. The heads of both natural and optional groupings set the tone and embody the honor rating of the group, so to say.

Honor has male and female aspects. When considered from this perspective, the male aspect is called honor, while the female aspect is called shame. Shame in this context refers to a person's sensitivity to what others think, say, and do with regard to his or her honor. In natural groupings, honor and shame—the male and the female—are fused, as in the family, village, or city. Such natural groupings have collective honor and shame. But in the moral division of labor, in the concrete activity of concrete people, honor and shame become gender specific, gender embedded. The male is to defend both corporate honor and any female honor embedded in the corporate honor. The female, on the other hand, symbols the shame aspect of corporate honor, that positive sensitivity to the good repute of individuals and groups. Figure 3 illustrates this point.

In order to understand persons in agonistic, honor-and-shame-based Mediterranean societies, it might be good to have an idea of childrearing practices that facilitate the formation of such persons. The comparative listing that follows presents a set of contrasts between traditional Mediterranean (and elsewhere) approaches to child rearing and parenting and emerging U.S. preferences in the same area. The purpose of the list is to provide general orientation, so that considerate readers of the New Testament might realize the contexts in which they might be situated and so that they might acquire an appreciation for the contexts of the persons about which they read.

Table 1: Contrasting Child Rearing Approaches

Mediterranean Preferences	Emerging U.S. Preferences
—Total unawareness of any sort of biological "givens" influencing the needs and behavior of the developing human being. Hence an attitude of basic distrust: a distrustful directive approach.	—A developing belief in biological "givens" influencing the needs and behavior of the developing human being. Hence an attitude of basic trust: a trusting, cooperative approach.
—The infant is seen as (a) being selfish and demanding; (b) wanting as much gratification and indulgence as s/he can get (usually too much).	—The infant is seen as (a) being immature and dependent; (b) wanting as much gratification and satisfaction as s/he needs (an adequate amount).
—To get gratification, the infant is perceived as behaving in ways that are self-willed, demanding, manipulative, cunning (thus confirming belief in inherent potential for badness).	—To get gratification, the infant is perceived as behaving in ways that are influenced by mechanisms whose function is to ensure that its needs are adequately met.
—Gratification of the infant is seen as leading to the danger of "spoiling" if more than the right amount is given.	—Gratification of the infant is seen as leading to satisfaction and contentment; "spoiling" is simply not a danger.
—The goal and obligation of parenting is to control and direct the child's behavior and to produce a "good" child (who will be obedient and conform).	—The goal and obligation of parenting is to enjoy a good relationship with the child, and help to produce a "whole," healthy person (who is likely to be sufficiently "good" also).
—Parents are to mold the child to a predetermined pattern; secure control by regulating habits, and training to accept authority and discipline.	—Parents are to satisfy the child's needs and develop a cooperative, mutually satisfying, affectionate relationship in which the potentialities of the child and parents unfold, blossom, and gradually mature. The developing capacities for self-regulation are respected and encouraged.

Mediterranean Preferences

—Parents are to teach "right from wrong" and demand obedience; extinguish "self-will," "bad" behavior and insist on and/or reinforce "good" behavior.

—Parents are right to ignore the child's point of view and to disregard the child's feelings and capacities. The child is to conform to the requirements of the adult world. In these circumstances, as the child's hostility and negativism become aggravated, unless they are repressed, parents are right to apply more force to control the child.

—Parental disapproval is rather frequent and may be reinforced by threats, punishments, and sometimes violence or inculcation of guilt.

—Outcome usually entails increased risk of conflict, frustration, and stress in unsatisfying relationships.

—For the individual, sensitivity may be blunted; externally imposed discipline may break down sooner or later in rebelliousness.

—In school, teachers are omniscient; teaching is one-way; total dependence of children on parents and elders.

—Less questioning of authority in general.

Emerging U.S. Preferences

—Parents are to teach avoidance of common dangers and gradually encourage the disposition to consider and respect the needs and feelings of others, through experiencing this consideration within the family.

—Parents are to try to understand the child's point of view and consider the child's feelings and capacities in their requests of the child; this would minimize hostility and negativism. Parents accept the child's feelings in the expectation that sufficient (self-)control will be achieved as appropriate to the child's age. (The options of exercising authority and sufficient force are still available if essential).

—Parents discourage inconsiderate behavior, but the quality of the relationships tends to make punishment inappropriate, and it may seldom or never be required.

—Outcome sought is mutual satisfaction in interpersonal relationships with joy and delight (sometimes) as a natural reward for health-promoting activities.

—For the individual, sensitivity is left intact; adequate self-discipline develops as appropriate to the age.

—In school some teaching is two-way; children learn things that elders never learned; less dependent.

—More questioning of authority in general.

These comparative lists have been culled from Cook, Peter S. "Childrearing, Culture and Mental Health: Exploring an Ethological-Evolutionary Perspective in Child Psychiatry and Preventive Mental Health with Particular Reference to Two Contrasting Approaches To Early Childrearing." *Medical Journal of Australia Special Supplement* 2 (1978): 3–14.

References and Suggested Readings

Abu-Hilal, Ahmad. "Arab and North-American Social Attitudes: Some Cross-Cultural Comparisons." *Mankind* 22 (1982):193–207.
Augsburger, David W. *Pastoral Counseling Across Cultures*. Philadelphia: Westminster Press, 1986.
Bourdieu, Pierre. "The Sentiment of Honour in Kabyle Society." In *Honour and Shame: The Values of Mediterranean Society*, ed. J. G. Peristiany, 191–241. Chicago: University of Chicago Press, 1966.
Davis, John. "Family and State in the Mediterranean." In *Honor and Shame and the Unity of the Mediterranean*. American Anthropological Association Special Publication #22, ed. David D. Gilmore, 22–34. Washington: American Anthropological Association, 1987.
Delaney, Carol. "Seeds of Honor, Fields of Shame." In *Honor and Shame and the Unity of the Mediterranean*, American Anthropological Association Special Publication #22, ed. David D. Gilmore, 35–48. Washington: American Anthropological Association, 1987.
_____. "The Meaning of Paternity and the Virgin Birth Debate." *Man* 21 (1986):494–513.
Gilmore, David D. "Anthropology of the Mediterranean Area." *Annual Review of Anthropology* 11 (1982):175–205.
_____., ed. *Honor and Shame and the Unity of the Mediterranean*. American Anthropological Association Special Publication #22. Washington: American Anthropological Association, 1987.
_____. "Introduction: The Shame of Dishonor." In *Honor and Shame and the Unity of the Mediterranean*, 2–21. American Anthropological Association Special Publication #22. Washington: American Anthropological Association, 1987.
Giovannini, Maureen J. "Female Chastity Codes in the Circum-Mediterranean: Comparative Perspectives." In *Honor and Shame and the Unity of the Mediterranean*, American Anthropological Association Special Publication #22, ed. David D. Gilmore, 61–74. Washington: American Anthropological Association, 1987.
Hall, Edward T. *The Silent Language*. Garden City, N.Y.: Doubleday & Co., 1959.
_____. *The Dance of Life: The Other Dimension of Time*. Garden City, N.Y.: Doubleday & Co., 1983.
Hanson, K. C. "How Honorable! How Shameful! Makarisms and Reproaches in Matthew's Gospel." *Semeia* 68 (1994[96]):83–114.
Hsu, Francis. "Passage to Understanding." In *The Making of Psychological Anthropology*, ed. George D. Spindler, 142–173. Berkeley, Calif.: U. of California Press, 1978.
Malina, Bruce J. *Christian Origins and Cultural Anthropology*. Atlanta: John Knox, 1986.
Malina, Bruce J., and Jerome H. Neyrey. *Calling Jesus Names: The Social Value of Labels in Matthew*. Sonoma, Calif.: Polebridge Press, 1988.

_____. "Conflict in Luke-Acts: Labelling and Deviance Theory." In *The World of Luke-Acts. Models for Interpretation*, ed. Jerome H. Neyrey, 97–122. Peabody, Mass.: Hendrickson, 1991.

_____. "The First-Century Personality: Dyadic, Not Individual." In *The World of Luke-Act: Models for Interpretation*, ed. Jerome H. Neyrey, 67–96. Peabody, Mass.: Hendrickson, 1991.

_____. "Honor and Shame in Luke-Acts: Pivotal Values of the Mediterranean World." In *The World of Luke-Acts. Models for Interpretation*, ed. Jerome H. Neyrey, 25–65. Peabody, Mass.: Hendrickson, 1991.

Moxnes, Halvor. "Honor and Shame." In *The Social Sciences and New Testament Interpretation*, ed. Richard L. Rohrbaugh, 19–41. Peabody, Mass.: Hendrickson, 1996.

Murdock, George Peter. *Theories of Illness: A World Survey*. Pittsburgh: University of Pittsburgh Press, 1980.

Neyrey, Jerome H. *Honor and Shame in the Gospel of Matthew*. Louisville, Ky.: Westminster John Knox, 1999.

Peristiany, J. G., and J. Pitt-Rivers, eds. *Honour and Shame: The Values of Mediterranean Society*. London: Weidenfeld & Nicholson, 1966.

Peristiany, J. G., ed. *Honour and Grace in Anthropology*. Cambridge: Cambridge University Press, 1992.

Pilch, John J. "Lying and Deceit in the Letters to the Seven Churches: Perspectives from Cultural Anthropology." *Biblical Theology Bulletin* 22 (1992):126–135.

_____. "'Beat His Ribs While He Is Young' (Sir 30:12): A Window on the Mediterranean World." *Biblical Theology Bulletin* 25 (1995):65–70.

_____. "Death with Honor: The Mediterranean Style Death of Jesus in Mark." *Biblical Theology Bulletin* 25 (1995):65–70.

Pilch, John J., and Bruce J. Malina, eds. *Handbook of Biblical Social Values*. 2d ed. Peabody, Mass.: Hendrickson, 1998

Pitt-Rivers, Julian. *The Fate of Shechem or the Politics of Sex: Essays in the Anthropology of the Mediterranean*. Cambridge: Cambridge University Press, 1977.

2

The First-Century Personality

The Individual and the Group

Honor and shame were pivotal values for the persons presented in the New Testament and in the Bible as a whole. Among those people, the virtuous man was the strong man who knew how to maintain and perhaps increase his honor rating along with that of his group. And the virtuous woman was the woman devoted to her husband and family, who knew how to safeguard the family's honor and teach her children accordingly. If we were to move from our consideration of these pivotal values to the individuals who embodied them, we would be moving from a discussion of a phase of social interaction to a sort of social psychology, to the self-image and mind-set of the honorable or dishonorable person.

The First-Century Personality

What sort of personality sees life nearly exclusively in terms of honor? For starters, such a person would always see himself or herself through the eyes of others. After all, honor requires a grant of reputation by others. So what others tend to see is all-important. Further, such individuals need others for any sort of meaningful existence, since the image such persons have of themselves has to be indistinguishable from the image held and presented to them by their significant others in the family, tribe, village, city, or ethnic group. In this sense, a meaningful human existence depends on a person's full awareness of what others think and feel about oneself, along with one's living up to that awareness. Literally, this is conscience. The Latin word *conscientia* and the Greek word *syneidesis* stand for "with-knowledge," that is, a knowledge with others, individualized common knowledge, commonly shared meaning, common sense. Conscience then refers to a person's sensitive awareness to one's public ego-image along with the purpose of striving to align one's behavior and self-assessment with that publicly perceived image. A person with conscience is a respectable, reputable, and honorable person. Respectability, in this social context, would be the characteristic of a person who needs other people in order to grasp his or her own identity. Conscience is a sort of internalization of what others say, do, and think about oneself, since these others play the role of witness and judge. Their verdicts supply a person with grants of honor necessary for a meaningful, humane existence.

Thus the honorable person would never expose his or her distinct individuality. One's unique personhood, one's inner self—with its difficulties, weaknesses, confusions, and inabilities to cope, as well as its distinctive, individual realm of hopes and dreams—is simply not of public concern or comment. Rather, persons of such enculturation know how to keep their psychological core hidden and secret. They are persons of careful calculation and discretion, normally disavowing any dependence on others. They are adept at keeping their innermost self concealed with a veil of conventionality and formality, ever alert to anything that might lead to their making an exhibition of themselves, to anything that would not tally with the socially expected and defined forms of behavior that have entitled them and their family to respect. Typically, for example, Paul tells the Corinthians that he rejects the opinions that men might form of him (1 Cor. 4:1–4), yet he seeks the approval of his significant others, the Corinthians in this case, for what he does (1 Cor. 9:1 ff.). Jesus, too, is depicted as a man of honor, "not regarding the face [= honor] of men" (Mark 12:14), yet concerned about "who . . . men say that I am" (Mark 8:27; see also Matt. 11:2–6, 7–14; 16:13–16).

Given this brief description of the first-century personality, what sort of individuals would you expect to find in the pages of the New Testament? Would such persons be like us and feel guilty when they did something wrong? Could they be said to have the kind of conscience we do? Our sort of conscience, as most people use the word, refers to the pain we feel within ourselves over some past specific action that we ourselves, individually and alone, judge to be "bad" because it was "wrong." Would our first-century persons be worried about past specific actions they themselves judged to be wrong? Or would they be worried about actions that they thought other people might say would be dishonoring? These sorts of questions are rather important, since they lead us to some sort of assessment of the group of foreigners who people our New Testament documents.

Consider the Apostle Paul, for example. For many Christians today, Paul is a perfect example of a person much like we conceive ourselves to be, affected by anxiety and guilt, by remorse and concern for atonement and spiritual development. For he must have been introspective, meditative, and habituated to examining his conscience before God. Did he not write, "So I find it to be a law that when I want to do right, evil lies close at hand. For I delight in the law of God, in my inmost self, but I see in my members another law at war with the law of my mind and making me captive to the law of sin which dwells in my members" (Rom. 7:21–23)? But is he pointing to some sort of internalized standard of morality; to some sense of personal guilt; to a self-punitive, self-critical reaction of remorse and anxiety after the transgression of some commandment of God? Certainly St. Augustine (d. 430) and, much later, Martin Luther, thought so. However, the general problem with their interpretation is that Paul believed that the Law was observable and that he himself did not transgress the commandments of God in the Law. As a matter of fact, in a brief autobiographical passage in Philippians 3, Paul himself tell us that "as to righteousness under the law," he considered himself "blameless" (v. 6; read the whole passage). In other words, he believed that during his Pharisaic period of life, he actually observed all that was required of him by the Law. Hence it was not guilt or anxiety relative to the Law that led him to Jesus groups or maintained his conversion to those groups. But how did he know he was blameless? Was it because his conscience did not bother him? Or was it because none of his significant others, none of his publics, accused him of acting shamefully, dishonestly, or disobediently? What sort of self-awareness does Paul reveal in his writings? What sort of self-awareness was typical of first-century Mediterranean man?

In order to generate some understanding of first-century personality, I have chosen two models from cultural anthropology that seem to fit the data in our documents. The first of these models deals with the nonindividualistic, strongly group-oriented, collectivistic self-awareness that seems to have been typical of the first-century people in our New Testament. The second sketches out the conception of the makeup of the individual that seems to have been characteristic of the Semitic subculture of that period and earlier. Taken together, the models should offer some understanding of the dynamics running between the individual and the group as we find them in the New Testament.

Group-Oriented Personality

Have you ever noticed how few people bother to read any first-century Mediterranean writings apart from the New Testament? For the most part, people who do in fact read and study the New Testament do so because they believe that it is the word of God, and that therefore it should be read. Yet if the New Testament lacked the contemporary religious imprint that it bears, how many persons in our culture would find it enticing, alluring, and interesting reading? Would they be moved by reading Plutarch, Josephus, Philo of Alexandria, Epictetus, Musonius Rufus, and other writers of that period? By our standards, first-century Mediterranean writings are generally boring. Perhaps the main reason for this is that the center of concern in those writings is not ours. For whenever we start to discuss some gossip, some person, or some social problem, almost invariably and inevitably our conversation takes on psychological undertones. We adopt a point of view that is psychological. Why do some of your friends take drugs? Why are some people in your school homosexual? Why that senseless suicide? Why is your aunt's or uncle's marriage on the verge of a collapse? Why don't you ever have fun? Why did your friend get invited on a date, but not you? Why do certain persons always get better grades, better jobs, make more friends? Why do certain people always keep their grades and salaries secret? How many of these kinds of questions will you answer without resorting to psychology; to questions of inner motivations that are quite personal; to reasons based on personality, childhood experiences, personality development, interpersonal ability in terms of poise, IQ, emotional control, personal story, highly personal reasons, and the like?

In our culture, we tend to consider a person's psychological makeup, his or her personality development from infancy on, as well as his or her individuality and uniqueness (personal reasons) as perhaps the most important elements in understanding and explaining human behavior, both our own and that of others. Yet if you carefully read the New Testament writings or any other writing from the same period, you will find an almost total absence of such information. One obvious reason for this state of affairs is that the people described in the New Testament, as well as those who described them, were not interested in or concerned about psychological or personality information. Otherwise we should find as much of such information in those writings as we might in a modern biography, novel, or newspaper. Since this kind of information is lacking, you might conclude that the first-century Mediterranean person did not share or comprehend our idea of an "individual" at all. And I believe you would be right.

What do we, in fact, mean by an "individual"? Clifford Geertz has observed that our conception of the individual as ". . . a bounded, unique, more or less integrated motivational and cognitive universe, a dynamic center of awareness, emotion, judgment and action organized into a distinctive whole and set contrastively both against other such wholes and against its social and natural background, is, however incorrigible it may seem to us, a rather peculiar idea within the context of the world's cultures." You might not have thought of yourself in these terms, but take the time to consider this description of an individual. In our culture we are brought up to stand on our own two feet, as distinctive wholes, distinctive individuals, male and female. We are motivated to behave in the "right" way, alone if necessary, regardless of what others might think or say. In our process of identity formation, we are led to believe and act as though we do so singly and alone, responsible only for our own actions because we consider each person a unique sphere of feeling and knowing, of judging and acting. When we relate to other people, we feel that they are as distinct and unique as we ourselves are. In addition to being unique and distinct persons, each of us lives within our unique social and natural environments. This is individualism, and this sort of individualism is rare in the world's cultures today. It was perhaps totally absent from the societies represented in the New Testament.

Instead of individualism, what we find in the first-century Mediterranean world is what might be called collectivism. Persons always considered themselves in terms of the group(s) in which they experienced themselves as inextricably embedded. We might describe such a psychological orientation as "dyadism" (from the Greek word meaning a pair, a twosome), as opposed to "individualism." The dyadic person is essentially a group-embedded and group-oriented person (some call such a person "collectivity-oriented"). Such a group-embedded, collectivistic personality is one who simply needs another continually in order to know who he or she really is. The person I described at the beginning of this chapter (you might read it again) is not an individualistic but a collectivistic personality. Such persons internalize and make their own what others say, do, and think about them because they believe it is necessary for being human to live out the expectations of others. Such persons would conceive of themselves as always interrelated with other persons while occupying a distinct social position both horizontally (with others who share the same status, moving from center to periphery) and vertically (with others who are above and below in social rank). Such persons need to test this interrelatedness, with the focus of attention away from self and on the demands and expectations of others who can grant or withhold recognition. Pivotal values for such persons would be honor and shame, not guilt.

Collectivistic personality is characteristic of individuals who perceive themselves and form their self-image in terms of what others perceive and feed back to them. They feel the need of others for their very psychological existence, since the image they have of themselves must agree with the image formulated and presented by significant others, by members of significant and person-sustaining groups such as family, tribe, village, even city and larger ethnic network. To paraphrase Geertz, our first-century person would perceive himself or herself as a distinctive whole in relation to other such wholes and set within a given social and natural background. Every individual is perceived as embedded in some other, in a sequence of embeddedness, so to say. If our sort of individualism leads us to perceive ourselves as unique because we are set apart from other unique and set-apart beings, then first-century persons would perceive themselves as unique because they were set with other like beings within unique and distinctive groups. If this all sounds a bit abstruse, consider the following situation. When you or almost any other American enter a crowded room, say at a college gathering or a friend's party, more often than not you will feel and imagine that your immediate task is to solve the problem of group presence, the problem of community. How can you move from your inner self out across the no-man's land of group presence and make contact with another separate and unique person? This sort of problem is typical of individualism. For the first-century person, the problem is the opposite. How can one who is permanently embedded, psychologically and socially, in a group of significant others differentiate himself or herself to act as an individual at all? The collectivistic personality is thus a person whose total self-awareness emphatically depends on such group embeddedness.

For the collectivistic personality, interpersonal behavior remains purely impersonal, without some sort of perception that he or she and another person are somehow attached to each other, somehow related to each other. In other words, a basic prerequisite for a truly interpersonal exchange is that I, as a collectivistic personality, and another human being mutually believe that we have some common personal bonds, from shared blood to mutual acquaintances to common ethnic heritage. We have to come to see that somehow we are "brothers and sisters" or "kinsmen." We thus perceive each other as members of the same group, an in-group. Should there be nothing in common between us except our common humanity—even the sort of common humanity expressed in the Stoic brotherhood of males under the fatherhood of Zeus who indwells select individual males—then our interaction would remain impersonal, like an interaction with a tree or a tennis ball or a goldfish. Such impersonal interaction characterizes behavior toward the out-group and its insignificant members.

To get a better feel for the type of personality I am describing, imagine your name to consist of only your family name and your family's place of origin. Your name, then, might be Smith of Chicago. (Note: This is only a device to get you to feel collectivistic personality. In the first century no one bore a family name with place of origin as their name. Most people in the first-century Mediterranean world were in fact geographically immobile.) As Smith of Chicago, you would, of course, be only one particular instance of Smith of Chicago; there would be others. Yet the name "Smith of Chicago" would directly refer to what all you Smiths of Chicago have in common, to what is typical of your unique group. Hence, should I get to meet and know you, Smith of Chicago, I would really get to know a representative of a category, an abstract category known as Smith of Chicago. And this category would consist of enduring, lasting, and fixed qualities; all Smiths of Chicago from time immemorial would presumably have the same qualities you have. I would, naturally, presume that what I see in you is typical of all Smiths of

Chicago, so if I got to know those qualities from you or any other Smith of Chicago, I would get to know all of you—by getting to know one of you. It is the group that is unique and individualistic, not the representative of the group.

Further, because both of us would refer to ourselves and perceive each other in terms of such specific group or category qualities, we would tend to believe and presume that human character as specified in unique and distinct groups and their individual components is fixed and unchanging. Every family, tribe, village, city, and ethnic group would be quite predictable, and so would the individuals who were embedded in and shared the qualities of some family, tribe, village, city, or ethnic group. Consequently, if anything in life is unpredictable, it is not the individual human being. Rather, unpredictability derives from something or someone beyond the control of the predictable and unchanging human beings we might know. So there is no need to look inside the individual human being, either oneself or any other. In other words, it would make no cultural sense at all to ascribe anything to personal and uniquely individual psychological motives or introspectively generated reasons and motivations. Another way to say this is that the collectivistic personality makes sense out of other people by means of "sociological" thinking, by means of reasons typical of the group to which the individual belongs and whose values the individual embodies. By our standards, such "sociological" thinking would be based on extremely poor sampling techniques. We would call such perceptions "stereotypes." Stereotypes are fixed or standard general mental pictures that various group members mutually hold in common and that represent their expectations and attitudes as well as the judgments of other group members.

For example, consider the following statements: "Cretans are always liars, evil beasts, lazy gluttons" (Titus 1:12). "Judeans have no dealings with Samaritans" (John 4:9). "O Jerusalem, Jerusalem, killing the prophets and stoning those who are sent to you" (Matt. 23:37; Luke 13:34). "Certainly you are one of them; for you are a Galilean" (Mark 14:70). "Can anything good come out of Nazareth?" (John 1:46). "Woe to you, Chorazin! woe to you, Bethsaida! . . . and you, Capernaum, will you be exalted to heaven?" (Matt. 11:21–24; Luke 10:13–15). "Is not this the carpenter, the son of Mary and brother of James and Joses and Judas and Simon, and are not his sisters here with us?" (Mark 6:3). Note how such statements derive their understanding of some person on the basis of family, village, or city in which individuals are embedded. The same sort of approach can be found in Paul when he talks of ethnic groups, of "Judeans and Greeks" (some [mis-]translations "Jews and Greeks") (e.g., Rom. 3:2–29; 9:24; 11:14; 1 Cor. 1:22–24; 9:20; 10:32; Gal. 2:13–15); in John's Gospel when the author speaks of the "Judeans" (some [mis-]translations: "Jews"); and in Revelation when the author stereotypes the post-Jesus groups of the cities of Asia Minor to which the seven letters are addressed (Rev. 2–3). During the same time period, Philo of Alexandria duly stereotypes his fellow inhabitants: "But the Egyptian is by nature an evil eyed person, and the citizens [of Alexandria] burst with envy and considered that any good fortune to others was misfortune to themselves" (*Flaccus* 29 LCL). Josephus, in turn, notes how Tiberians have "a passion for war" (Josephus, *Life* 352); Scythians "delight in murdering people and are little better than wild beasts" (Josephus, *Against Apion* 2.69 LCL). Earlier, Cicero observed that the Carthaginians were frauds and liars due to their ports being visited by too many merchants. Then there were the Campanians who are so arrogant due to the fertility and beauty of their land. And the Ligurians were hard and wild because they were just like all other people who struggle to make mountain soil productive (*Agrarian Laws* 2.95).

Thus to get to know one member of the group is to get to know the whole group. While many in our society do in fact make judgments of this sort, a culture that does not go beyond general "sociological" criteria would lack individualism in our sense of the word. And, it seems, all the various societies of the first-century Mediterranean world evidenced such a collectivistic culture.

Consider the characteristic ways of explaining behavior in our documents. Whenever anything significant happens, be it an occasion of joy or a human problem or crisis, the collectivistic personality inevitably ascribes it to standard, "sociological," stereotypical causes (e.g., by citing a maxim or proverb: "For where your treasure is, there will your heart be also" [Matt. 6:21]) or to rather obvious, external, precipitating events (like Mark's "the girl got up and walked; for she was twelve years old" [5:42]; or the notice that Jesus found Peter and Andrew "casting a net into the sea; for they were fishermen" [Matt. 4:18]). At the conclusion of the book, there are exercises in which I will ask you to verify this point by considering a large sampling of "for" or "because" statements in the New Testament. None of these statements, to my knowledge, contains psychological, introspective, uniquely personal sorts of explanations, explanations that would be typically personal in our culture. It would seem that the New Testament (like the Bible in general) simply lacks any uniquely personal, individualistic motives or introspectively generated explanations for human behavior. Such explanations would be quite beside the point for the collectivistic personality. Rather, the individual was symptomatic and representative of some group.

From this viewpoint, responsibility for morality and deviance is not on the individual alone but on the social body, the group in which the individual is embedded. It is because something is amiss in the functioning of the social body that individual deviance crops up. Thus, for example, Paul stigmatizes whole groups, Judeans and Greeks (Rom. 1–3) or Galatians (Gal. 3:1) and sees some socially infecting *hamartia* (later called "original" sin in Latin) behind individual sinful actions. Mourning, the public protestation of the presence of evil, is a group reaction to deviance in its midst, as in 1 Cor. 5:1 ff.; 2 Cor. 12:21; Rev. 18:7–15.

Undoubtedly the moral norms we find in the New Testament have relevance for individual conduct, but in all such moral descriptions and listings, the individual is not the main concern. Such descriptions were written from the viewpoint of the supra-individual, objective horizon of the social body. Examples of such descriptions are the various sin lists (e.g., Mark 7:21–22 and parallels); lists of vices and virtues (e.g., Gal. 5:16–24); and household codes (e.g., Eph. 5:21–6:9; Col. 3:18–4:l; 1 Tim. 2:8–3:15). The main problem is to keep the family, the tribe, the village, and the ethnic group sound, corporately and socially. In the post-Jesus communities, the main problem was to keep the post-Jesus group, the individual church, in harmony and unity, in sound state (e.g., 1 Cor. 12; Rom. 12:3–21). The individual as such, our collectivistic personality, is expendable (e.g., "It is expedient for you that one man should die for the people, and that the whole people should not perish" [John 11:50]; excommunication procedures in 1 Cor. 5:5, 13; Rom. 16:17; and Paul's own willingness to be cut off from Christ for his people, Rom. 9:3). Further, the soundness of the group, like the behavior of the collectivistic personality individually, is heavily determined by its impact on surrounding groups and by the expectations of outsiders. (Read, for example, 1 Thess. 4:12; 1 Cor. 6:6; 10:32–33; 14:23; Rom. 12:17–18; Col. 4:5; 1 Tim. 3:7). Post-Jesus group members have to be at least as good as the outsiders are, and in this sense outsiders set the norm for the group.

Given this emphasis on collectivistic personality and its concomitant honor and shame values, one of the chief implications we can deduce from these facts is that first-century people did not know each other very well in the way we know people, that is, psychologically, individually, intimately, and personally. Again, this is due to the fact that they knew or cared little about psychological development, psychological motivations, and introspective analyses. Jesus himself, as presented in the Gospels, is a good example in this regard. Of the twelve men he chose, we are told that one betrayed him, one denied him, and the rest quibbled a lot and eventually abandoned him in a crisis situation. Paul himself constantly had problems with the allegiance of the various groups he gathered, for example, the Galatians and the Corinthians. All this simply indicates what poor judges of individual character, of individual psychology, people in such cultures are. This is not because they are obtuse or unobservant. Rather, it is because such abilities are culturally unimportant; there are no cultural cues of perception highlighting this feature.

Conditions under which it would be advantageous to know people well as individuals are left out of cultural focus, so to say. For if one had to know other individuals very well, it would mean that people were idiosyncratic, inconstant, moody, devious, changeable, and unpredictable. It would mean, in sum, that people were not sensitive to their honor, to their conscience, to the image other people held of them and their group. So for the people of the New Testament period, if human beings are anything, it is certain that they are not "psychologically unique worlds," at least not to other human beings. For only God knows the human heart (Luke 16:15; Acts 1:24); can see what is secret (Matt. 6:4, 6, 18); can disclose what is in the heart (1 Cor. 14:25); tests our hearts (1 Thess. 2:4); searches the hearts of men (Rom. 8:27); and hardens the heart of whomever he wills (Rom. 9:18). That Jesus is said to have discerned what people had in their hearts is very significant in this regard (e.g., Luke 5:22; 9:47). However, it was culturally assumed that only God knew the individual heart, and yet this is not an expression of despair. It simply means that people do not have to know what is in another's heart because the uniquely personal is culturally defined as not very interesting, and it would have nothing to do with human relations anyway. It is what comes out of the heart that counts, the fruits that reveal the inmost quality of the tree (e.g., Mark 7:21–22; Matt. 7:16–20, and see below). Yet what in fact emerges from the heart is, as we might expect, stereotypical and culturally predictable.

If you were a student of psychology and were to evaluate the people presented in the New Testament, you would probably say that they were rigid and highly controlled personality types, or that they were fearful of others, or that they interacted in standardized and conventional ways almost all the time. You would categorize them as anti-introspective, or not at all psychologically minded. The whole point is that in this aspect of their culture, they were not like we are at all. So to infer psychological states of some person or other on the basis of our documents (e.g., the psychology of Jesus or Paul) would be a highly questionable and obviously anachronistic enterprise. There simply is not enough information in the document for this sort of inference.

In sum, the primary emphasis in the culture we are considering is on collectivistic personality, on the individual as embedded in the group, on behavior as determined by significant others. Groups are unique and distinct. On the other hand, individual behavior was certainly evaluated, even if from a stereotypical point of view. Such evaluation presupposes some set of categories for perceiving and assessing behavior. Now, what set of categories does the New Testament employ to function as a nonintrospective model of the individual human being?

The Makeup of Human Beings:
A Three-Zone Model

Collectivistic personality seems to have been common throughout the various cultures of the first-century Mediterranean world, and not only there. At a rather high level of abstraction, these cultures were quite similar. Yet at a lower level of abstraction, at the level of the subcultures in the area, there were notable differences. Among these differences is the manner of articulating personality perception, that is, the way in which people described the workings of the individual human being. Greek and Roman philosophers and their followers talked of the makeup of humans in terms of body and soul; in terms of intellect, will, and conscience; in terms of virtues and vices that fazed a person's immortal soul or some indwelling deity. Such ideas and terminology are absent from the biblical writings. How then did the largely Semitic biblical authors perceive the stereotyped, nonintrospective makeup of the collectivistic personalities they described and interpreted in their writings?

As I mentioned previously, descriptions of human behavior in the New Testament depict persons and events concretely, from the outside, so to say. They avoid introspection as uninteresting and evaluate behavior on the basis of externally perceptible activity and in terms of the social functions of such activity. Now, what is the individual framework of typically human behavior, the makeup of the individual in himself or herself? Again, an individual is perceived as a socially embedded and interacting whole, a living being reacting to persons and things on the outside. The main framework of perimeters or boundaries of this interaction between the individual and the world outside the individual is described metaphorically, for the most part, using parts of the human organic whole as metaphors. Thus, most obviously, human beings are endowed with a heart for thinking, along with eyes that fill the heart with data; a mouth for speaking, along with ears that collect the speech of others; and hands and feet for acting. More abstractly, human beings consist of three mutually interpenetrating yet distinguishable zones of interacting with persons and things in the human environment: the zone of emotion-fused thought, the zone of self-expressive speech, and the zone of purposeful action.

To put it in other words, human beings are perceived as fitting into their rightful place in their environments, physical and social, and acting in a way that is typically human by means of their inmost reactions (eyes-heart) as expressed in language (mouth-ears) and/or outwardly realized in activity (hands-feet). These three zones comprise the nonintrospective makeup of human beings and are used to describe human behavior throughout the Bible, from Genesis to Revelation. They are typical, in the first century, of the Semitic subculture of the Mediterranean world and perhaps underlay the philosophical accretions of the Greek and Roman worlds as well. Be that as it may, our concern here is with the biblical writings, and it is to them that we turn to verify this three-zone model. This model was invented and discovered by Bernard de Géradon some time ago, and in what follows, many of his observations will be presented.

To begin with, it might be useful to recall that Semitic descriptive approaches tend to be highly synthetic rather than analytic—more like flood-lights than spotlights. A floodlight covers a whole area at one time, and movement of the light might intensify exposure in a given part of the area, yet the whole area always remains in view. Similarly, specific words covering one of the three zones would stand for the whole zone, while always keeping the total functioning human being in view. Here is a representative list of such words and the zones to which they refer:

1. *Zone of emotion-fused thought:* eyes, heart, eyelid, pupil, and the activities of these organs: to see, know, understand, think, remember, choose, feel, consider, look at. The following representative nouns and adjectives pertain to this zone as well: thought, intelligence, mind, wisdom, folly, intention, plan, will, affection, love, hate, sight, regard, blindness, look; intelligent, loving, wise, foolish, hateful, joyous, sad, and the like.

   In our culture, this zone would cover the areas we refer to as intellect, will, judgment, conscience, personality thrust, core personality, affection, and so forth.

2. *Zone of self-expressive speech:* mouth, ears, tongue, lips, throat, teeth, jaws, and the activities of these organs: to speak, hear, say, call, cry, question, sing, recount, tell, instruct, praise, listen to, blame, curse, swear, disobey, turn a deaf ear to. The following nouns and adjectives pertain to this zone as well: speech, voice, call, cry, clamor, song, sound, hearing; eloquent, dumb, talkative, silent, attentive, distracted, and the like.

   In our culture, this zone would cover the area we refer to as self-revelation through speech: communication with others, and the human person as listener who dialogues with others in a form of mutual self-unveiling, and so on.

3. *Zone of purposeful action:* hands, feet, arms, fingers, legs, and the activities of these organs: to do, act, accomplish, execute, intervene, touch, come, go, march, walk, stand, sit, along with specific activities such as to steal, kidnap, commit adultery, build, and the like. The following representative nouns and adjectives pertain to this zone: action, gesture, work, activity, behavior, step, walking, way, course, and any specific activity; active, capable, quick, slow, and so forth.

   In our culture, this zone would cover the area of outward human behavior: all external activity, and human actions on the world of persons and things.

It seems almost impossible for us to tell whether persons using this model were explicitly aware of it. It seems more likely that the model served as an implicit pattern, an unarticulated set of significant areas working much like the grammar of a native speaker who knows no explicit, articulated grammar. Yet whenever writers (or speakers in the document) describe human activity, they inevitably have recourse to the three zones, at times emphasizing only one or two of them, with the other(s) always in view in the background.

The idea is that all human activities, states, and behaviors can be and are in fact chunked in terms of these three zones. Now, when all three zones are explicitly mentioned, then the speaker or writer is alluding to a total and complete human experience. For example, it is to such a total and complete experience that "John" alludes when he writes, "That which was from the beginning, which we have *heard*, which we have *seen* with our *eyes*, which we have *looked* upon and *touched* with our *hands*, concerning the word of life . . . that which we have *seen* and *heard* we *proclaim* also to you, so that you may have fellowship" (1 John 1:1–3 [emphasis added here and in following passages in this chapter]). Similarly, the law of limited retribution in Exodus 21:24, restated in Deuteronomy 19:21, and cited in part in Matthew 5:38, basically refers to limiting retribution within the whole range of human interactions covered by each zone: "*eye* for *eye*, *tooth* for *tooth*, *hand* for *hand*, *foot* for *foot*." The statement looks to righting restrictions put on individual social rights. If this legal formula derives from and expresses the three zones that make up a human being, it would obviously not be meant literally and concretely (except by persons who do not understand the culture or by persons in the culture who are at the concrete stage of cognitive development, i.e., children and adults who are retarded by nature or by choice or experience).

A few more examples: "There are six things which the LORD hates, seven which are an abomination to him: haughty *eyes*, a lying *tongue*, and *hands* that shed innocent blood, a *heart* that devises wicked plans, *feet* that make haste to run to evil, a false *witness* who breathes out lies, and a man who sows discord among brothers" (Prov. 6:16–19). In this seven-patterned proverb (patterned much like the seven days of creation in Genesis 1), we have two complete descriptions of the totally wicked person in terms of three zones, followed by the worst type of person in that culture, one who breaks up bonds of loyalty in a family of blood. Or again, note how the prophet Elisha symbols his total living self as he lies on the child he seeks to resuscitate: "his *mouth* upon his mouth, his *eyes* upon his eyes, and his *hands* upon his hands" (2 Kings 4:34). Or consider the description of the linen-clothed man in Daniel in what is obviously meant to be a total description: "His face like the appearance of lightning, his *eyes* like flaming torches, his *arms* and *legs* like the gleam of burnished bronze, and the sound of his *words* like the noise of a multitude" (Dan. 10:6). This is a statement of the total and complete function of the person described. The author of Revelation, perhaps taking his cue from Daniel, describes his celestial vision of the Son of man as follows: "His *eyes* were like a flame of fire, his *feet* were like burnished bronze, refined as in a furnace, and his *voice* was like the sound of many waters; in his right *hand* he held seven stars, from his *mouth* issued a sharp two-edged sword, and his *face* was like the sun shining in full strength" (Rev. 1:14–16). Again, we have a description of function in terms of three zones, a portrayal of how this being relates to those he comes into contact with—a functional picture. Note also how the final section of the Sermon on the Mount (Matt. 6:19–7:27), dealing with the righteousness of disciples, covers the three zones: the first block of material deals with the eyes-heart (Matt. 6:19–7:6), the second with mouth-ears (Matt. 7:7–11), and the last, exhorting section with hands-feet (Matt. 7:13–27).

As previously mentioned, at times only two of the zones are mentioned, leaving the third in the background. Thus, for example: "You have heard that it was said, 'You shall not *commit adultery* [hands-feet].' But I say to you that every one who *looks* at a woman lustfully has already committed adultery with her in his *heart* [eyes-heart]. If your right eye causes you to sin, pluck it out and throw it away; it is better that you lose one of your members than that your whole body be thrown into hell [eyes-heart]. And if your right hand causes you to sin, cut it off and throw it away; it is better that you lose one of your members than that your whole body go into hell [hands-feet]" (Matt. 5:27–30). Notice the chiastic pattern in this passage (a pattern in the form of the Greek letter *X*, thus: a, b, b', a'). Just as one cannot commit adultery with one's physical and literal hands and feet or with one's physical and literal heart, so too the right eye that needs to be plucked out and the right hand that needs to be cut off are not physical and literal eyes and hands. Rather, the parable urges that one consider the zones or spheres of activity that prove to be an obstacle to proper interpersonal behavior and "cut out" such activities. In this passage, only two of the zones are mentioned, thus emphasizing the relationship between the head and the hands and feet, between one's interior, innermost self and one's outward activity. Mark 7:14–23 is much like this passage from Matthew. The basic argument about uncleanness and the heart is about the relationship between one's interior, innermost self and outward activity: activity flows from the heart, and it is the heart that needs realigning. The same holds for speech: "For out of the abundance of the *heart* the *mouth* speaks" (Matt. 12:34, and see Matt. 13:13–17).

The Makeup of Human Beings and God

A tradition in the late Israelite writing, *Pirqe Aboth* 2:1, exhorts, "Know what is above you: an all-seeing *eye*, an all-hearing *ear* and a book in which all your *actions* are recorded." The eye, ear, and recording of actions obviously pertain to God. Since statements about God, like statements in the physical sciences, derive from analogies based on human behavior, it follows that biblical descriptions of how God functions will take the shape of analogies drawn from perceptions of how human beings function.

Consider idols. Idols, of course, have "*mouths*, but they speak not, they have *eyes*, but they see not, they have *ears*, but they hear not" (Ps. 135:16–17); they "cannot either *see* or *hear* or *walk*" (Rev. 9:20). Now, what about God? "He who planted the *ear*, does he not *hear?* He who formed the *eye*, does he not *see?* He who *chastens* peoples, does he not *chastise?*" (Ps. 94:9–10). Throughout the Bible, we read repeatedly about how God "is wise in *heart* and mighty in *strength*" (Job. 9:4); the prophets continually insist that "the *mouth* of the Lord has spoken"; and the story tellers of Israel never tire of describing what God has done by "thy mighty *hand*, and . . . thy outstretched *arm*" (1 Kings 8:42). Obviously none of this means that for our authors, God has physical and concrete eyes and ears or hands and feet. Like the zones themselves when applied to humans, the physical and concrete bodily organs stand symbolically for a sphere and style of human ability and interaction. And when these zones are applied to describe God, the difference between God and human persons is notably underscored. Everything about God is simply beyond human beings, including God's concern for his own. As Paul puts it in a hymn he cites: "What no *eye* has seen, nor *ear* heard, nor the *heart* of man conceived, what God has *prepared* for those who love him" (1 Cor. 2:9).

The specific way in which the difference between God and humankind is highlighted is by the fact that in God's behavior, the three zones work in harmony. What God conceives in His heart and speaks with His mouth is good and effectively takes place. People are not consistently effective, nor do they evidence harmony among the three zones. Thus relative to God we find "For he *spoke*, and it *came to be*" (Ps. 33:9); "I, the LORD, have *spoken*, and I will *do* it" (Ezek. 36:36)—no gap between speech and action; "Has he *said*, and will he not *do* it? Or has he *spoken*, and will he not *fulfil* it?" (Num. 3:19). Another major difference between God and humankind is that God alone knows the human heart: "Man *looks* on the outward *appearance*, but the LORD *looks* on the *heart*" (1 Sam. 16:7; and the passages cited above relative to collectivistic personality). And of course, God alone makes and acts on a scale that is incomparable. A perusal of Genesis 1–2:4 reveals God, six times, speaking, making, and seeing—the three zones. For example, "God *said*, 'Let there be light'; and there *was* light. And God *saw* that the light was good . . . God *said*, 'Let there be lights' . . . God *made* the two great lights, . . . And God *saw* that it was good" (Gen. 1:3–4, 14–18). Notice the harmony between what God says, does, and judges or thinks; and notice how effective this harmony of the interrelated zones is. At the close of this passage (Gen. 1:26), the earthling is described as the image and likeness of God, somewhat like God, yet somewhat unlike God. How? Why? Again, consider the three zones. The earthling, like God, has a heart that plans, thinks, judges, chooses; speech that expresses what is in the heart; and activity that realizes what the heart has devised and what speech has expressed. Yet the earthling is unlike God, imperfect, since what a human being plans often never takes effect, what a human being says often does not agree with what is in the heart, and what a human being does often turns out to be ineffective, incomplete. In sum, human beings experience discord among the three zones, something typically human. Yet, like God, human beings too function in terms of the three zones.

If you think this description is exaggerated, consider Ben Sirach's retelling of Israel's past:

> He gave them authority over everything on earth. He clothed them with *strength* like his own, and made them in his own image. He filled all living things with dread of man, making him master over beasts and birds. He shaped for them a *mouth* and *tongue*, *eyes* and *ears*, and gave them a *heart* to think with. He filled them with knowledge and understanding and revealed to them good and evil. He put his own light in their heart to show them the magnificence of his *works*. He set knowledge before them, he endowed them with the law of life. He established an eternal covenant with them and revealed his judgments to them. Their *eyes* saw his glorious *majesty* and their *ears* heard the glory of his *voice*. He said to them, 'Beware of all wrongdoing'; he gave each a commandment concerning his neighbor. Their ways are always under his *eye*, they cannot be hidden from his *sight*. Over each people he has set a governor, but Israel is the Lord's own portion. . . . All their *works* are as the sun to him, and his *eyes* rest constantly on their *ways*. (Sir. 17:2–19)

In the New Testament, moreover, we find an interesting application of this three-zone model to God. Without doubt, the motive behind this new application was the experience of Jesus and the question of Jesus' relationship to God. Jesus referred to God as "Father" and "my Father," that is, Patron. There are many passages telling us what the Father does, and in these passages the Father functions like God in terms of three zones. However, there are specific passages that mark off the Father relative to Jesus as Son, and in these passages the Father functions in terms of the eyes-heart zone: He is the Father of lights (James 1:17; 1 John 1:5) who is invisible (1 Tim. 1:17) and inaccessible (1 Tim. 6:16). No one has *seen* the Father (John 6:46). Yet the Father "*sees* in secret" (Matt. 6:18), *knows* our *hearts* (Luke 16:15), *loves* the world (John 3:16), *judges* each one impartially according to his *deeds* (1 Pet. 1:17), and the like. "Of that day or that hour no one *knows*, not even the angels in heaven, nor the Son, but only the Father" (Mark 13:32). Relative to God, Jesus "is my *beloved* Son, with whom I am well pleased" (Matt. 3:17; 17:5).

Further, relative to God, Jesus as Son is revealer of the Father: "All things have been delivered to me by my Father; no one *knows* a son except a father, and no one *knows* a father except a son" (Matt. 11:27). This revelation of the Father is described in terms of the mouth-ears function. After all, Jesus is the *word* of God (John 1:1 ff.); "in these last days he has *spoken* to us by a Son" (Heb. 1:2). "Everyone who is of the truth hears my *voice*" (John 18:37). What the Father wants of the house of Israel is that it heed Jesus, "*listen* to him" (Matt. 17:5). As resurrected Lord, Jesus' command is that his disciples *teach* others to *observe* "all that I have *commanded* you" (Matt. 28:20), in sum, a word that is to be realized. However, note that as a human being, Jesus manifested three zones like every other human being. The Gospels present "all that Jesus began to *do* and *teach*" (Acts 1:1) and often reveal dimensions of his heart ("I am gentle and lowly of *heart*" [Matt. 11:29]). Thus in terms of the three zones, Jesus is truly human; yet in relation to the Father, he is the Son who reveals the Father, the mouth-ears of God.

Finally, the hands-feet zone applied to God invariably alludes to the Spirit of God. The word "spirit" literally means wind, the main observable energy source of the ancient world apart from human and animal power. The wind runs a range from a cool refreshing breeze to a destructive hurricane or tornado. Wind is power, and the holy wind ("holy Spirit") always connotes power, activity, doing, effectiveness. Many of the prophets of the Bible assert that "the *hand* of the LORD" was upon them (1 Kings 18:46 = Elijah; 2 Kings 3:15 = Elisha; Isa. 8:11; Ezek. 3:22). The same holds for the inaugurating New Testament prophet, John the Baptist: "For the hand of the Lord was with him" (Luke 1:66). Jesus claims to do good for others by the *finger* of God: "But if it is by the *finger* of God that I cast out demons, then the kingdom of God has come upon you" (Luke 11:20). Thanks to God's Spirit, "many signs and wonders were done among the people by the *hands* of the apostles" (Acts 5:12). On Pentecost day, this same Spirit appears in the form of "tongues as of fire," since the effect of his enabling activity was speech (Acts 2:1–4). In first-century physics, wind, water, and fire have the properties of liquids in contemporary perception. So, like water, wind and fire can be "poured out" (the Latin root word translated "infuse," means "to pour out over," while the Latin root word translated "inspire," means "to blow out over"). Hence the Spirit of God can be poured out on all people (Acts 2:17), and water can symbolize the outpouring of the Spirit in baptism. This sort of "poured-out-over" Spirit can subsequently permeate the hearts and mouths of human beings, that is, influence all three zones, not only a person's hands and feet. So the persecuted Jesus followers can "say whatever is given you in that hour, for it is not you who speak, but the Holy Spirit" (Mark 13:11). And the charisms effected by the Spirit in 1 Corinthians 12 are all mouth-ears and hands-feet charisms; beyond them lies "love," which is the eyes-heart quality of group attachment (1 Cor. 13).

In sum, it would seem that the distinctive post-Jesus group conception of God in terms of the Trinity has its roots in the three-zone model of the human being typical of the culture we are considering. It is a sort of replication—the application of the same pattern to another area—of the model of what constitutes the human being applied to experience of God, undoubtedly due to the experience of Jesus. Further, the conceptions of God in the Bible in general are likewise rooted in the three-zone model of humankind's makeup.

Summary

According to the perceptions of the group of foreigners we are studying in our New Testament documents, it would seem that a meaningful human existence depends on people's full awareness of what others think and feel about them, and their living up to that awareness. Conscience is sensitivity to what others think about and expect of a person; it is another word for shame in the positive sense (just like mind is another word for heart). As a result, the person in question does not think of himself or herself as an individual who acts alone regardless of what others think and say. Rather, the person is ever aware of the expectations of others, especially significant others, and strives to match those expectations. This is the group-embedded, group-oriented, collectivistic personality, one who needs another simply to know who he or she is.

Since collectivistic personality derives its information from outside of the self and, in turn, serves as a source of outside information for others, anything unique that goes on inside of a person is filtered out of attention. Individual psychology, individual uniqueness, and individual self-consciousness are simply dismissed as uninteresting and unimportant. Instead, all motivations, motives, and attitudes derive from culturally shared stereotypes, from generalities perceived to inhere in certain groups, ranging from one's family to one's village or city to one's nation. These stereotypes, too, derive not from psychological considerations of an individualistic type but from obvious and apparent group traits and behavior. People spend much of their concern on their honor rating within significant groups and in assessing the honor rating of their group relative to others.

Just as society consists of a number of interpenetrating yet distinct groups comprised of interpenetrating yet distinct individuals, so too the individual is perceived to consist of interpenetrating yet distinct zones of activity. The existence and function of these zones is verified and validated on the basis of outside, external, concrete observations chunked in terms of three areas: eyes-heart, mouth-ears, and hands-feet. In more abstract terms, eyes-heart is the zone of emotion-fused thought; mouth-ears is the zone of self-expressive speech; and hands-feet is the zone of purposeful activity. Just as individuals act in terms of these three zones, so do groups.

This cultural model of human makeup is applied analogically to God. God, too, gets described in terms of these three zones. In the New Testament, due to the central significance of the experience of Jesus, the three zones of the God-model are further refined in terms of specific activity ascribed to the Father, the Son, and the Spirit.

The following listing offers a summary set of contrasts between individualistic U.S. persons (not all are such) and traditional, group-embedded, dyadic Mediterraneans. The purpose of the list is to provide a general orientation, so that considerate readers of the New Testament might have at hand a comparative tool for access to the contexts in which both the readers and those they read about might be situated.

Table 2: Contrasting
U.S. Persons with Ancient Mediterraneans

Mediterranean Preferences	U.S. Preferences
General Attitudes	
—People put high value on conformity.	—People put high value on independence.
—Authoritarian attitudes are the social norm.	—Authoritarian attitudes are a matter of personality.
—Superiors make decisions autocratically and paternalistically.	—Managers (and parents) make decisions after consulting with subordinates.
—Subordinates are more satisfied with superiors who give orders and directions and maintain their social distance.	—Subordinates are more satisfied with superiors who allow for participation in decision making and play down social distance.
—Subordinates prefer superiors who make decisions either autocratic-paternalistically, or in majority-rule fashion.	—Subordinates prefer superiors who make decisions in a consultative and give-and-take style.
—Subordinates (employees) fear to disagree with superiors and are reluctant to trust each other.	—Subordinates (employees) are less afraid to disagree with superiors and show more cooperativeness.
Attitudes toward Status Differences	
—High-status people are of a different kind than low-status people.	—High-status and low-status persons are all "people like me."

Mediterranean Preferences	U.S. Preferences
—A few should be independent, most dependent.	—All should be interdependent.
—The basic fact of power precedes questions of morality; the legitimacy of power is ascribed, like status itself.	—The use of power must be legitimated and subject to norms of good and evil.
—Power-wielders are entitled to privileges and must look as mighty as possible.	—All persons have equal rights; the powerful should downplay their might and not look the part.
—Societal upheaval is always due to some "underdog," who must be punished by force and shame.	—Societal upheaval is always due to some systemic feature. The system needs fine-tuning, while deviants require rehabilitation.
—To change the social situation, dethrone those in power.	—To change the social situation, redistribute power.
—There is always latent conflict between the powerful and the powerless.	—There is always latent harmony between the powerful and the powerless.
—Since low faith in outgroup persons is the norm, the powerless will never unite and/or cooperate.	—The powerless can unite and cooperate on the basis of solidarity.

Group Orientation vs. Individualism

—People born into extended families that protect them in exchange for loyalty, commitment, in-group solidarity.	—Everyone is supposed to take care of himself or herself and his/her immediate family.
—The individual is emotionally dependent on organizations and institutions, with identity based in the social system.	—The individual is independent of organizations and institutions, with identity based in the individual.
—Private life is invaded by in-group, kin group, and organizations to which one belongs; opinions are predetermined; individual conformity and group acceptance are foremost; group membership is ideal.	—Individuals have a right to a private life and to their own opinions; individual initiative and achievement are foremost, with leadership as ideal.
—Social relations predetermined in terms of in-groups, with need for prestige within the in-groups.	—People are thought about in general terms, with need to make specific friendships.

Mediterranean Preferences	U.S. Preferences
—Value standards differ greatly for in-group and out-group members; particularism is the norm.	—Value standards are to apply to all human beings; universalism is the goal.

Ideological/Religious Outlooks

—Religion is part and parcel of the political system and the family system.	—Religion is separate from the political system and family system.
—Activist religion with emphasis on doing symbolically significant things.	—Pragmatic or introvert, meditative religions.
—Collectivist conversions.	—Individual conversions.
—Worship lays stress on group identity and shared group history.	—Worship lays stress on the world of the independent actor.
—Ideological, theory-oriented thinking is popular.	—Pragmatic, empirically oriented thinking is popular.
—Activities more structured, with more explicit (written) rules and with a larger number of specialists involved in details, seeking organizational uniformity.	—Activities are less structured, with fewer explicit (written) rules, with more generalists or amateurs. Specialists are more involved with strategy, with pluriform organizations.
—Acquiescence in the possession of absolute truth.	—Ongoing search for relative truth.
—Belief in inequality of sexes.	—Belief in equality of the sexes.
—Appeal of "tough" religious currents, philosophies, and ideologies.	—Appeal of "tender" religious currents, philosophies, and ideologies.
—Sympathy for the successful achiever, heroes who endure pain, hardship, suffering.	—Sympathy for the unfortunate, heroes who do good for the sake of other, less fortunate persons.

On the Gender Division of Labor

—Machismo (showy masculinity) is the ideal.	—Gender equality of opportunity and reward is the ideal.
—Gender roles in society are to be clearly differentiated.	—Gender roles in society should be fluid.
—Males must behave assertively, and females must always be caring.	—Males need not be assertive but can also take caring roles; females too can be assertive.
—Males should dominate in all social settings.	—Differences in gender roles should not mean differences in power.

These comparative lists have been culled from:

Hofstede, Geert. *Culture's Consequences: International Differences in Work-Related Values.* Cross-Cultural Research and Methodology Series 5. Beverly Hills, Calif.: Sage, 1984.

Malina, Bruce J. "Dealing with Biblical (Mediterranean) Characters: A Guide for U.S. Consumers." *Biblical Theology Bulletin* 19 (1989):127–141.

———. "Mary—Woman of the Mediterranean: Mother and Son." *Biblical Theology Bulletin* 20 (1990):54–64.

———. "Is There a Circum-Mediterranean Person? Looking for Stereotypes." *Biblical Theology Bulletin* 22 (1992):66–87.

References and Suggested Readings

De Géradon, Bernard. "L'homme a l'image de Dieu." *Nouvelle Révue Théologique* 80 (1958):683–695.

Geertz, Clifford. "'From the Native's Point of View': On the Nature of Anthropological Understanding." In *Meaning and Anthropology*, ed. Keith H. Basso and Henry A. Selby, 221–237. Albuquerque: University of New Mexico Press, 1976.

Hanson, K. C. "Sin, Purification, and Group Process." In *Problems in Biblical Theology: Essays in Honor of Rolf Knierim*, ed. H. T. C. Sun, *et al.*, 167–91. Grand Rapids: Wm. B. Eerdmans Publishing Co., 1997.

Hui, C. Harry, and Harry C. Triandis. "Individualism-Collectivism: A Study of Cross-Cultural Researchers." *Journal of Cross-Cultural Psychology* 17 (1986):225–248.

Malina, Bruce J., "Dealing with Biblical (Mediterranean) Characters: A Guide for U.S. Consumers." *Biblical Theology Bulletin* 19 (1989):127–141.

———. "Mother and Son." *Biblical Theology Bulletin* 20 (1990):54–64

———. "Is There a Circum-Mediterranean Person? Looking for Stereotypes." *Biblical Theology Bulletin* 22 (1992):66–87.

———. "Power, Pain, and Personhood: Asceticism in the Ancient Mediterranean World." In *Asceticism*, ed. Vincent L. Wimbush and Richard Valantasis, 162–77. New York: Oxford University Press, 1995.

———. "The Mediterranean Self: A Social Psychological Model." In *The Social World of Jesus and the Gospels*, 67–96. London: Routledge & Kegan Paul, 1996.

Malina, Bruce J., and Jerome H. Neyrey. *Portraits of Paul: An Archaeology of Ancient Personality*. Louisville, Ky.: Westminster John Knox, 1996.

Pierce, Claude Anthony. *Conscience in the New Testament: A Study of Syneidesis in the New Testament.* Studies in Biblical Theology 15. London: SCM Press, 1955.

Pilch, John J. "Healing in Mark: A Social Science Analysis." *Biblical Theology Bulletin* 15 (1985):142–150.

———. "The Health Care System in Matthew: A Social Science Analysis." *Biblical Theology Bulletin* 16 (1986):102–106.

———. "Sickness and Healing in Luke-Acts." In *The Social World of Luke-Acts: Models for Interpretation*, ed. Jerome H. Neyrey, 181–210. Peabody, Mass.: Hendrickson, 1991.

———. *Healing in the New Testament: Insights from Medical and Mediterranean Anthropology*. Minneapolis: Fortress Press, 2000.

Prochaska, James O., with John C. Norcross. *Systems of Psychotherapy: A Transtheoretical Analysis*. 3d ed. Pacific Grove, Calif.: Brooks/Cole, 1994.

Saunders, George R. "Men and Women in Southern Europe: A Review of Some Aspects of Cultural Complexity." *Journal of Psychological Anthropology* 4 (1981): 413–434.

Selby, Henry A. *Zapotec Deviance: The Convergence of Folk and Modern Sociology.* Austin: University of Texas Press, 1974.

Sharabi, Hisham, with Mukhtar Ani. "Impact of Class and Culture on Social Behavior: The Feudal Bourgeois Family in Arab Society." In *Psychological Dimensions of Near Eastern Studies,* ed. L. Carl Brown and Norman Itzkowitz, 240–256. Princeton, N.J.: Darwin Press, 1977.

Triandis, Harry C. "Cross-Cultural Studies in Individualism and Collectivism." In *Nebraska Symposium on Motivation 1989,* ed. R. A. Diensbier and J. J. Berman, 41–133. Lincoln: University of Nebraska Press, 1990.

Triandis, Harry C., et al. "An Etic-Emic Analysis of Individualism and Collectivism." *Journal of Cross-Cultural Psychology* 24 (1993):366–383.

3

The Perception of Limited Good

Maintaining One's Social Status

The group of foreigners on whom we eavesdrop as we read the New Testament writings comes from the first-century Mediterranean world. Now, another significant feature of this first-century Mediterranean world is that it is a nearly perfect example of what anthropologists call classic peasant society: a set of villages socially bound up with administrative preindustrial cities. To understand our foreigners and their concern with honor and shame, it is important to formulate some adequate model of peasant society and the types of perceptions such a society generates. Right from the beginning it is important to note that the term "peasant" in the phrase "peasant society" refers to persons, regardless of their occupation, who have been enculturated in and continue to be members of a peasant society. The "peasant" mentality of peasant society members is typical of beggar and king, of smallholder and large landowner, of prophet and scribe. This "peasant" mentality is a societal characteristic, not a status or occupational feature.

Ruralized Society

Preindustrial cities are invariably found in ruralized societies. What I mean by ruralized society is that great landowners set the agenda for the empire on the basis of their interests, values, and concerns. This point should be clearer from the following considerations. It is a truism among urban historians that the United States at present is an *urbanized* society. Urban areas contain most of the national population, and urban agendas determine national policies. Urban concerns dominate the goals, values, and behaviors of the five percent of the population that is engaged in agricultural production. Our urbanized society is quickly developing into one with a global outreach. Before it became urbanized, the United States became an urban society over the period marked by the rise of industrialization to the end of the Second World War. An *urban* society, in this perspective, is one in which a significant proportion of the population lives and works in urban centers, following an agenda quite different from rural society yet in somewhat

81

tandem rhythms. In urban societies, urban agendas compete with rural ones in determining national policies. Urban and rural agendas foster conflicting goals, values, and behaviors. Before the waves of immigration at the end of the nineteenth century and the first quarter of the twentieth, the United States was essentially a *rural* society, with rural agendas determining national policies and rural concerns dominating the goals, values, and behaviors of the ninety-five percent of the population living on the land and the five percent living permanently in cities. However, when a handful (about two percent of the population) of elite city inhabitants are the overwhelming owners of the land in an empire, when these great landowners set the agenda for the empire on the basis of their interests, values, and concerns, the society is best characterized as *ruralized*. Now, it is ruralized societies that support peasant ways of thinking and being.

Kinship

As is well known, such ruralized societies had two focal social institutions, realized in the spatial and architectural arrangements called the house and the city. The first, basic institution was kinship; the second was politics. Kinship is the symboling of biological processes of human reproduction and growth in terms of abiding relations, roles, statuses, and the like. Kinship is about naturing and nurturing human beings interpreted as family members (and "neighbors" in nonmobile societies). In ruralized societies, the kinship group was the economic and religious unit as well: the ancient Mediterraneans knew domestic economy and domestic religion (but at the family level, no economy or religion separate from kinship). For example, domestic religion used the roles, values, and goals of the household in the articulation and expression of religion: religious functionaries of domestic religion were household personages (notably fathers and, inside the household, mothers, as well as oldest sons and ancestors); focus was on the deity(ies) as source of solidarity, mutual commitment, and belonging mediated through ancestors, who were expected to provide well-being, health, and prosperity for the kin group and its patriarchs to the benefit of family members. The house had its altars and sacred rites (focused on the family meal and the hearth as symbols of life) with father (patriarch) and mother (first in charge at home) officiating. Deities were tribal and/or household ones (e.g. lares, penates, God of Abraham, Isaac, Jacob, etc.) as well as ancestors who saw to the well-being, prosperity, and fertility of the family members. There was much concern about inheritance and the legitimacy of heirs. Domestic religion seeks meaning through belonging: an ultimately meaningful existence derives from belonging, for example, to a chosen, select, holy people. In well-ordered societies, it is belonging within the proper ranking of one's well-ordered society (often called hierarchy). In societies in some disarray, it is belonging to a proper kin and/or fictive kin group. In the domestic economy kinship concerns for naturing and nurturing are replicated in the production and sustenance of new life in agricultural pursuits, a family affair for nonelites. The in-group/out-group pattern marking kinship boundaries serves as a marker between families as well as between the kin group's political unit and the rest of the world.

Politics

The second, equally focal, institution in the ancient Mediterranean world was politics—the symboling of social relations in terms of vertical roles, statuses, and interactions. Politics was about effective collective action, the application of force to attain collective goals. The roles, statuses, entitlements, and obligations of the political system were available to properly pedigreed persons from only the "best" families and were hence tied up with the kinship system. The political unit was likewise an economic and religious one: the ancient Mediterranean knew political economy and political religion (at the political level, there was no economy or religion separate from politics). Political concerns for effective collective action on behalf of the in-group were replicated in the application of force on out-groups, largely in the interest of fundamental domestic economic concerns: acquisition of more land, labor, animals, and the like. Political religion, in turn, employed the roles, values, and goals of politics in the articulation and expression of religion: religious functionaries were political personages; focus was on the deity(ies) as source of power and might, expected to provide order, well-being, and prosperity for the body politic and its power wielders (elites) to the benefit of subjects. In monarchic city-territories of the eastern Mediterranean, temples were political buildings and temple sacrifices were for the public good; the deity of the temple had a staff similar to the one a monarch had in the palace (major domo = high priest; officials of various ranks and grades = priests, levites, temple slaves, and the like). "Democratic" cities controlled by local elites altered monarchic temples into democratic ones, now owned and run by city councils or noble council members, with sacrifice offered according to the wishes of the sacrificing entity.

City and Country

The great landowners shaped the agenda of daily life for society at large. These great landowners, the "best" people" or "aristocrats," generally had two places of residence. One was a house in the countryside, on the land that provided this elite person with power and wealth. The other was a house built as part of a cluster of such houses of other land-owning elites in a central (or nodal) place, the city. Just as smallholders lived in houses clustered together (usually for support and protection) in towns and villages, so too lived the large holders. Their housing clusters, however, formed the center of what the ancients called a *polis* (Greek), *urbs* and *civitas* (Latin), or *ir* (Hebrew).

The ancient city, in fact, was a bounded, centralized set of selective kinship relationships concerned with effective collective action and expressed spatially in terms of architecture and the arrangement of places. The centralized set of social relationships among elites took on spatial dimension by means of territoriality. That is, these elites claimed dominance of their central place and its surround. This is simply one dimension of the effective collective action of a political institution. Large numbers of people were required to support the elites and their concerns both in the country and in the city. Resident city support consisted of retainers that constituted the non-elite, central-place population.

In other words, the first-century Mediterranean *civitas* or *polis* was really a large, ruralized central place in which properly pedigreed "farmers/ranchers" displayed and employed their unbelievable wealth in competitions for honor among each other. Large holders thus found it in their interest to live near other large holders in central places that likewise provided them with organized force (an army) to protect their interests from the vast masses of other persons. The elite united to promote and defend their collective honor in face of the out-group in annual rites of war, which if carried off successfully, brought them more land and/or the produce of that land. They equally participated in the continual, if seasonal, activity of extortion called taxation. Thus an honor rating rooted in kinship brought them the power that brought them further wealth.

Yet for elites, the city house was a secondary dwelling. It was not a private place like the dwellings of the city non-elite. Rather the elite city house was multifunctional, a place of constant socializing and economic and sometimes political intercourse, and not simply a place of habitation. For these elites, living together essentially served the purpose of daily challenge-riposte interaction in the pursuit of honor.

The primary elite residence was the country estate, a place of residence and subsistence (family plus land and buildings for production, distribution, transmission, reproduction, and group identification). Non-elite farmers and tenants imagined their limited holdings in terms of the ideal, the elite country estate. These country houses were spacious, centrally heated, with a swimming bath, library, works of art, and the like. They were situated on vast agricultural estates worked by slaves in the West and largely by tenants in the East. At one time in the first century A.D. fully half of what is today Tunisia belonged to only six owners. Elite estates of twenty-five hundred acres, with farm buildings covering forty-five acres, would not be unusual.

The Preindustrial City

Thus the basic human environment into which first-century Mediterranean persons—Israelites, Romans, Greeks, or otherwise—were born was composed predominantly of agricultural and/or fishing villages socially tied to preindustrial cities. The preindustrial cities in question replicated the political institution with its embedded religion and economics. Thus the cities usually served as the administrative, religious, and market center for the villages or towns under their symbolic power. Jerusalem, Corinth, Ephesus, and even Athens and Rome were typical preindustrial cities at this time. The only difference between Rome and the other cities of the area was that Rome served as *the* central city, the imperial hub, to which all other cities were politically tied. Each individual city, in turn, had a larger or smaller number of villages or towns under its sway. What resulted from this arrangement was a complex of inward-looking, closed systems that interfaced or touched on each other: the village system, the city system, the empire system, and above all of these, the cosmic system.

If you want to imagine what I am talking about, think of the usual Tinker Toy-like model of a molecule composed of connected atoms. The empire was much like the total molecule, while the villages and preindustrial cities to which the villages were socially attached were like atoms, closed circles in which people faced inward, for the most part. Yet each unit of the empire—cities and villages—stood in relation to some other unit that could and did influence its attached surrounding units. What happened in a village could sometimes influence the city, while what happened in the city always influenced the connected villages. Furthermore, the influences were not of equal weight.

On the other hand, what happened in the imperial city of Rome reverberated throughout the system, while influences from subordinate cities and villages could be brought to bear on Rome. Consequently, all these human social arrangements called villages, towns, cities, and empire were perceived to be closed and complete within themselves, yet nonetheless related to each other in terms of space (the Mediterranean world), of time (the first century), and of social interaction (mutual influence among villages, towns, cities, and imperial center). To borrow an expression from biology, this sort of relationship among communities in the Mediterranean world (and peasant societies in general) might be called *symbiotic. Symbiosis* refers to the living together in more or less close union of two or more dissimilar organisms in a mutually beneficial relationship. In our case we have dissimilar social arrangements in close union that worked to effect mutual benefits. But the larger units always benefitted more than the smaller, to be sure. Rome was *the* city, with the rest of the Mediterranean world its surrounding tenancy holdings, its suburbs, if you will. Yet for the Israelite towns and villages of Judea, Galilee, and Perea, Jerusalem was *the* city, with the rest of the country much like its tenancy holdings.

What was life like in the preindustrial city? A city like Jerusalem depended on food, supplies, and raw materials from the outside for its existence. Revelation 18:12–13 offers a list of what was normally imported for this religious and administrative center: "gold, silver, jewels and pearls, fine linen, purple, silk and scarlet, all kinds of scented wood, all articles of ivory, all articles of costly wood, bronze, iron and marble, cinnamon, spice, incense, myrrh, frankincense, wine, oil, fine flour and wheat, cattle and sheep, horses and chariots, and slaves." The city, then, was a market center. And if we cross off the exotic imports, Jerusalem would depend on the villages of Palestine for wine, oil, flour, wheat, cattle, sheep, cloth, fish, and the like.

The preindustrial city contained no more than ten percent of the entire population under its direct and immediate control. And of this ten percent that constituted the preindustrial city population, less than two percent belonged to the elite or high status. The city itself was characterized by rigid social segregation marked by quarters or wards, through which ran streets that were no more than mere passageways for people and for animals used in transportation. The majority of the city-dwellers (the remaining eight percent plus) were engaged in handicraft manufacturing, for the most part, and clustered in guilds that inhabited their own sections of the city. The city house was the workplace, and producers sold directly to their customers.

In their city section, the small merchants or craftsmen, the day laborers or teamsters, were not much different from the villagers, since the life of the city elite was normally quite closed off from that of the low-status city resident, often by a wall. The preindustrial city had no classes based on wealth, surely no middle class at all. On the other hand, below the low-status city-dweller stood the lowest-status group of beggars and slaves.

The elite or high-status persons of the preindustrial city consisted of individuals, at times literate, who held positions in the political, political-religious, and political-economic institutions of the society. Thus these elites, assisted by their slaves, operated the administrative and religious institutions of the society, along with the wealthy absentee landowners who resided in the city. In the New Testament, the Sadducees and Herodians belonged to Jerusalem's elite. The members of the city's elite derived their status through birth; they belonged to the right families, and thus enjoyed power, property, and certain highly valued personal attributes, with their position legitimated by the Old Testament writings, for the most part. This is quite clear for the priestly Sadducees, while the princely Herodians would get their legitimation from the sacred writings of the Romans: Roman law, with the Roman prefect in the country to enforce it.

For our purposes, perhaps the most important role of the elite is that of the bearers of the culture's "Great Tradition," the embodiment of the norms and values that give continuity and substance to the ideals of Israelite society. To find the ideal forms of social norms (marriage and household, education, religion, government, economics) most closely approximated in reality, we would have to look to the literate city elite, since elites were best able to fulfill the exacting requirements of the sacred writings. This, again, should be obvious for Israel's Temple priesthood, its scribes, and the well-born of the city. As bearers of the Great Tradition, the city elite had political control, with two principal functions: exacting taxes (especially for the Temple, its city, and the city elite) and maintaining order through a police force and a type of court system that supported the order spelled out by the rules of sacred scripture, the Torah, which was the law of the house of Israel.

The reason for my describing the preindustrial city, even if briefly, is that in peasant society, the non-elite (the remaining ninety-eight percent of the population consisting of city non-elites and villagers) formed a sort of replication of the preindustrial city elite and stand in symbiotic social relationship to it. The movement set under way by Jesus of Nazareth, as we read about it in the Synoptic Gospels, is essentially a village movement, a movement running through the countryside. Eventually, according to Matthew, Mark, and Luke, Jesus does come to the political, political-religious, and political-economic center of Israel, the preindustrial administrative city of Jerusalem. The city elites perceive a threat in this movement, and they annihilate its central symbolic figure. On the other hand, after Jesus' resurrection, the post-Jesus movement group gradually makes its way throughout the Mediterranean world as a city phenomenon, from Jerusalem through the cities of the empire to Rome itself. Yet, as we see from Paul, even in its preindustrial city expression the post-Jesus movement group does not make any great impact on the city elites.

Hence, by and large, in reading the New Testament we deal with ruralized societies, first with town and village communities in the Synoptics and with non-elite, preindustrial city groups in Paul and the writings of the Pauline school. From what has been said previously, we might model the populations of the first-century Mediterranean world in terms of four categories: the elites, the city non-elites, the villagers, and the lowest non-elites. Post-Jesus

groups arise within the middle two categories: the city non-elites and the villagers, largely from the house of Israel. What these two groups have in common is that they are the bearers of the culture's "Little Tradition," that is, a
simplified and often outdated expression of the norms and ideals embodied
by the city elites. To quantify the difference somewhat, we might say that the
city non-elites are usually once or twice removed, while the villagers are two
or three times removed, from "where it's at," "it" being the lifestyle, norms,
and values held by the Great Tradition of the city elites. What this means for
our New Testament documents is that city elites like the Sadducees, Herodians, and Jerusalemite scribes who belonged to the Sanhedrin would be
"where it was at," the trendsetters, the closest approximations of the ideals
and values of Israelite society. The non-elite Jerusalemites would be somewhat removed in practice and understanding from the elite expression of the
Great Tradition, yet feel capable of mediating that tradition to the countryside at large, even to the world at large—and this is where the Jerusalem
Pharisees would fit in. On the other hand, Israelite villagers would be several
times removed from the city expression of the ideals and values of Israelite
society, living them out in antiquated and often "incorrect" and incomplete
form when measured by the city elite normal. For example, Galilean "bandit"
groups could model themselves on the outdated aspirations of the Maccabees
of the past (about 170 B.C.), while Jesus could very easily be perceived as a
prophet of old—something quite passé in city circles.

There is no such thing as a grass roots movement in peasant societies. Villagers and, to a lesser extent, city non-elites, are what they are (low-status
peasants) precisely because they draw on and develop their cultural forms by
imitating customs and values of other, more highly placed members of their
wider society. Since these low-status imitators imperfectly comprehend what
they see and hear about city elites, what they acquire from city elites is
reworked, simplified, and cut down so that these elements can be made to fit
the less complex arrangements of village or non-elite existence. Normally, by
the time novel city elements are successfully incorporated into non-elite and
eventually village culture, city elite life has changed and moved on; hence villagers always appear old-fashioned to city-dwellers, while city non-elites
seem behind the times to city elites.

What this social arrangement implies for New Testament reading is that
the Sadducees, Herodians, and their scribes ought to be imagined as the city
elite trendsetters. Jerusalemite Pharisees and their scribes would belong to
the city non-elite, with their rural expression in the Pharisee villages. The
social bandits of Galilee would be typical of ordinary village life, as would
those joining the reform movement set under way by John the Baptist and
taken up by Jesus.

Limited Good: A Basic Cue of Perception

Given the symbiotic social arrangement between village and preindustrial city, along with the sectional and divided structure of the preindustrial city itself, the overwhelming majority of persons living in the first-century world (about ninety-eight percent, if not more) would find themselves subject to the demands and sanctions of power-holders outside their social realm. Their lot was an unquestioned, if uneasy, acceptance of dominance by some supreme and remote power, with little control over conditions that governed their lives. This means that for the most part (exceptions will be listed below), the people presented in the pages of the New Testament would see their existence as determined and limited by the natural and social resources of their village, their preindustrial city, their immediate area and world, both vertically and horizontally. Such socially limited and determined existence could be verified by experience and lead to the perception that all goods available to a person are, in fact, limited. Thus extensive areas of behavior are patterned in such a way as to suggest to one and all that in society as well as in nature—the total environment—all the desired things in life, such as land, wealth, prestige, blood, health, semen, friendship and love, manliness, honor, respect and status, power and influence, security and safety—literally all goods in life—exist in finite, limited quantity and are always in short supply.

Further, not only is it obvious that all conceivable good things in life are finite in number and limited in quantity, but it is equally apparent that there is no way directly within a person's power to increase the available quantities. It is much as though the obvious fact of land shortage and/or housing opportunity in a densely populated area applied to all other desired things in life: simply not enough to go around. The good things constituting life, like land itself, are seen as inherent in nature, there to be divided and redivided, if possible and necessary, but never to be increased.

Since all good exists in limited amounts that cannot be increased or expanded, it follows that individuals, alone or with their families, can improve their social positions only at the expense of others. Hence any apparent relative improvement in someone's position with respect to any good in life is viewed as a threat to the entire community. Obviously, others are being deprived and denied something that is theirs, whether they know it or not. And since there is often uncertainty as to who is losing—it may be my family and I—any significant improvement is perceived not simply as a threat to other individuals or families alone, but as a threat to all individuals and families within the community, be it village or city quarter.

To understand our first-century group of foreigners, however, imagine there being a gasoline shortage in the United States, with gasoline always in short supply. To buy gas would require waiting in long lines at those select service stations that happen to be open when a truckload unpredictably arrives. How would you feel about finding an open station recently supplied with gasoline? How would you feel about people who jumped their place in line? U.S. persons tend to believe all goods in life are limitless. So in the event of any sort of shortage, they blame the persons in charge of the manufacture and distribution of the product in question. Most Americans know that price-fixing and price-gouging are part of the ideal free enterprise system.

Be that as it may, to understand the first-century Mediterranean, apply the image of a gasoline shortage to all the good things, persons, relationships, and events of your life; imagine them to be in short supply at all times, just like gasoline. How would you maintain your standard of living, and your self-image that so frequently depends on that standard of living in our society? Could you get ahead without making enemies? What or who would there be to help you out when you are faced with a need?

To return to the first century and its perception of all goods in life as limited, within the limited and finite social arrangements of the village or city quarter, community stability and harmony among individuals and families can develop and be maintained only by keeping to the existing arrangements of statuses. Thus most people would be interested in maintaining things just the way they are. Honorable persons would be greatly concerned about maintaining stability and harmony; they would be much interested in preserving their inherited status. So what honorable persons do is work at preserving their status in two chief ways: (1) by using a sort of personal defensive strategy toward others with whom they do not want to get involved and (2) by striking up selective dyadic alliances with those with whom they do want to get involved. We shall now consider each of these approaches and their implications for the New Testament.

The Honorable Person's Defensive Strategy

Status refers to a person's social position relative to other human beings in the same social system. We reveal our status by the social roles we play—by the way we act, feel, and think. These roles, abstractly considered, consist of entitlements and obligations, the entitlements we believe we have in our interactions with others, and the obligations others have toward us in respecting our rights. Naturally, we have a corresponding obligation to acknowledge the entitlements of others. Status in the first-century Mediterranean world derived mainly from birth and was symboled by the honor and prestige already accumulated and preserved by one's family. In chapter 1, I noted the gender division of labor typical of Mediterranean society. Both males and females share the family's honor and prestige, yet males represent the family to the outside, while females dominate the inside. What the good wife wants most is an honorable husband and honorable sons. What she is expected to support is her husband's (and sons') realization of the image of the honorable man.

The honorable man, the first-century male ideal, is one who knows how to live out and live up to his inherited obligations. He neither encroaches on others nor allows himself to be exploited or challenged by others. He works to feed and clothe his family. He fulfills his community and ceremonial obligations. He minds his own business in such a way as to be sure no one else infringes on him, while looking for possible advantages for himself. In sum, he does not seem to be outstanding, but he knows how to protect his entitlements bound up with his inherited status.

Moreover, honorable persons, male and female, feel they are entitled to fulfill their inherited roles and are hence entitled to economic and social subsistence. The right to subsistence—to the preservation of family status in all the dimensions of the ideal person's role—is the active moral principle in peasant societies. In other words, the only time our first-century villagers or non-elite city dwellers will rebel is when their subsistence is taken away. And should this happen, rebellion is not to achieve some higher standard of living or some new social status but only to return to normal subsistence levels. For example, it was the loss of subsistence due to fixed percentage taxation that spawned the Galilean social banditry that Josephus writes about. (The name for a social bandit of this kind was "thief"; Barabbas was one of these, and Jesus was crucified between two such "thieves.")

For our ideal first-century person, what was basic to human living itself was the maintenance and defense of one's valuable self-image as well as the social image of the broader family along with the married couple and their children. Thus the whole family was concerned about its honor. To deprive persons of honor in word and/or deed is what the biblical vocabulary for interpersonal sin is about, as we have previously seen. How did honorable people, males and females, behave at a more concrete level?

To demonstrate to their fellows that they do not in fact encroach on the good of others, ideal honorable persons maintain a culturally predictable, transparent, socially open existence. What this means is that they live in a way that allows others to know what they are up to. Being collectivistic personalities, they themselves need feedback from others as well. One way of showing this openness, to reveal that they are no threat to others, is to allow children to roam freely in and out of their house, workplace, or any other situation that might harbor a secret threat to others. Children serve as village or neighborhood communication links. To be hostile to children means to wish to pull something over on others, to intend to close the shutters of one's existence on others. (Note the ready availability of children in the village settings of Matt. 18:2; Mark 9:36; Luke 9:47.) Another form of signaling such openness—giving others the opportunity to check up if they wish—is to keep the door to one's courtyard and/or house open when the village or neighborhood is up and about. (Note the Gospel scenes of people parading through houses where Jesus is present, e.g., Mark 2:15–16; 7:24b; Matt. 26:6–7.) Honorable persons lead a defensive existence. They avoid the appearance of presuming on others, lest such presumption be interpreted as trying to take something that belongs to another. (Note Jesus' response to one who wants him to intervene in a family matter:"Man, who made me a judge or divider over you?" [Luke 12:14].) In other words, honorable persons, "good" persons, embody a sort of cultural self-deprecation that indicates that they seek nothing that might even remotely belong to another. Thus John the Baptist predictably proclaims his unworthiness in Mark 1:7 (see also Acts 13:25). Persons hoping for some benefaction likewise express characteristic unworthiness, whether they in fact are or are not worthy (Matt. 8:8; see also Matt. 10:37–38; 22:8; Luke 15:19, 21). This point of view moves honorable persons to refuse to give credit to others outside the in-group or family for anything in their life. To give credit to others is to admit borrowing from outsiders, hence to confess that they have taken something not rightfully theirs, that they have consciously upset the community balance and the honorable self-image they try so hard to maintain (see Mark 9:38–40 and perhaps Gal. 1:12 ff.—Paul's protest of being indebted to no man). It is because of perceived community imbalance that "a prophet is not without honor, except in his own country, and among his own kin, and in his own house" (Mark 6:4), that is, within his in-group, his closed society. The closed community has ready arguments for rejecting an achiever (see Matt. 11:19; Luke 7:34).

Further, honorable persons never admit to initiating bonds or alliances with others; such things either "just happen" or they are "asked by another." They fear that the admission of asking someone who is not somehow already indebted to them may be interpreted as presuming or imposing on others, trying to get something to which they may not be entitled. For example, day laborers have to be "asked" to work and do not seek a job; after all, they have their honor, too (Matt. 20:7: "no one has hired us" in the parable of the vineyard). People become Jesus' disciples because he asks them (Mark 1 :17, 20; 2:14; 10:21). No one seeks out Jesus for discipleship, since that would be presumptuous and require a put-down (perhaps Luke 9:57–58, 61–62 were originally such put-downs). The same holds for the growth of post-Jesus groups; people have to be asked, so some have to be sent (Mark 6:7–11; Matt. 10:7–16; Luke 10:1–12; Rom. 10:15). In this vein, note the many summary statements in the Gospels pointing to how people come to Jesus, seeking him out for healing and help, which he does not volunteer without being asked (e.g., Mark 1:32–33, 45b; 3:7–8, etc.). Finally, honorable persons never compliment others. And they do not express gratitude to equals or to higher-status persons until a transaction is over. If a compliment is given, there is denial that there is any reason for the compliment. For the person who compliments is guilty of aggression, of a negative challenge. To compliment others is to tell them to their face that they are rising above the level that spells security for all and to suggest that they may be confronted with sanctions. The denial of compliments given is the denial of cause for anyone to envy the one complimented (see the next chapter). For example, when a man comes up to Jesus and says, "Good Teacher, what must I do to inherit eternal life?" Jesus repudiates the compliment, as any honorable man would: "Why do you call me good? No one is good but God alone" (Mark 10:17–18).

Furthermore, to express gratitude to higher-status persons after some positive interaction means to call a halt to an initiated, open-ended, reciprocal relationship. A heartfelt "thank you" signifies that our relationship of mutual obligation is closed and finished, since I cannot and will not repay you. Among equals, such "gratitude" is shameful, but with higher-status persons it is honorable, provided that no more interactions with those same persons are foreseen or expected. Thus most people in the Gospels do not thank Jesus after he heals them; rather they praise God from whom good health comes, further implying that they might have to interact with Jesus again should illness strike later (see Mark 2:12; Matt. 9:8; 15:31; Luke 5:26; 7:16; 13:13; 18:43; 19:37; Gal. 1:24). To thank Jesus would mean that the relationship is over (e.g., Luke 17:16, where the Samaritan thanks Jesus, intimating that he believes his leprosy is healed for good, as one might expect from a Messianic healer; not so the others, who might need Jesus' services again).

So much for the personal defensive strategy characteristic of honorable persons. Now let us consider the type of dyadic alliances they might use with those with whom they intend to get involved.

The Honorable Person's Dyadic Alliances

With the perception of all good as limited, our first-century honorable persons found that hard work, thrift with a view to future acquisition, and personal skills and abilities were human qualities quite necessary for maintaining one's status but useless for getting ahead. Given the limitations on land and resources, along with the lack in inanimate sorts of energy to power technology, additional hard work, development of one's abilities and skills, or achieving goals simply did not produce any significant gain in wealth or influence, in power or broader loyalty. In a village where farms and shops are small, as well as in a preindustrial city where family industry is limited, wealth is accumulated extremely slowly, if at all. There are few ways, if any, for a landless tenant farmer to become a smallholder, for a smallholder to become a large landowner, for petty shopkeepers, merchants, or craftsmen to become wealthy of and by themselves within their limited social environments. Now, if to move beyond one's limited share in life would lead to challenges and reprisals of all sorts, how is an honorable person in need, in trouble, or in dire straits to find rescue from some difficult situation? In the common Greek of the first century, "salvation" meant rescue from a difficult situation; it was not a specifically God-oriented word, just as our word "redemption" when used of trading stamps is not a God-oriented word. Our first-century honorable persons were certainly interested in salvation in a whole range of forms, depending on the need that befell them and their families. Where would they look for salvation if crops failed, if a family member took ill, if bride wealth was needed for a marriage, if taxes proved too high? The culture provided them with traditional but limited forms of cooperation with both their village peers and with outsiders of equal or higher social standing.

Perhaps the most significant form of social interaction in the limited-good world of the first century is an informal principle of reciprocity, a sort of implicit, nonlegal contractual obligation, unenforceable by any authority apart from one's sense of honor and shame. By means of this principle of reciprocity, the honorable person selects (or is selected by) another for a series of ongoing, unspecified acts of mutual support. This is what George Foster calls the "dyadic contract." He defines it as an implicit contract informally binding pairs of contractants rather than groups (recall that "dyad" means a pair, a twosome). In our limited-good world, such contracts can bind persons of equal status (colleague contracts) or persons of different statuses (patron-client contracts). These informal contracts function side by side with the formal contracts of society, such as buying and selling, marriage, Israel's inherited covenant with God, and the like. However, the dyadic contract crosscuts the formal contracts of the culture, serving as the glue that holds individuals together for long or short terms, and enabling the social interdependence necessary for life.

Dyadic contracts are initiated by means of the positive challenges we spoke of previously. For example, the acceptance of an invitation to supper, of a small gift, or of a benefaction like healing was equivalent to a positive challenge requiring a response. It signaled the start of an ongoing reciprocal relationship. To accept an invitation, a gift, or a benefaction with no thought to future reciprocity implies acceptance of imbalance in society. Such an action would damage the status quo. Within a closed system, this does not happen without grave repercussions, for in reality there are no free gifts, just gifts that mark the initiation or continuance of an ongoing reciprocal relationship. Thus in Luke 5:27–32, Jesus invites Levi, a toll collector, to follow him. Levi accepts and then reciprocates by inviting Jesus to a feast with his friends. Each invitation is a positive challenge, a gift that requires repayment. Such positive challenges and appropriate responses will continue indefinitely, embracing a range of goods and services, provided that an exactly even balance between two partners is never struck. It is this sort of dyadic contractual relationship that bothers Jesus' critics when he eats with "sinners and tax collectors" (see also Mark 2:15–16; Matt. 11:19). Now, if a balance in reciprocity were struck, or if one's partner called a halt to responding with a verbal display of gratitude (for example, "Thank you very much"), that would signify the end of the ongoing reciprocity. This sort of reciprocity among equals is a symmetrical one between closely located persons of the same social status, hence a colleague contract.

I might mention, by the way, that even buying and selling involve reciprocal obligations of a symmetrical sort, for in the context of limited good, the seller always does the buyer a favor by selling to him or her. It is always a seller's market. Thus, even if an entire village consists of the same sort of producers (e.g., fishermen), or an entire preindustrial city quarter contains artisans producing the same merchandise (e.g., tentmakers), all are assured of their clientele because of previous dealings with them; hence such small merchants are not in competition with each other, as they would be in our society.

A patron-client contract, on the other hand, is very similar to a colleague contract in that it is initiated by means of a positive challenge, a positive gift or request for aid. But it ties persons of significantly different social statuses, hence the goods and services in the ongoing reciprocal relationship will be different. The relationship is asymmetrical since the partners are not social equals and make no pretense to equality. We might say that with equals in colleague contracts, persons provide themselves with all they need, at peak periods of demand, of the kinds of goods and services to which they themselves also have access. The patron-client contract, on the other hand, provides things not normally available in the village or city neighborhood, things that at times are badly needed. Both sorts of relationship require imbalance for continuance, and both can be discontinued with varying degrees of sanction. What patrons offer is "favors." A favor refers to some object, good, or action that is either unavailable at all or unavailable at a given time.

Patron-client relationships seem to be implied in the Gospels when people approach Jesus for "mercy" (e.g., Matt. 9:27: blind men; 15:22: Canaanite woman; 17:15: father of an epileptic; 20:30: blind men again). Furthermore, all positive relationships with God are rooted in the perception of patron-client contracts. For example, the charisms listed by Paul in 1 Corinthians 12 and Romans 12 are gifts from God naturally requiring repayment in the forms of loyalty, obedience, honor, and submission. Such gifts coming from the God as heavenly patron, that is Father, look to long-term continuance. The theological vocabulary of grace is all about favors offered by our Patron "who art in heaven." However, there are forms of patron-client contracts of a shorter term, of a noncontinuing kind. For example, vows to God like the Nazirite vow Paul made (Acts 18:18; see Acts 21:23–24 for others, and Num. 6:1–21 for the rules) are such short-term contracts. Once the patron, God, grants the request and the client complies by fulfilling his vow, a balance is struck and the relationship for this purpose is terminated.

Persons who know how to put prospective clients into contact with the patrons those clients need are called brokers (the Greek name for broker is "mediator"). In the Gospels, Jesus for the most part acts as broker, putting people in contact with their heavenly Patron/Father, the God of Israel. When he sends out his disciples, Jesus commissions them as brokers with the same task he has. And throughout the New Testament, God is described for the most part with the analogy of "patron" in a typical Mediterranean patron-client relationship with those who worship Him.

All in all, our first-century foreigners made their way through life by attempting to strike up dyadic contracts that they felt might be helpful. Over time, a person would build contractual relationships with fellow villagers and friends in other communities, occasionally dropping those that no longer served and developing new ones that offered promise. Every person worked out or tried to work out similar ties with more powerful persons, that is, with human and nonhuman patrons. Their approach was pragmatic and eclectic, based on trial and error, and done in a spirit of "nothing ventured, nothing gained," so typical of traditional peasant society. Thus honorable persons looked for ways to interest and obligate potential partners whom they felt could help them, and in so doing committed themselves to carry out the terms of the contract with those who, in effect, accepted their offer. By means of a greater or lesser number of such contractual ties with both peers and superiors, typical persons of the first-century Mediterranean maximized their interests and security posture in the uncertain world in which they lived.

From the viewpoint of the dyadic contract, Jesus' call to others to follow him in the Gospels is an instance of an individual initiating reciprocal relationships with other individuals. At times Jesus meets with a refusal, as in the case of the greedy young man (Mark 10:17–31; Matt. 19:16–30; Luke 18:18–23). The important thing to note is that the dyadic contract obliges no wider group than the individuals (and perhaps their embedded females and children) who made the contract. Consequently, it would be quite normal for the disciples of Jesus to squabble with and challenge each other, since they have ties to Jesus and not to each other (e.g., Luke 9:46; 22:24). Further, Jesus makes appeals to individuals on a dyadic basis, as in the following example: "Come to me, all who labor and are heavy laden, and I will give you rest" (Matt. 11:28). The teacher-disciple relationship is equally dyadic (Matt. 10:24). Finally, the factions in the church of Corinth seem to have derived from dyadic relationships to individual apostles (1 Cor. 1:12). I might point out here, incidentally, that Paul's solution to the problem posed by such dyadism, much like the solution envisioned in Matt. 23:8–10, is to point out that obligations owed to Jesus have to be paid back not to Jesus, but to others in dyadic relation with Jesus, that is, one's fellow post-Jesus group members. The result is a sort of polyadic relationship ("poly-" means many): a number of people in equivalent social statuses organized around a single interest and mutually obligated in terms of this single interest, much like a guild or Roman burial association.

Limited Good and the Accumulation of Wealth

How would our honorable first-century foreigner look upon profit making or the accumulation of wealth? From all that we have considered so far, most people in the first-century Mediterranean world worked to maintain their inherited status, not to get rich. The goal of life in a closed society such as theirs is contentment derived from preserving one's status, not acquisition or achievement. With such a goal in mind, it would be impossible to attempt to convince such people that they might improve their social standing with more work. For this reason, you will find no capitalist or communist work ethic in the New Testament. Nor will you find any program of "social action" aimed at the redistribution of wealth or anything of the sort. The closest thing to this sort of conception in first-century Judea would be the Zealot movement that arose about the time of the Judean uprising against Rome about A.D. 66. However, like all peasant movements, the Zealots were not after the reshaping of society but rather the restoration of the political subsistence economy to which all peasants believe they are entitled.

On the contrary, in the closed type of society we are considering, the honorable persons would certainly strive to avoid and prevent the accumulation of capital, since they would see it a threat to the community and community balance, rather than a precondition to economic and social improvement. Since all goods are limited, one who seeks to accumulate capital is necessarily dishonorable; the operative dirty word in this regard is "greed." A person could not accumulate wealth except through the loss and injury suffered by another. A fourth-century Mediterranean proverb says, "Every rich person is either unjust or the heir of an unjust person," or "Every rich person is a thief or the heir of a thief." The outlook was the same in the first century.

• By and large, only the dishonorable rich, the dishonorable non-elites, and those beyond the pale of public opinion (such as city elites, governors, and regional kings) could accumulate wealth with impunity. This they did in a number of ways, notably by trading, tax collecting, and money lending. At bottom, the trader, the tax collector, and the money lender (at interest, of course) were all the same: they made profit by defrauding others, by forcing people to part with their share of limited good through extortion. The money lender could have his debtors imprisoned, the purpose of imprisonment being to put pressure on the debtor's family to pay off the money due (e.g., Matt. 5:25–26; Luke 12:57–59). During the ministry of Jesus, the Romans collected their own taxes in Judea, while the Herodians did so in Galilee. However, there were toll collectors, like Levi, who collected indirect taxes (similar to the taxes we pay on liquor, food, and gasoline, that is, sales taxes). In the process, the toll collector would collect as much as he could squeeze from the people over and above what the Romans demanded, then pay his share to the Romans and pocket the rest (e.g., Luke 3:13; 19:1–9). Finally, the trader, the intercity import-export merchant of the preindustrial city, was often a freedman or city non-elite person secretly subsidized by wealthy Roman citizens or other elites. Traders bought needed commodities in one place and sold them in another at monopoly prices, getting as much as they could regardless of their own costs. All these forms of capital accumulation were perceived to be forms of usury. Technically, *usury* means making money by allowing another to use one's money, much as our bank loans and other modern lending institutions do. In the first century they would all be considered dishonorable and immoral forms of usury. Trading, in turn, meant making money by investing in some goods purchased abroad with the hope (and certainty) of selling for a much higher price at home (e.g., Luke 19:12–27). The trader, like the money lender and the tax collector, was considered basically godless. For example, in James 4:13–16, traders talk as follows: "Today or tomorrow we will go into such and such a town and spend a year there and trade and get gain." (Read the whole passage. The criticism in the passage is that traders do not trust in God, but in their own devices.)

Thus, in ruralized, preindustrial societies, profit and gain normally refer to something that accrue to a person by fraud or extortion, that is, something other than wages, customary rent, reciprocal lending, or direct sale from producer to consumer. Paul reminds his readers that "wages are not reckoned as a gift" (Rom. 4:4), yet some wealthy persons would defraud wage earners by reneging on what they owed (James 5:1-6). Such greed was typical of the "lovers of money," those who sought capital accumulation, a thoroughly dishonorable line of conduct (see 1 Tim. 3:8, 13; 6:5, 6; Titus 1:7, 11; 1 Pet. 5:2; 2 Pet. 2:15; Jude 1:11, 16; note also Mark 10:19: "Do not defraud"; 1 Cor. 6:7–8; Matt. 20:1–15).

Now, the honorable man would not want to be branded as "greedy," hence the accumulation of capital, the profit motive, was closed to him. This is typical of a limited-good, closed society with its contentment and status-maintenance orientation. In such a society, the saying "For you always have the poor with you" (Mark 14:7; Matt. 26:11; John 12:8) is a cultural truism, something obvious to any thinking, reasonable person in the first-century Mediterranean world. But there is more to it than meets the eye. For who in fact are the poor in a limited-good society?

In peasant societies, "poor" is not exactly a designation of social rank or a reference to the lowest standing in a series of such ranks. As a matter of fact, being "poor" is not primarily an expression of "class" or economic rank at all. The culture that we study has its prime focus and pivotal value in kinship, in belonging, and in the social order based on honor and shame. The status into which one is born, regardless of how high or low, is normally honorable. Peasants consider all persons in their society as "equal." Money is not the determiner of one's social standing or status ranking as it is in our society; rather, birth is. Then what does being "poor" refer to? If we consider the data presented in the New Testament, we find two sets of usages of the word. First of all, there is a series of passages in which the word "poor" is used without further description. From such passages we simply cannot get any idea of what the authors are referring to except by sticking our own ideas into their words (e.g., Matt. 19:21; 26:9, 11; Mark 10:21; 14:5, 7; Luke 18:22; John 12:5–8; 13:29; Rom. 15:26; 2 Cor. 6:10; 8:9; 9:9; Gal. 2:10).

On the other hand, there is also a series of passages in which the word "poor" is used in the company of other words that describe the condition of the person who is labeled "poor." Thus, Luke 4:18 has a quote from Isaiah in which the poor are those imprisoned, blind, or debt-ridden. Matthew 5:3 ff., along with Luke 6:20–21 have the poor ranked with those who hunger, thirst, and mourn (a mourner is one afflicted with evil who by mourning protests the presence of evil). Matthew 11:4–5 lists the blind, the lame, lepers, the deaf, and the dead with the poor, while Luke 14:13, 21 has the maimed, the lame, and the blind. Further, Mark 12:42–43 and Luke 21:2–3 speak of a poor widow, and Luke 16:20–22 tells of the poor Lazarus who was full of sores, hence ill, leprous. Finally, James 2:3–6 points out the shabbily dressed poor man as truly powerless, while Revelation 3:17 considers the poor to be wretched, pitiable, blind, naked—something like the list in Matthew 25:34 ff., where we find the hungry, the thirsty, the stranger, the naked, and the imprisoned.

⟡ Now, if we were to take all these adjacent descriptions of the poor and group them in terms of what they have in common, it would seem that being classified as poor was the result of some unfortunate turn of events or some untoward circumstances. Poor persons seem to be those who cannot maintain their inherited status due to circumstances that befall them and their families, such as debt, being in a foreign land, sickness, death of a spouse (widow), or some personal physical accident. Consequently, the poor would not be a permanent social standing but a sort of revolving category of people who unfortunately cannot maintain their inherited status. Thus day laborers, landless peasants, and beggars born into their situation were not poor persons in first-century society. And "poor" would most certainly not be an economic designation. Furthermore, the opposite of rich would not necessarily be poor. To repeat, in the perception of people in limited-good society, the majority of people are neither rich nor poor, just equal in that each has a status to maintain in some honorable way. Personal assessment is not economic but a matter of lineage. Thus, in this context, rich and poor really refer to the greedy and the socially ill-fated. The terms do not characterize two poles of society as much as two minority categories, the one based on the shameless drive to expand one's wealth, the other based on the inability to maintain one's inherited status of any rank.

Limited Good and Personal Causality

If ordinary first-century persons always had the socially ill-fated poor with them, so did they always have the greedy rich—if not in their village or city quarter then somewhere else, to be sure. As pointed out above, honorable persons would seek out patron-client contracts with those of higher status, especially to provide goods and services not normally available in the village or city neighborhood. When faced with some abnormal crisis, they would attempt to tap the proper higher-status resource in a variety of ways. This could be done far more easily than in our individualistic society, for higher-status persons were dyadic personalities as well. They too needed to live up to the ego-image provided by others and sanctioned by public opinion. Clients would repay their patrons by such intangibles as public praise, concern for their reputation among those of the client's status, and informing patrons of plots and machinations of others—in sum, by continually adding to the name and honor of their patrons. In the highly stratified, status-conscious social system of the first-century world, elites had a rightful place. The obvious inequality of persons and social statuses that we notice was considered normal, useful, and God-given. After all, we do not have control over our family of birth or its status, wealth, and prestige. These we inherit according to God's good pleasure. (You might also consider that social distinction is discrimination only when your society claims that all persons are legally equal. No first-century society ever asserted the legal equality of all males, much less of all persons.)

The honorable higher-status person, then, like the lower-status person, was expected to live out and live up to that socially ascribed self-image. And this entailed the obligation of serving as patron for clients of lower social strata. This arrangement enabled members of any given closed system to seek and often gain access to other systems—for example, the tenant farmer to the landowner, the village artisan to some city-dweller, and both of these to some local administrative office holder, to the emperor, to the gods, or to God. The centurion of Capernaum, who "built us our synagogue" in Luke 7:1–10, was such an available patron. Paul's appeal to the emperor in Acts 25:25 is an instance of seeking the salvation available to a Roman citizen. From a limited-good perspective, an individual faced with an unusual crisis might achieve a solution to it by tapping sources perceived to stand outside his or her stratum or system. If such a maneuver succeeds, the success might be envied by one's peers within the closed system, but it is not seen as a direct threat to community stability, for no one within the community loses anything. Still, such success has to be made known publicly and explained to others.

In other words, what needs explanation to prevent community recrimination and reprisal is success found at the boundaries of one's closed system and the systems adjacent to it. Positive results from contacts at these boundaries were attributed to luck, good fortune, or providence. For example, finding a lost sheep or a lost coin (Luke 15:6–9) and the joy accompanying it requires public explanation to prevent suspicion of theft. Male children—an economic asset in most ranks of first-century society—are normally ascribed to God (Luke 1:13). Note also the parables of the kingdom in Matthew 13:44 (treasure in a field); 13:45 (finding a pearl); 13:47–48 (dragnet and fish). In all of these, the situation of the kingdom is compared to the activity of people who find success due to luck or good fortune. On the other hand, parables dealing with prayer to patrons of various sorts (for example, Matt. 7:7–8 [beggar's behavior]; Luke 18:1–5 [widow and judge]; Luke 18:9–14 [God and the Pharisee and publican]; as well as the prayers of various people to Jesus, for example, Mark 10:46–52 [the blind beggar Bartimaeus]; Mark 10:35–41 [the request of James and John]) indicate how one might have recourse to a higher status patron ranging from a local prestigious person to a local king or to some god or to God.

This last-mentioned point is rather significant for understanding a very fundamental cue of perception shared by our group of foreigners. As pointed out many times previously, in limited-good societies, hard work, acquisition of goods, and human abilities simply cannot bring forth the power and commitment needed to rescue a person from an abnormal, difficult situation. Another way to say this is that an individual's manipulation of his or her available world of things, of "its," is simply nonproductive and insufficient for adequate rescue from very difficult situations. Such human manipulation of the available world of things is technology, and first-century technology, even if it were applied exhaustively, yielded no significant increase in power, wealth, influence, or anything else. Consequently, apart from luck or good fortune, the only source of help would lie in the manipulation of the available world of visible and nonvisible persons, of "thou's," of higher-status persons who were able to provide relief in unusual situations (peer and colleague contracts take care of usual needs). Furthermore, if luck and fortune ultimately derive from God or the gods, then the divinity too becomes a "thou" worthy of manipulation. What I mean is that if in order to succeed in life, it is obvious to all that technology, hard work, and technical abilities are all a waste of time and highly threatening to others even if they could be applied, then all that is left for the individual is to learn how to manipulate other individuals to one's advantage. Such manipulation requires awareness and skill, since most often the person offering the most good will be one of a higher status. This cultural fact—that success in life derives from manipulating persons— leads to some conclusions typical of the limited-good outlook.

The first conclusion, an important cue of perception, is that *every effect that counts in life is caused by a person.* Consequently, when something significant happens, positive or negative, the question to ask is, "Who did it?" (not "What did it?" as we ask in our culture). It further follows that some persons are more powerful than others, as can readily be proved by the effects caused by various persons. The key to success, then, is to get to know the power of the persons with whom an honorable person can actually or potentially interact and to use those persons for one's own ends, for salvation from a difficult situation. Take sickness and pain, for example. In this cultural context, since sickness is something that counts in a person's life, who would cause it? If it is not caused by me or some other human being who might punch, stab, or otherwise hurt me, then it must be caused by some nonhuman person, a nonhuman "thou." And if it is person-caused, even by nonhuman persons, then every healing is in effect wiping out the influence of another person and is hence an exorcism. And, of course, every exorcism implies a healing, that is, restoring a person to a previously held social position.

So honorable people have to learn how to succeed with the persons with whom they might come into contact, specifically by means of the "sociological" thinking mentioned in the previous chapter. The persons with whom one interacts are both the human and nonhuman beings that populate one's world of social interactions. What all this indicates is that in the first-century Mediterranean world, social structures in general (such as kinship-rooted economics), as well as concrete expressions of those structures (such as farming, along with an actual good harvest or bad, drought, famine, adequate rain, and the like), are perceived as created, maintained, controlled, and governed by various persons, human and nonhuman, depending on the dimensions of the effects. The parable of the weeds sown in the wheat by an enemy (Matt. 13:24 30) points to a human person. But the grand dimensions of human experience, such as weather, health, life and its transmission, political power, and so on, are far above and beyond any individual human being's control or grasp. These are ascribed to nonhuman persons. Thus people in our period perceived God, gods, and their agents—spirits, demons, angels—as necessary to maintain the equilibrium both of society and its pursuits in social and physical environments, most often regardless of what honorable human beings themselves might do. For example, Plutarch explains the fate of those responsible for the death of Julius Caesar as follows: "However the great guardian genius [literally: 'great demon'] of the man, whose help he had enjoyed through life, followed upon him even after death as an avenger of his murder, driving and tracking down his slayers over every land and sea until not one of them was left, but even those who in any way soever either put hand to the deed or took part in the plot were punished" (*Lives: Caesar* 69.2, LCL). Josephus tells us that in a battle with Sulla and royalist troops outside of Bethsaida Julias, his horse stumbled in a marshy spot, and he broke his wrist; "and my success on that day would have been complete had I not been thwarted by some demon" (*Life* 402 LCL).

In other words, for the first-century Mediterranean person, nearly all the social realities singled out in our modern textbooks and courses in sociology, social psychology, and the natural sciences would be perceived as due to persons, visible and nonvisible. To us their reports sound like references to "religious" (or superstitious) phenomena. The reason for this is that "religion" dealt with respect for those who controlled human existence. And those who controlled human existence were the nonhuman and human persons above us to whom we owe a debt of honor and respect.

Thus the surest and most common sources of help and security available to people of the first-century Mediterranean society were persons of the same rank as well as and especially higher-ranking human and nonhuman beings who controlled their existence to a large extent. The key to success was to learn how to manipulate the available persons. The patron-client contract looks to one phase of this sort of manipulation in the relationship between superiors and subordinates. Our first-century villagers and city non-elites believed that they had a moral right to subsistence and to reciprocal interaction with the more fortunate elites of their society, ranging from the local wealthy landowner to the gods or God. So long as these elites allowed the lower ranks their subsistence, it did not matter how much they took in taxes, tribute, sacrifice, and the like. And so long as these elites allowed lower-status persons to interact with them in patron-client relationships, it did not matter how unbalanced they might be in prestige and power, since all were "equal" anyway.

Limited Good
and the Structured Social World

Before concluding this chapter, we might consider the general structure of the social world experienced by those foreigners whom we study when we read the New Testament. The perception of limited good leads to the perception of personal causality. The dyadic contract was one important way for persons to make their way in a world in which what persons caused determined everything important in life. This world of persons consisted of a set of ranks that embraced all persons, in fact all of reality, reaching up to the cosmos, with God at the top. Given the obvious principle that to harm or help one person it took another person, human or nonhuman, the first-century Mediterranean social world would be inhabited by persons standing in vertical relationship to each other and within limited, closed, horizontal systems somewhat as follows:

1. *God*: On top was God, whom the Mediterranean world knew as "the Most High" (e.g., Luke 1:32, 35; 2:14; 6:35). Semites in general, and Israelites in particular, believed that all things are possible with God (e.g., Matt. 19:26; Mark 10:27; Luke 1:37; Luke 18:27). Roman and Greek elites believed that God himself was limited: he could not make a square circle, make rivers run backward, cause the oceans to overrun land, and the like.

2. *Gods or sons of God or archangels*: These comprised a sort of heavenly bureaucracy in charge of a segment of the cosmos or at work doing the bidding of God. Satan (a Persian name for "spy, a secret service agent"), or the devil (the Greek translation of Satan), was originally God's secret service agent, as in Job 1; by the first century this negative person leads a sort of palace revolt against God, and, in this, Satan likewise involves humans (e.g., see Luke 4:6). At this rank we ought to include the stars, whether individually or in constellated forms. First-century persons believed stars were living beings, intelligent and powerful, exercising great impact on lands over which they move. Beings at this level can influence everything below them, but not God. They are controlled by God.

3. *Lower nonhuman persons*: These include suprahuman forces that have effect on human beings and their world; these are called angels (a sky servant,

in origin a Semitic term for an agent from the heavenly court, a sort of heavenly factotum), spirits (a sky power, a Semitic term for suprahuman power
known by its effects), or demons (the Greek word for such suprahuman powers; Romans called them *genii* or geniuses). These, too, could influence at will
everything below them, but not those above them. They get their orders
from those above them, ultimately all under God's control.

4. *Human beings*: This level comprises the world of humankind in structured society, running along a scale from emperor to slave for the empire,
from king and high priest to slave in Israel. In this pyramidal structure, persons of higher rank could influence all below them at will, but not vice versa.

5. *Beings lower than humans*: If creatures lower than humankind affect
human beings, that is due to their being manipulated by others up and down
this ladder of persons who use them to their own advantage.

Meaningful survival clearly entailed maintaining one's place on this ladder.
For their own well-being and security—or simply because that is their
nature—each higher-type person attempts to manipulate the lower and looks
to noninterference from horizontal colleagues. For lower-ranking persons to
gain effective influence on some higher being, an intermediary broker-type
person, a sort of go-between, is necessary to act as a social lever. The broker,
of course, must in some way relate to or come from the same sphere as the
higher being whom one wishes to influence, or from a sphere above that
being. God, being on the top of the status ladder, has all others under effective control.

Summary

The first-century Mediterranean world might be characterized as a peasant society, that is, a ruralized society consisting of preindustrial cities along
with surrounding villages over which the cities exercise control and influence.
The majority of the people of the time lived in villages or in artisan quarters
of the preindustrial city. For this majority (and, it seems, for the minority
elite as well), the main perception in life was that all goods are limited. This
perception lies behind the behavior considered necessary for an adequate
human existence. The basic need for security in a threatening and threatened
world, prismed through the image of limited good, revealed the sources of
power and influence, of wealth and loyalty, at the interfaces of one's closed
system as well as among select members of one's peer group. Behavior at this
boundary, horizontally considered, entailed reciprocal obligations with one's
colleagues. Vertically considered, such behavior took the shape of the patron-
client system. Both colleague relationships and patron-client relationships
entailed reciprocal obligations that might be called dyadic contracts.

Honorable persons in the world of limited good were those who knew how to preserve their inherited status. In their quest to maintain this important self-image, honorable persons knew how to use their colleagues as well as a range of powerful and socially superior human and nonhuman persons to meet life's problems. This, of course, implied the need for knowledge of patrons, a sort of popular political science. The human patron-client system had a comparable nonhuman system in the beings that controlled human existence, resulting in a cosmic patron-client system that embraced the human as well. So honorable persons also knew how to manipulate the available nonhuman powerful persons to help in meeting life's problems. This likewise implied a need for knowledge of cosmic patrons, a sort of popular and personalistic natural science, along with a knowledge of God.

References and Suggested Readings

Elliott, John H. "Patronage and Clientism in Early Christian Society. A Short Reading Guide." *Forum* 3, no. 1 (1987):39–48.

_____. "Temple Versus Household in Luke-Acts: A Contrast in Social Institutions." In *The Social World of Luke-Acts: Models for Interpretation*, ed. Jerome H. Neyrey, 211–240. Peabody, Mass.: Hendrickson, 1991.

Hanson, K. C. "The Galilean Fishing Economy and the Jesus Tradition." *Biblical Theology Bulletin* 27 (1997):99–111.

Hanson, K. C. and Douglas E. Oakman. *Palestine in the Time of Jesus: Social Structures and Social Conflicts*. Minneapolis: Fortress Press, 1998, 99–129.

Malina, Bruce J. "Patron and Client: The Analogy behind Synoptic Theology." *Forum* 4, no. 1 (1988):1–32.

_____. *The New Jerusalem in the Revelation of John: The City as Symbol of Life with God*. Zacchaeus Studies. Collegeville, Minn.: Liturgical Press, 2000.

Moxnes, Halvor. *The Economy of the Kingdom: Social Conflict and Economic Relations in Luke's Gospel*. Philadelphia: Fortress Press, 1988.

Oakman, Douglas E. *Jesus and the Economic Questions of His Day*. Queenston, Ont.: Edwin Mellen Press, 1986.

_____. "The Countryside in Luke-Acts." In *The Social World of Luke-Acts: Models for Interpretation*, ed. Jerome H. Neyrey, 151–180. Peabody, Mass.: Hendrickson, 1991.

_____. "The Ancient Economy in the Bible: BTB Readers Guide." *Biblical Theology Bulletin* 21 (1991):34–39.

_____. "Was Jesus a Peasant? Implications for Reading the Samaritan Story (Luke 10:30–35)." *Biblical Theology Bulletin* 22 (1992):117–125.

Potter, Jack M., May N. Diaz, and George M. Foster, eds. *Peasant Society: A Reader*. Boston: Little, Brown & Co., 1967.

Rohrbaugh, Richard L. *The Biblical Interpreter: An Agrarian Bible in an Industrial Age*. Philadelphia: Fortress Press, 1978.

_____. "The City in the Second Testament: BTB Readers Guide." *Biblical Theology Bulletin* 21 (1991):67–75.

_____. "The Pre-Industrial City in Luke-Acts: Urban Social Relations." In *The*

Social World of Luke-Acts: Models for Interpretation, ed. Jerome H. Neyrey, 125–151. Peabody, Mass.: Hendrickson, 1991.

_____. "A Peasant Reading of the Parable of the Talents/Pounds: A Text of Terror?" *Biblical Theology Bulletin* 23 (1993):32–39.

Scott, James C. *The Moral Economy of the Peasant.* New Haven, Conn.: Yale University Press, 1976.

Sjoberg, Gideon. *The Preindustrial City: Past and Present.* New York: Free Press, 1960.

Wolf, Eric R. *Peasants.* Englewood Cliffs, N.J.: Prentice-Hall, 1966.

4

Envy—The Most Grievous of All Evils

Envy and the Evil Eye in the First-Century Mediterranean World

In Mark's story of Jesus' arrest and death, the author reports that Pilate "perceived that it was out of envy that the chief priests had delivered him [Jesus] to death" (Mark 15:10; Matt. 27:18 repeats Pilate's assessment). Yet few Bible readers take the assessment very seriously. Few readers consider the cause of Jesus' death to be something so relatively unimportant in our society as envy. Perhaps envy, however, was not so unimportant in the first-century Mediterranean world. In the Israelite tradition, for example, envy was the cause of that paramount and inescapable negative feature of human existence: death. "Through the devil's envy, death entered the world" (Wisd. Sol. 2:24). Philo, an émigré Israelite who lived in Alexandria, insisted that envy was "the most grievous of all evils" (*Special Laws* III.1.2). Once we learn how first-century Mediterraneans perceived envy, it will become apparent that envy was indeed a significant characteristic of ancient Mediterranean living.

The Social Roots of Envy

In the previous chapter, we took a long look at the ancient Mediterranean belief that all goods in life were limited. Before that, we noted that first-century Mediterraneans lived in a ruralized society, with wealth and well-being attached to the land. And at the beginning of this book, we considered honor and shame as pivotal values in the ancient (and modern) Mediterranean world. It seems that the configuration of the perception of limited good and concern for honor and shame, coupled with life in ruralized society, produces preoccupation with envy. The point here is not that the ancients envied and we do not. We do, indeed, experience envy, yet we are not preoccupied with it nor do we ascribe significant events to it.

If we begin with our own, twenty-first-century Western experience, when does a person feel envious? When do we envy another, or when does another envy us? Invariably the feeling of envy surfaces only when we compete with another person who wins out over us in possessing some thing or in entering into some relationship that is in extremely restricted supply: a unique role (class president, best student); a unique relationship (best friend, male or female); a single, available job; a single bargain (new car sale); and the like. You will notice that envy emerges only in situations of highly curtailed, drastically limited valuable objects. We envy other people when they are in possession of some highly restricted valuable object that we ourselves would like to have. And similarly, others envy us should we come into possession of some highly limited valuable object. Of course persons winning possession of rare, valuable objects or relationships consider themselves fortunate and elated in their new possession.

It would seem that envy is a feeling of begrudging that emerges in face of the good fortune of others relative to some restricted good that is equally of interest to us. We might say that we only envy our social equals in similar social circles, yet in U.S. perception, we can all aspire to becoming prominent persons. And we find little difficulty in looking at eminent persons as beneath contempt. This description, of course, befits individualistic U.S. society. U.S. persons believe they may rise (and fall) in social standing; hence all persons are potentially social equals. What of persons in the ancient Mediterranean? You will notice that Mark's report of Pilate's appraisal of the reason for Jesus' being put to death pits an individual over against a group, Jesus over against the high priests, who are envious of Jesus. When groups envy others, either single individuals or other groups, it is a good indication that we are dealing with a collectivistic, group-oriented society rather than an individualistic society. In collectivistic societies, people stay in the status in which they were born. Social standing is determined by birth, one's ethnic group in general, and one's status within that ethnic group. There is little, if any, social mobility, upward or downward. Even when elites are dispossessed and defamed by their elite peers, they remain elites at the lowest levels of elite statuses.

Furthermore, just as honor and shame work differently in individualistic societies compared to collectivistic ones, so does envy. You will recall that shame in the ancient Mediterranean (and in collectivistic societies) is a publicly rejected claim to worth. A person asserts some value or feature as honorable (I am a great scholar, athlete, public speaker, worker), and the public refuses to acknowledge the person's worth, even rejects him or her. This is shame marked by socially perceived disgrace. To be shamed by others breeds intense rage and inflicts a profound wound on the persons who are disgraced, together with those associated with them, particularly family members. Whether it is a bumper sticker on a car or a sign on a Roman cross, it becomes humiliation for everyone in the in-group. The ordinary reaction of collectivistic persons is to inform the group in which they might be embedded of the refusal of acknowledgment with a view to planning revenge on the new or traditional enemy responsible for the dishonor.

In collectivistic societies, shame works only for those individuals who feel an allegiance to others and to the social system in general, with a capacity to care about their social standing. In the Mediterranean world, there were alienated, unallied persons such as beggars, the dispossessed elites, or the conquered and exiled. If people are alienated, the effort to shame them is irrelevant and may only be a badge of honor. Thus to be crucified by conquering Romans who likewise crucified many of one's fellow Israelites would not be shameful to fellow ethnics. But to be handed over by one's fellow Israelites for crucifixion by out-group Roman authorities would be public shame, indeed.

In individualistic societies, where honor and shame are highly psychologized and bear deeply introspective resonance, shame is a denial of personal worth by some significant person (mother, father, teacher, relative, sibling). The person who is shamed believes he or she is simply not worthy to be alive, to be a person, to exist. This introspective sense of being shamed diminishes a person's self-worth and often activates urges of self-destruction as the only proper answer to one's lack of self-worth. This sort of reaction would rarely be found in the Mediterranean, past or present. As I was recently told by a Mediterranean informant after we both witnessed an incident of public shaming, "If I felt the urge to commit suicide, I would kill somebody." This, in a nutshell, is a typical anti-introspective, collectivistic reaction to being shamed.

Envy and Honor Concerns

Now, the experience of envy described by persons in the first-century Mediterranean shares the same collectivistic social playing field as the honor and shame interactions described previously. While honor and shame are basic values and primary concerns, the honor that other people cannot see, perceive, and experience is simply no honor. It does not exist. Hence the need to do something to show one's honorable status was imperative. The Bible translators' words for behaviors that demonstrate honor include *to glorify, to acquire glory,* and *glory. Glory* refers to the external items people have that reveal their status, their honor. To glorify is to trot out, parade, and show by some external act what sort of person one is and what sort of group one belongs to. For example, "The heavens are telling the glory of God" (Ps. 19:1); the devil took Jesus "to a very high mountain, and showed him all the kingdoms of the world and the glory of them" (Matt. 4:8; see Luke 4:6); "In a multitude of people is the glory of a king, but without people a prince is ruined" (Prov. 14:28); "For a man ought not to cover his head, since he is the image and glory of God; but woman is the glory of man" (1 Cor. 11:7). These are many instances of glory, of the external and visible showing the nonvisible social standing of the persons involved.

Ancient Mediterraneans were absorbed with honor concerns, much as modern U.S. persons are taken by wealth in its many forms. "Love of honor" (*philotimia*) as a driving behavioral force in the world of Jesus is no different from modern concerns for a better paying job, a raise, greater profit, or any other shape the "love of wealth" takes in our economic-focused society. Aristotle attempted to explain "for what reason, and of whom, and in what frame of mind, men are envious" in his very Mediterranean experience (*Rhet.* 2.10.1). The motive, he states, is "love of honor," that is, a drive to prominence through attention-getting and eye-catching behavior:

> It is equally clear for what reason, and of whom, and in what frame of mind, men are envious, if envy is a kind of pain at the sight of good fortune in regard to the goods mentioned; in the case of those like themselves; and not for the sake of a man getting anything, but because of others possessing it. For those men will be envious of others who are or seem to be like them. I mean like in birth-status, family relationship, age, moral habit, reputation, and possessions. And those will be envious who possess all but one of these features. That is why those who attempt great things and succeed are envious, because they think that every one is trying to deprive them of their acquisitions. The same is true for those who are honored for some special reason, especially for wisdom or happiness. And those driven to prominence are more envious than the unambitious. And so too, those who are excessively appreciative of their own wisdom, for they are driven to prominence in wisdom; and, in general, those who wish to be prominent in anything are envious in regard to it. And the small-minded, because everything appears great to them. (*Rhetoric* 2.10.1–3)

Aristotle presumes that readers know what he and his world meant by "love of honor," a common term found throughout Greek literature. "Love of honor" was a frequently mentioned and highly prized quality from Homer to Augustine. Xenophon, for example, described the Athenians as passionate for praise: "Athenians excel all others not so much in singing or in stature or in strength, as in love of honor, which is the strongest incentive to deeds of honour and renown" (*Mem.* 3.3.13). Similarly, Augustine looks back on Rome and describes what seems to him the pivotal value that drove Romans in all their endeavors—the love of praise: "For the glory that the Romans burned to possess, be it noted, is the favourable judgment of men who think well of other men" (*City of God* 5.12). For love of praise, the Romans overcame vices common to other peoples: "He (God) granted supremacy to men who for the sake of honor, praise and glory served the country in which they were seeking their own glory, and did not hesitate to prefer her safety to their own. Thus for one vice, that is, love of praise, they overcame the love of money and many other vices" (5.13). Xenophon valued "love of honor" so highly, he identified it as one of the chief things that distinguish not only humans from animals, but noble humans from ordinary folk.

"Honor" for the ancients meant primarily prominence from renown and reputation. Hence they engaged in various competitions that brought victory and thus fame. Competitions could be as innocent as rivalry at plays, dances, and songs at festivals, or as deadly as quarreling, feuding, and warring. Hence, it is not surprising that "love of honor" in competitive contexts is translated by scholars as "rivalry" or "aspiration" or simply "ambition." But at heart, it is a drive to prominence, a passionate quest for honor.

Yet, say Aristotle and many other ancient informants, this "love of honor" produces envy. Since the ancients were intensely desirous of fame and honor and thought that all things existed in limited supply, envy naturally follows love of honor. Hence, Aeschines remarks in one of his speeches how his client was put upon "by men who were envious and wished to bring insult upon his honorable name" (*Embassy* 111). Isocrates describes a famous Greek army that was filled with gods and the sons of the gods, "men who were not of the same temper as the majority of mankind nor on the same plane of thinking, but full of pride and passion and envy and ambition" (*Panathenaicus* 81–82). Similarly, Plutarch describes how the envy that springs up in someone while listening to a lecture arises from "ambition": "Now while envy in other matters is engendered by certain untrained and evil dispositions of a man, the envy that is directed against a speaker is the offspring of an unseasonable desire for repute and ambition" (*Listening to Lectures* 39E). Among the ancients, then, desire for fame, glory, and honor not only spurred individuals to excellence but pricked others to envy their success.

As previously noted, fame, glory, and honor have to be made tangible in concrete, perceivable objects and behaviors. The mediating concrete, perceivable objects and behaviors are "goods," that is, persons, things, and people doing things on one's behalf. For first-century people, the need for expressing one's honor with goods is rooted in a social system in which all goods are perceived as limited. This means that there are only so many goods to go around to show one's collectivistic glory.

Envy and Limited Good

Envy, in collectivistic cultures, clearly presupposes the perception of *limited good*. As noted previously (see p. 89 ff.) the perception of limited good is the socially shared conviction that the resources enabling a community to realize its range of needs are in finite supply and that any disruption of the social equilibrium can only be detrimental to community survival. Persons believe that in their social, economic, and natural universe—in sum, in their total environment—all goods exist in finite, limited quantity and are always in short supply. This literally includes all desired goods in life: land, wealth, prestige, blood, health, semen, friendship and love, manliness, honor, respect and status, power and influence, security and safety. And it is clear to all that a person has no direct power to increase the available quantities.

Since all good exists in limited amounts that cannot be increased or expanded, individuals, alone or with their families, expressing their honor attainments in some concrete way, can do so only by utilizing goods at the expense of others. Hence any expression of good fortune in terms of any good in life is viewed as a threat to one's rival groups or even to the entire community. Some are thus being deprived and denied something that is theirs, though they may not be aware of it. Because of this uncertainty about who is losing—it may be my in-group and I—expressions of improvement may be perceived as threats to other single individuals or families alone as well as to all individuals and families within the community, be it village or city quarter. After all, some person in our "egalitarian" society is stepping out of line, claiming to be better than us, and acting pretentiously. Community stability and harmony among individuals and families can develop and be maintained only by keeping to the existing arrangements of statuses. Thus most people would be interested in maintaining things just the way they are. It is this perspective in which envy is rooted.

When one shows something truly illustrious, others believe it impinges on their terrain, and they become envious. While a number of ancient Mediterranean observers agree about the nature of envy and its social dimensions, no ancient observer realized that the way the game of envy was played always presupposed that all goods in life are limited. Without the perception of limited good and the use of goods to express one's good fortune, envy does not emerge. The perception of limited good seems to be a necessary condition for envy to come forth in ruralized societies concerned with honor and shame. Thus, for example, in the United States, should a friend get a new car and tell you about it, as a rule you do not feel envious since you too can acquire a new car. And the same with new clothes, a new house, marriage, and children. So long as the good fortune in question is readily accessible to all, there is little concern about envy. On the other hand, in a society where the perception of limited good is a common social perception, envy will be institutionalized. Mediterranean envy concerns acquire institutional shape because honor and shame are pivotal values that need to be concretized and externalized. Under such conditions in a subsistence-based, ruralized society, patterns of envy will be well-known, commented on, and frequently observed in ways that do not happen in guilt-oriented, urbanized societies with perceptions of limitless good.

For first-century persons in the Mediterranean culture area, envy was a value that directed a person to begrudge another the possession of some singular quality, object, or relationship that gave or expressed honor. It was the limited nature of the honor-bearing quality, object, or relationship in question and the social status of the possessor that triggered envy. Plutarch observed how envy surfaces among social equals only when another seems to enjoy apparent prosperity (*On Envy and Hate* 537A). People of higher social standing are beyond envy. "Supreme and resplendent good fortune often extinguishes envy. For it is hardly likely that anyone envied Alexander or Cyrus when they had prevailed and become masters of the world" (*On Envy and Hate* 538A). Aristotle, writing several centuries earlier, likewise observed, "Envy is defined as a kind of distress at apparent success on the part of one's peers" (*Rhetoric* 2.10.1). He too stated that only social equals can really be envious by noting what they share in common: "I mean those like themselves in terms of birth, relationship, age, disposition, reputation, possessions" (2.10.2). He then discusses those who are envied: "It is evident, too, whom people envy . . . they envy those near to them in time and place and age and reputation, whence it has been said 'Kinship, too, knows how to envy'" (2.10.5). Most typically, then, envier and envied are social equals. Cicero echoes this commonplace when he says, "People are especially envious of their equals, or of those once beneath them, when they feel themselves left behind and fret at the other's upward flight" (*De Or.* 2.52.209). Envy interactions thus replicate honor interactions in that challenges for honor can take place only among equals. So too feelings of envy.

Such observations are quite significant. For if Israel's high priests delivered Jesus to death out of envy, it means that in Pilate's outsider observation, Jesus was a social equal of the high priests. This, of course, may simply derive from the Roman sense of superiority to all out-groups. The "natives" are all the same status to the foreigner authorities.

In the Israelite tradition, there is a relevant description of envy in the so-called "Testament of Simeon," part of a document called *The Testament of the Twelve Patriarchs*. This document antedates Jesus' career by a century or two. It is called a testament because it has the form of the last words of Israel's patriarchs directed to their "heirs," their descendants. In the ancient world, a final testament is a document describing the final concerns of a dying person—much like our wills. Since U. S. society has economics as its focal social institution, however, wills most commonly deal with the disposition of a dying person's property. But since the ancient Mediterranean had kinship as its focal social institution, testaments are full of advice for a person's heirs. Moreover, in the United States persons about to die are said to see their whole lives flash before their eyes. Not so in the ancient Mediterranean world. What is distinctive of final words in the Mediterranean (and elsewhere) is that the person about to die is believed capable of knowing what is going to happen to persons near and dear to him (or her). Dying persons are prescient because they are closer to the realm of God (or gods), who knows all things, than to the realm of humans, whose knowledge is limited to human experience. Thus Xenophon tells us, "At the advent of death, men become more divine, and hence can foresee the forthcoming" (*Cyrop.* 7.7.21). In the *Iliad* (16.849–50) the dying Patroculus predicts the death of Hector at the hands of Achilles, and the dying Hector predicts the death of Achilles himself (22.325). Similarly, in Sophocles' play *The Women of Trachis* the dying Heracles summons Alcmene so that she may learn from his last words "the things I now know by divine inspiration" (*Trachiniae* 1148). Vergil finds it normal to have the dying Orodes predict that his slayer will soon meet retribution (*Aeneid* 10.729–41). Plato too reports that Socrates made predictions during his last moments, realizing that "on the point of death, I am now in that condition in which men are most wont to prophesy" (*Apol.* 39c; cf. Xenophon, *Anab.* 30). Cicero reports concerning Callanus of India: "As he was about to die and was ascending his funeral pyre, he said: 'What a glorious death! The fate of Hercules is mine. For when this mortal frame is burned the soul will find the light.' When Alexander directed him to speak if he wished to say anything to him, he answered: 'Thank you, nothing, except that I shall see you very soon.' So it turned out, for Alexander died in Babylon a few days later" (*De Divinatione* 1.47).

The Israelite tradition equally shared this belief, as is clear from the final words of Jacob (Genesis 49) and Moses (Deuteronomy 31–34; see also 1 Samuel 12; 1 Kings 2:1–17; Joshua 23–24). This belief is behind the well-known documents called "testaments" written around the time of Jesus (e.g., *Testament of Moses*; see also *Jub.* 22:10–30, 1 Macc. 2:47–70; Josephus, *Antiquities* 12.279–84). So here in one section of *The Testament of the Twelve Patriarchs*, Simeon is on the point of death and knows what is going to happen to his children. Here is a large segment of his deathbed advice to them, with the words for envy italicized:

> 1. The copy of the words of Simeon, what things he spoke to his sons before he died, in the hundred and twentieth year of his life, in the year in which Joseph died. For they came to visit him when he was sick, and he strengthened himself and sat up and kissed them, and said to them:

2. Hear, O my children, hear Simeon your father, what things I have in my heart. I was born of Jacob my father, his second son; and my mother Leah called me Simeon, because the Lord heard her prayer. I became strong exceedingly; I shrank from no deed, nor was I afraid of anything. For my heart was hard, and my mind was unmoveable, and my bowels unfeeling: because valor also has been given from the Most High to men in soul and in body. And at that time I was *envious* of Joseph because our father loved him; and I set my mind against him to destroy him, because the prince of deceit sent forth the *spirit of envy* and blinded my mind, that I regarded him not as a brother, and spared not Jacob my father. But his God and the God of his fathers sent forth His angel, and delivered him out of my hands. For when I went into Shechem to bring ointment for the flocks, and Reuben to Dotham, where were our necessaries and all our stores, Judah our brother sold him to the Ishmaelites. And when Reuben came he was grieved, for he wished to have restored him safe to his father. But I was angry with Judah in that he let him go away alive, and for five months I continued vengeful against him; but God restrained me, and withheld from me all working of my hands, for my right hand was half withered for seven days. And I knew, my children, that because of Joseph this happened to me, and I repented and wept; and I besought the Lord that He would restore my hand unto me, and that I might be kept from all pollution and *envy*, and from all folly. For I knew that I had devised an evil deed before the Lord and Jacob my father, on account of Joseph my brother, in that I *envied* him.

3. And now, children, take heed of the spirit of *deceit and of envy*. For *envy* rules over the whole mind of a man, and does not allow him either to eat, or to drink, or to do any good thing: it ever suggests to him to destroy him that he *envies*; and he that is *envied* continues to flourish but he that *envies* fades away. Two years of days I afflicted my soul with fasting in the fear of the Lord, and I learned that deliverance from *envy* comes by respect for God. If a man flee to the Lord, the evil spirit runs away from him, and his mind becomes easy. And henceforward he sympathizes with him whom he *envied*, and condemns not those who love him, and so ceases from his *envy*.

4. And my father asked concerning me, because he saw that I was sad; and I said, I am pained in my liver. For I mourned more than they all, because I was guilty of the selling of Joseph. And when we went down into Egypt, and he bound us as a spy, I knew that I was suffering justly, and I grieved not. Now Joseph was a good man, and had the Spirit of God within him: compassionate and pitiful, he bore not malice against me; nay, he loved me even as the rest of his brothers.

Take heed, therefore, my children, of all *misdirected zeal and envy*, and behave in the integrity of your heart, keeping in mind the brother of your father, that God may give to you also grace and glory, and blessing upon your heads, even as you saw in him. All his days he reproached us not concerning this thing, but loved us as his own self, and beyond his own sons; and he glorified us, and gave riches, and cattle, and fruits freely to us all. Do you then also, my beloved children, love each one his brother with a good heart, and remove from you the *spirit of envy*, for this makes the soul savage and destroys the body; it turns one's purposes into anger and war, and stirs up unto blood, and leads the mind into frenzy, and does not allow prudence to act in men: moreover, it takes away sleep, and causes turmoil to the soul and trembling to the body. For even in sleep some malicious *envy*, deluding him, gnaws at his soul, and with wicked spirits disturbs it, and causes the body to be troubled, and the mind to awake from sleep in confusion; and as though having a wicked and poisonous spirit, so it appears to men. . . .

6. Behold, I have foretold you all things, that I may be clear from the sin of your souls. Now, if you remove from you your *envy*, and all your stiffneckedness, as a rose shall my bones flourish in Israel, and as a lily my flesh in Jacob, and my odor shall be as the odor of Libanus; and as cedars shall holy ones be multiplied from me for ever, and their branches shall stretch afar off. . . .

8. And Simeon made an end of commanding his sons, and slept with his fathers, being an hundred and twenty years old. And they laid him in a coffin of incorruptible wood, to take up his bones to Hebron. And they carried them up in a war of the Egyptians secretly: for the bones of Joseph the Egyptians guarded in the treasure-house of the palace; for the sorcerers told them that at the departure of the bones of Joseph there should be throughout the whole of Egypt darkness and gloom, and an exceeding great plague to the Egyptians, so that even with a lamp a man should not recognise his brother.

9. And the sons of Simeon bewailed their father according to the law of mourning, and they were in Egypt until the day of their departure from Egypt by the hand of Moses.

It is easy to see that the description of envy in this document is much like that found in other Mediterranean authors. Simeon recounts his role in the selling of his half-brother, Joseph. He envied his father's love for young Joseph. Love, parental attachment to children shown in various outward ways, was a limited good. The author of this document, however, like his other Mediterranean contemporaries, is unaware of limited good. Instead he ascribes the emergence of envy to an evil spirit. This evil spirit provoked envy in this patriarch. And the envy revealed itself in Simeon's anger and plans to kill his brother. Envy leads to murder (as in the story of Cain and Abel). But Simeon's plans were thwarted by God, who had Joseph sold and moved to Egypt.

In the next paragraph, we have a description of envy. Once it emerges, it controls the human heart, suppresses appetite, suggests plans for harming the envied person. The envier dwindles away; the envied person prospers. Reverence for God, who providentially disposes benefactions among human beings, assuages envy and enables the envier to develop positive feelings for the one previously envied.

In greater detail, we learn about envy's impact on heart and body: it leads to anger and war, blood feud and mental frenzy, suppressing caution. It makes one sleepless, anxious, nervous, and convulsive. And even in sleep, dreams are troubled while awaking is fearsome.

In the end, Simeon expresses the wonderful outcome produced by the absence of envy among his children: conquest over enemies with ensuing peace and prosperity. It is important to note that what Simeon describes is in-group envy, envy toward one's kin. There is little concern about envying an enemy or an outsider. After all, in situations where outsiders incite envy, it is quite appropriate to be outraged, even to kill them.

Why would people think it is quite right to envy outsiders? The reason is that persons who are envied stand out from the rest of the community. They stand above their fellows. The social deviance involved in possessing something perceived as singular is that the one possessing the unique item stands out or stands above his or her proper social status and/or the group in general. The one who is envious becomes negatively disposed towards the person with the singular possession and is often seized by the desire to deprive the other person of that possession—often in the name of the group. It is right to cut down anyone standing about his/her status—but not one's own kin.

Observing Envy

It might be good to recall, once more, that ancient Mediterraneans were anti-introspective and not psychologically minded at all. That means that terms for internal states invariably entail corresponding external actions. It is only from the actions that one can actually know the internal states of another (and oneself). Although Aristotle calls envy a "*lype*" (distress, grief, pain) (*Rhetoric* 2.10.1), it is a very dangerous phenomenon because it rarely stays at the level of emotion but emerges in observable behavior. What sort of behaviors, then, point to the presence of envy?

As we might assume, envious people reveal their internal feelings in a number of ways. Among these, scholars have noted ostracism, gossip and slander, feuding, litigation, and homicide. Yet all would agree that the prevalence of envy in ancient Mediterranean society was rather strongly underscored by belief in the evil eye.

To begin with, consider the first set of envy-rooted behaviors. *Ostracism* is a type of shunning that entails temporary banishment. It was a social mechanism developed in classical Athens whereby a person who gained too much prominence was banished from the city for a limited time. Although allowed to return, the overachieving, envied person was nevertheless out of the public's eye and unable to exercise "love of honor" in competition with others. Ostracism thus necessarily resulted in a lowering of the honor standing of the envied and banished person.

Some examples of such ostracism are involved in behaviors in which prophets are rejected by their own in-groups: "And Jesus said to them, 'A prophet is not without honor, except in his own country, and among his own kin, and in his own house'" (Mark 6:4: note the list of in-groups; see also Matt. 13:57; Luke 4:24; John 4:43). John reports that Jesus' followers were ejected from the synagogue, a form of such ostracism (John 9:22; 12:12).

Gossip is essentially "critical talk about absent third parties." Plutarch provides the modern reader with a unique report by a native informant on the relationship of gossip and envy: "Since it is the searching out of troubles that the busybody [i.e., gossiper] desires, he is possessed by the affliction called 'malignancy,' a brother to envy and spite. For envy is pain at another's good, while malignancy is joy at another's sorrow" (*Talkativeness* 518C). Reputations are easily ruined by gossip. In the Gospels, questions about Jesus' factual origin would be rooted in envy: "Coming to his own country he taught them in their synagogue, so that they were astonished, and said, 'Where did this man get this wisdom and these mighty works?'" (Matt. 13:54–57; see Luke 4:22). John, in turn, reports the same tradition and appropriates it as follows: "They said, 'Is not this Jesus, the son of Joseph, whose father and mother we know? How does he now say, I have come down from heaven'?" (John 6:42).

Feuding refers to the challenge-riposte interactions so common in the ancient Mediterranean and described previously. Challengers are frequently motivated by envy. Consider all the passages in the Gospels in which Jesus' challengers seek "to test him." Such testing episodes point to envy as their trigger. The questions are to put down the successful Jesus a few pegs. Such challenge-riposte scenarios often describe the persistent state of "enmity" that existed between individuals or families in antiquity. When Jesus asks his followers to "pray for your enemies," he has such feuding partners in mind.

Among elites, those feuding often conducted their attacks through *litigation*, by taking persons to court, if possible. Litigation in antiquity was not about justice, about getting at the truth of a case, such as is often portrayed on contemporary TV shows. Rather litigation, as noted previously, is about shaming one's opponent, thus reducing him (or her) to public pity.

Finally, an envious person might resort to physical violence and even *homicide* to reduce the status of the person envied. Israelite tradition ascribed Cain's murder of Abel to envy; the same was true of Saul's attempts to slay David. In Luke's special tradition, Jesus' own town mates seek to put him to death after an interaction that demonstrates their envy toward him (Luke 4:16–30). The same is true in Pilate's assessment of the high priests who want Jesus killed (Mark 15:10). Thus, envy is no empty emotion.

Evil Eye: Proof of Envy

As a rule, people in the Mediterranean were (and are) very watchful of those who might envy them by attention to the *evil eye*. Evil-eye belief refers to the conviction that certain individuals, animals, demons, or gods have the power to cause some negative effect on any object, animate or inanimate, on which they may look. Evil eye works voluntarily or involuntarily. The negative effects it can cause are injuries to the life or health of others, to their means of sustenance and livelihood, or to their honor and personal fortune.

Basic to this belief was the notion that certain individuals, animals, demons, or gods had the power of injuring or casting a spell on every object, animate or inanimate, on which their glance fell. Through the power of their eye, which could operate involuntarily as well as intentionally, such evil-eye possessors were thought capable of damaging or destroying their unfortunate victims. In fact, though, such negative effects derived not simply from the power of their eye but from the condition of their heart, since eyes and heart worked in tandem. A number of ancient Mediterranean informants have noted how the effects of the evil eye correlate with envy, a quality of the heart. The eye served to express the innermost dispositions, feelings, and desires of the heart. Numerous biblical passages illustrate this connection of eye and heart (Deut. 28:65; 1 Kings 9:3; Job 30:26–27; 31:1, 7, 9, 26–27; Ps. 73(72):7; Prov. 15:30; 21:4; 44:18; Isa. 6:10; Lam. 5:17; Sir. 22:19; 1 Cor. 2:9). Ephesians 1:18, for instance, speaks of "eyes of the heart" (cf. also *1 Clem.* 36:2). Jeremiah 22:17 refers to eyes and heart intent on dishonest gain, bloodshed and the practice of oppression and violence. To understand the ancient Mediterranean perspective on the evil eye, consider how they viewed the relationship between light and the eyes.

For the ancient Mediterranean, light was the presence of light, and darkness was the presence of darkness. That is, both light and darkness were positive entities, having no relationship to any source of light or darkness other than themselves. Thus the sun did not "cause" daylight nor did the moon or stars "cause" light at night. Day and night were simply the structured framework in which the sun and moon operated. Notice that in Genesis, the sun, moon, and stars were created after the creation of light and darkness (Gen. 1:3–5, 14–19). While the sun and moon marked the changing of the seasons, they had no influence on the seasons any more than they influenced day or night. The relative darkness of winter was due to the cloudy sky, not to the low path of the sun. In fact the sun was noted for its warmth rather than its light. Light was present due to the presence of light itself, not the presence of the sun. This meant that the onset of celestial light over the land was the dawn, and the coming of celestial darkness over the land was dusk (not sunrise and sunset).

In the story of creation, the creation of light set light itself apart from preexisting darkness, just as the creation of land (earth) set it apart from everpresent water (Genesis 1). Note that light (day) was created before the sun, and night before the moon. Dawn (morning) and dusk (evening) occur independently of the sun as well. The presence of light and land (earth) allowed for the coming of earthlings. Earthlings, human and otherwise, are created from earth, animated with the breath of life (Gen. 2:7), and endowed with the light of life (Job 33:30; Ps. 56:14), or "living light" as opposed to the light of the sky. Thanks to their living light, animate beings can see.

Sight consists of light emanating from the eyes of living beings. Just as the main humanly controlled source of light is fire, so too it is because the eyes are made of fire that humans see. As Jesus says, "The eye is the lamp of the body" (Matt. 6: 22). Aristotle observed, "Sight (is made) from fire and hearing from air" (*Problems* 31, 960a); "[V]ision is fire" (*Problems* 31, 959b); "Is it because in shame the eyes are chilled (for shame resides in the eyes), so that they cannot face one?" (*Problems* 31, 957b). The eye emits light that has an active effect on the objects on which its glance falls. "Man both experiences and produces many effects through his eyes; he is possessed and governed by either pleasure or displeasure exactly in proportion to what he sees," one of Plutarch's dinner guests observes (Plutarch, *Quaestionum convivialium* 5.7, 681A).

Similarly, the Israelite tradition believed God's sky-servants (angels) were made of fire. Hence when they appear to humans, they look like brilliant light. The fact that celestial bodies, such as stars or comets, emanate light means that they are alive. Stars, whether constellated or not, are living animate entities, as all ancients believed. That is why they move while the earth stands still at the center of creation. Since all living beings have light, light and life go hand in hand. In this perspective, all light and life have their origin in the creative work of God alone; they can be handed on by human beings, but not created by them.

Envy thus proceeds from the heart through the eyes. The usual suspects thought to harbor evil-eye abilities were family enemies, strangers, outsiders, and deviants, as well as the physically deformed, disabled, and the blind. Strangers and outsiders were presumed to be envious of the good things locals and insiders enjoyed; the socially deviant (criminals, traitors) were envious of those not caught and labeled as deviants, while the crippled and the blind were envious of those enjoying good health. Resident out-groups were stereotypically believed to be afflicted with the evil eye. Philo stereotypes the Egyptians as an envious and evil-eyed people in his writing against Flaccus: "But the Egyptian," he states, "is by nature an evil eyed person, and the citizens burst with envy and considered that any good fortune to others was misfortune to themselves" (*Flaccus* 29).

This association of evil eye and envy is typical of ancient Mediterraneans. Israelite tradition, for example, is full of warnings against persons with the evil eye. "[The person with] a good eye will be blessed, for he shares his bread with the poor" (Prov. 22:9), but "evil is the man with an evil eye; he averts his face and disregards people" (Sir. 14:8). "An Evil-eyed man is not satisfied with a portion and mean injustice withers the soul" (Sir. 14:9). "An Evil-eyed man begrudges bread and it is lacking at his table" (Sir. 14:10; cf. also Sir. 18:18; Tobit 4: 7, 17). "Remember that an evil eye is a bad thing. What has been created more evil than the eye? It sheds tears from every face" (Sir. 31:13). The glance and even the presence of such an individual were to be avoided because he or she was thought to have the power of injuring and destroying with his/her eye. "A fool," says Israelite wisdom, "is ungracious and abusive, and the begrudging gift of an Evil-eyed person makes the eyes dim" (Sir. 18:18). "Do not consult with an Evil-eyed man about gratitude or with a merciless man about kindness" (Sir. 37:11). "The evil eye of wickedness obscures what is good, and roving desire perverts the innocent mind" (Wisd. Sol. 4:12).

In the Bible envy manifests itself both on the tribal (Gen. 26:14; Isa. 11:13) and familial levels (Gen. 30:1; 37:11). As noted previously, it is associated with the worldview that prosperity occurs only at the expense of others, hence that the few who prosper are wicked. Their prosperity must have been obtained by social oppression and will be punished by Yahweh in the end (Job 5:2; Ps. 37:1; 73:3; Prov. 3:31; 23:17; 24:1, 19; 27:4). The situations in which suspicion of an evil eye occurs in the Old Testament vary from famine and the begrudging of food to the starving (Deut. 28:53–57) and the sharing/non-sharing of food in general (Prov. 23:1–8; Sir. 31:12–31), to the lust after wealth (Prov. 28:22), the miserly unwillingness to share with those in need (Deut. 15:7–11; Sir. 14:3–10; 18:18; Tobit 4:1–21), the consultation of inappropriate counselors for advice (Sir. 37:7–15), evil-eye fascination at the time of Enoch (Wisd. Sol. 5:10–15), protection of fields with an anti-evil-eye device (Let. Jer. 69), and control of the evil eye and other socially disruptive passions (Tobit 4:1–21). Further implicit traces of evil-eye belief in the Old Testament can be found in passages that refer to the envy, hatred, greed, or covetousness of the eye or heart (e.g., Gen. 4:5; 30:1; 37:11; Exod. 20:17; 1 Sam. 2:32; 18:8–9; Ps. 73:3; Prov. 23:1; Jer. 22:17) or to protective amulets (e.g., Judg. 8:21, 26; Isa. 3:20) customarily used against the evil eye.

In the New Testament, references to the evil eye involved similar social and moral overtones. Jesus himself, according to the Gospels, made mention of the evil eye more than once. Matthew's Sermon on the Mount contains one such instance that we shall consider later in more detail (Matt. 6:22–23; cf. Luke 11:34–36, which is located in a different setting). This precedes a later mention of the evil eye by Jesus in the parable of the laborers in the vineyard (Matt. 20:1–16). On another occasion, according to the Gospel of Mark, Jesus, in a dispute with the Pharisees over the issue of purity (Mark 7.1–23), lists the evil eye (Mark 7:22) among a group of evil things (Mark 7:23) that emerge from the human heart and thereby pollute a person. Finally, among the explicit references to the evil eye is Paul's reference in his conflict with his opponents at Galatia: "O foolish Galatians, who has injured you with the evil eye?" (Gal. 3:1). This letter contains several indications that Paul had been accused by his detractors of having had an evil eye. Paul defends himself ("You did not shield your eyes from me and my portrayal of the Christ" [Gal. 3:1b]; "You did not spit in my presence"[Gal. 4:14]; "You would have plucked out your eyes and given them to me" [Gal. 4:15]) and counters this charge with an evil-eye accusation of his own: "It is not I, but rather my opponents who have the evil eye." "It is they," he implies to his Galatian readers, "and not I who have injured your children with their malignant envy and have caused divisions within your community" (Gal. 4:17–18; 5:20, 26). In Galatians we have evidence of the way in which evil-eye accusations were employed by rivals to label and publicly discredit their opponents through appeal to the court of public opinion.

Protection against the Evil Eye

Because the dangerous evil eye was believed to lurk everywhere, vigilance was required of all persons in all walks of life. No one and no sphere of activity was immune from injury from the baleful glance. The evil-eye possessor, in fact, could afflict not only his/her friends and relatives but even him/herself (Plutarch, *Quaest. conviv.* 682A-F). Particularly vulnerable, however, were children (Plutarch, *Quaest. conviv.* 680D, 682A, 682F), and then also domestic residences, fields and animals, work sites, food and means of livelihood; that is, everything necessary for the continued existence of the family unit.

Ancient Mediterraneans used a range of protective amulets to protect themselves, their houses, their shops, and the public places they frequented. Among these a common protective device was a staring eye worn as amulet or carved into a wall or put into mosaic flooring. The eye served as a mirror to reflect the evil eye back on its possessor. Equally effective was a phallus, worn around the neck, inscribed in stone or hanging from the wall. An unexpected meeting with an epileptic, a lame man, or a stranger, sources of evil-eye effects, could be protected against by spitting. Other personal protective measures included avoiding eye contact altogether, concealing prized possessions, covering one's women and children, denying any improvement in one's economic situation, and wearing a variety of protective devices (strings of knots, red or blue colored cloth, sacks of herbs such as rue or garlic, amulet jewelry inscribed with anti-evil-eye symbols such as an eye under attack or miniature phalluses, phylacteries, horns, crescent moons, or bells).

The most common way to keep envy at bay was to use devices designed to ward off the effects of the evil eye, such as tattoos, seals and signet rings, incantations, and the like (see Judg. 8:21, 26; Isa. 3:20). The purple tassels at the bottom of one's cloak served this purpose (Luke 8:44). The pregnant Mary could travel alone to visit her cousin—a very unusual behavior in this culture—since the child in her womb served to defend and protect her from all harm. The leaping of Elizabeth's own fetus in her womb can be interpreted as a recognition of Jesus' apotropaic (evil-thwarting) powers and abilities (Luke 1:39–41). Another way to deal with envy is to confront envious persons and accuse them of harboring the "evil eye." As Elliott (1990) notes,

> Beyond spitting, the ancients employed a veritable arsenal of devices and methods for warding off the dread evil eye. The underlying principle was that of homeopathic magic and *similia similibus*, the use of "like against like." Such practices attested in art, artifacts, and architecture as well as literature, included the hanging of bullae around the necks of children; the wearing of *fascina* (replicas of phalluses), engraved amulets, and cloth of red or blue color; the manual gestures of the *digitus infamis* (extended middle finger of a fisted hand—the American "high sign"), the *manus cornuta* (extended second and fifth fingers of the fisted hand), and *manus fica* (thumb inserted between second and third fingers of fisted hand); and an array of similar designs and devices on public monuments and private home, thresholds, shops and graves—all for the purpose of distracting, deflecting or counteracting the omnipresent threat of the evil eye.

One of the participants in Plutarch's "Table Talk" named Patrocleas is said to have remarked,

> Envy, which naturally roots itself more deeply in the mind than any other passion, contaminates the body too with evil. When those possessed by envy to this degree let their glance fall upon a person, their eyes, which are close to the mind and draw from it the evil influence of the passion, then assail that person as if with poisoned arrows; hence, I conclude, it is not paradoxical or incredible that they should have an effect on the persons who encounter their gaze. . . . What I have said shows why the so-called amulets are thought to be a pro-

tection against envy; the strange look of them attracts the gaze, so that it exerts less pressure upon its victims. (681 F-82)

Apart from evil-eye influences, persons envied for possessing some singular quality, object, or relationship can defend themselves from envy in various ways.

Protection against Envy

Scholars have listed various types of behavior undertaken by people who fear the envy of others and seek to reduce their own visibility and vulnerability: (1) *concealment*, (2) *denial*, (3) a conciliatory *bribe*, and (4) *true sharing*.

We begin with *concealment* or *secrecy*. In a society like that in which Jesus lived, a personal self-disclosure may result in ridicule, hostility, gossip, envy, and conformity pressures to change. As we know, in ancient Mediterranean society interpersonal relations are characterized by competition, rivalries, and conflicts of opinion. In this limited-good world, where anything gained, whether new wealth, position, honor or whatever, was always believed to come at someone else's expense, one could never appear grasping or self-aggrandizing in public without raising immediate suspicion. The much-discussed "messianic secret" motif so prominent in Mark (1:25, 34, 44; 3:12; 5:43; 7:24, 36; 8:30; 9:9, 30; 14:61; 15:32) can be seen in this light. Having been born to the low social status of a village artisan, Jesus could not claim to be anything more than a village artisan without being viewed as grasping in the extreme. The Gospel authors allow their readers to know what the true social standing of Jesus is (Mark 1:1, a son of God; Matt. 1:1, Jesus Messiah; Luke 1:32, son of the Most High; John 1:1, the Word of God). But Jesus prefers concealment to ward off envy. He thus further shows himself to be an honorable person by trying to keep any talk of his being an extraordinary personage out of public notice. Note especially his silencing of demons who, given their higher position in the cosmic hierarchy, are readily able to identify this unexpected status for Jesus (see Mark 1:25, 34; 3:12). Boasting, the opposite of concealment, openly invites envy. "It is the glory of God to conceal things, but the glory of kings is to search things out" (Prov. 25:2).

Denial might be the simple rejection of a compliment. Few Bible readers pay attention to Jesus' rejection of the label "Good" when the greedy (i.e., rich) man addressed him as "Good teacher" (Mark 10:17). Yet one ancient informant explains how dangerous praise could be. Aulus Gellius tells of certain people who work spells by voice and tongue: "For if they should chance to bestow extravagant praise upon beautiful trees, plentiful crops, charming children, fine horses, flocks that are well fed and in good condition, suddenly, for no other cause than this, all of these die" (*Attic Nights* 9.4.8, referring to Pliny the Elder, *Natural History* 7.16). While claims to worth needed public acknowledgment in the world of Jesus, words of praise could kill. Hence we would expect people to be wary of compliments and other public expressions of a person's superior worth. Thus Jesus simply avoids envy by refusing the compliment "Good Teacher." He properly responds, "Why do you call me 'good'? No one is good but God alone" (Mark 10:18).

A *conciliatory bribe* is a gift bestowed on others so as to ward off or reduce sentiments of envy. It is a type of forced sharing of something to placate those who would be envious of the rising prominence of some person. It takes little imagination to realize that the stories of the feeding of the crowds in the Synoptic Gospels work as conciliatory bribes (Mark 6:32–44; 8:1–10; Matt. 14:13–21; 15:32–39; Luke 8:10–17; John 6:1–15). Instead of being envious of Jesus and thwarting him in his task of proclaiming the forthcoming theocracy, the crowds are duly astonished and enable him to continue his work.

True sharing was a way of leveling wealth and thus reducing envy. In the Gospels, instances of such true sharing took the form of almsgiving and temple tithing. In the stories in Acts, we learn of Jesus-group members who being "possessors of lands or houses sold them, and brought the proceeds of what was sold and laid it at the apostles' feet; and distribution was made to each as any had need" (Acts 4:34–35). But spectacular instances of such sharing in the Roman Empire involved wealthy aristocrats who funded projects in their cities, just as monarchs who did the same in the lands they controlled (e.g., King Herod the Great rebuilt the Jerusalem temple as well as a number of "cities" in his kingdom). Such public works on behalf of the people were called "liturgy."

Envy Is Not Jealousy

English speakers often confuse envy and jealousy. In antiquity, not only are two different words involved (as today), but the words referred to different realities. We have already noted that envy refers to the sentiment of begrudging the success of another. Jealousy, on the other hand, is the sentiment of concern for the well-being of whom or what one holds dear. It might be useful to note that the word "jealousy" is in fact a transliteration of the word "zeal." Jealousy has two dimensions. The first is a sort of defensive jealousy that emerges when the well-being of whom or what one holds dear is threatened. The second is assertive jealousy that surfaces in rivalry or competition that benefits one's in-group.

Defensive jealousy is, by far, the common reference for the words "jealous" and "zeal" in the Bible. A "jealous God" (Exod. 20:5; 34:14; Deut. 4:24;

6:15; 9:9; Josh. 24:19) is attached to and concerned for his status and his clients; a "jealous husband" is attached to and concerned for his social standing and for his wife (Num. 5:14, 30). Jealousy is a form of protectiveness that would ward off the envious and their machinations. It should not be confused with envy. Thus defensive jealousy or zeal refers to the latent emotional disposition and corresponding, activated behavior that an honorable person is expected to exhibit towards that to which he or she is perceived to possess exclusive access. Jealousy and zeal thus refer to a value that serves as a means for preserving and maintaining honor.

Within a context of honor and shame and a perception of limited good, zeal/jealousy refers to the concern for maintaining possession and control over that to which one claims to have honorable and exclusive access. Envy, in contrast to zeal/jealousy, constitutes the desire to possess another or the resentment of the honorable and exclusive possession of another. From the perspective of envy, zeal/jealousy is the expected, honorable response of a person perceived to have been dishonored, afflicted, violated, or otherwise injured by envious intentions and/or actions. Thus, in the Old Testament, limited goods capable of generating zeal/jealousy include God (Num. 25:11, 13; 1 Kings 19:10, 14; 2 Kings 10:16), who is, himself, an agent of jealousy (Exod. 20:5, 34:14; Deut. 5:9, 6:15); God's name (Ezek. 36:6); God's household (Ps. 69:9); God's holy Torah (Gal. 1:14); God's holy land (Ezek. 36:5, Joel 2:18; Nah. 1:2); God's holy city and mountain (Zech. 1:14); and God's holy remnant (1 Kings 19:31; Isa. 26:11). In the New Testament both Jesus-group members and outsider Israelites are called "jealous/zealous" (Acts 5:17, 13:45; Rom. 11:11; 2 Cor. 7:7, 9:2; 2 Pet. 1:10, 3:14).

Assertive jealousy or zeal is the motivating force behind fair competition and friendly rivalry. Of course it entails a challenge to others. In the following passage from Aristotle on zeal (*zelos*), I translate the word "competitiveness." Traditionally the word is translated "emulation," a term not in popular use today. Consider now what Aristotle has to say about this sort of assertive jealousy:

> Let us assume that competitiveness is a feeling of pain at the evident presence of highly valued goods, which are possible for us to obtain, in the possession of those who naturally resemble us—pain not due to the fact that another possesses them, but to the fact that we ourselves do not. Competitiveness therefore is virtuous and characteristic of virtuous men, whereas envy is base and characteristic of base men; for the one, owing to competitiveness, fits himself to obtain such goods, while the object of the other, owing to envy, is to prevent his neighbor possessing them. Necessarily, then, those are competitive who hold that they have a claim to goods that they do not possess; for no one claims what seems impossible. Hence the young and

high-minded are competitive. And so are those who possess such advantages as are worthy of honorable men, which include wealth, a number of friends, positions of office, and all similar things. For, believing it their duty to be good, because such goods naturally belong to those who are good, they strive to preserve them. And those are competitive, whom others think worthy of them. Honors obtained by ancestors, kinsfolk, intimates, nation, or city make men competitive in regard to such honors; for they think that these honors really belong to them and that they are worthy of them. And if highly valued goods are the object of competitiveness, it necessarily follows that the virtues must be such and all things that are useful and beneficial to the rest of mankind, for benefactors and virtuous men are honored; to these we may add all the goods which our neighbors can enjoy with us, such as wealth and beauty, rather than health. It is also evident who are the objects of competitiveness ; for they are those who possess these or similar goods, such as have already been spoken of, for instance, courage, wisdom, authority; for those in authority, such as generals, orators, and all who have similar powers, can do good to many. And those whom many desire to be like, or to be their acquaintances or friends; those whom many or ourselves admire. . . . (*Rhetoric*, 2.11.1–4)

Such assertive jealousy occurs in the New Testament list of vices. What makes assertive jealousy a negative quality in the in-group is that it necessarily leads to the dishonor of others, since all goods are limited. Hence early post-Jesus groups were to avoid such competitiveness among themselves (2 Cor. 12:20; Gal. 5:20; James 3:16).

Envy Is Not Hate

A first-century Mediterranean informant, Plutarch, authored a brief essay on envy and hate. He begins by observing that the source of the pain of persons who feel envy as well as persons who feel hate is "the fortunate man." We do not harbor goodwill toward persons we hate or envy. How do the two differ? Hate, he says, arises when people think they have been wronged or treated unjustly; the objects of hate are those given to wickedness and wrongdoing, people "deserving of hate." We can hate people as well as animals that we find repulsive (he mentions weasels, beetles, toads, and snakes). Animals, too, can hate their natural enemies. On the other hand, animals by all indications are not envious of each other. The reason for this is that "they have no notion of another's good or ill fortune, nor are they affected by glory or disgrace, things by which envy is most exasperated" (*On Envy and Hate* 537B). So envy is a typically human experience.

People who hate others readily admit the fact, but not so people who envy: "Men deny that they envy as well; and if you show that they do, they allege any number of excuses and say they are angry with the fellow or fear or hate him, cloaking and concealing their envy with whatever other name occurs to them for their passion, implying that among the disorders of the soul it alone is unmentionable" (*On Envy and Hate* 537E).

Envy Enters the Ten Commandments

Philo interestingly begins his treatment of the second half of the Ten Commandments (from the prohibition of adultery to the end) in such a way that might lead a reader to believe that the root of transgressions against neighbor was envy, "the most grievous of all evils." Paul lists envy among the vices of Gentiles in the famous list that opens his letter to the Romans: "They were filled with every kind of wickedness, evil, covetousness, malice. Full of envy, murder, strife, deceit, craftiness, they are gossips, slanderers, God-haters, insolent, haughty, boastful, inventors of evil, rebellious toward parents, foolish, faithless, heartless, ruthless" (Rom. 1:29–31). The list is simply a disguised listing of the Ten Commandments of Israelite tradition. The following reveals the numerals that serve as skeleton to the list: (1) evil, covetousness, (2) malice, envy, (3) murder, strife, (4) deceit, malignity, (5) gossips, slanderers, (6) haters of God, (7) insolent, haughty, (8) boastful inventors of evil, disobedient to parents, (9) foolish, faithless, (10) heartless, ruthless.

Why a disguised Ten Commandments? Josephus reports that in the Israel of his day, just as it was forbidden to utter the sacred name of YHWH, the most sacred name of the tribal God of Israel, so too it was forbidden to utter the "Ten Words" given on Sinai to Israel. It is true that these were the very Ten Words "which Moses has left inscribed on the two tables," yet "these words it is not permitted us to state explicitly, to the letter." Josephus notes that these Ten Words have "power" (*Ant* 3.90). After all, these very words, "the Ten Commandments which God himself gave to his people without employing the agency of any prophet or interpreter" (Philo, *Special Laws* III.2.7) were the direct words of the God of Israel himself, hence full of power. They must not be repeated verbatim, but they could be written verbatim. Since these words were put in amulets (*tephilin*) and doorpost amulets (*mezuzoth*) by no command of God (unlike the *Shema* of Deut. 6:4 ff.), it seems their presence there, "to the letter," was to serve as apotropaic, a prophylactic device to ward off hostile power, the evil eye, and the like.

While it was forbidden to recite the Ten Words in the exact wording and order as found in the Torah passage recounting the Sinai incident, first-century Israelites did not refrain from quoting them. They simply disguised them or reordered them. In the Synoptic tradition, for example, Jesus offers a listing to the Greedy Young Man as follows: "You shall not kill, You shall not commit adultery, You shall not steal, You shall not bear false witness, Honor your father and mother, and, You shall love your neighbor as yourself" (Matt. 19:18–19; Mark 10:19 omits love of neighbor as does Luke 18:20, who inverts adultery and killing). There are further truncated listings. For example, in the Sermon on the Mount the antitheses (Matt. 5:21–36) cover five of the ten commandments.

In the list of evils proceeding from the heart, Mark 7:21–22 has three parallel categories of three "evils," concluding with pride and foolishness, an Israelite designation for having other gods before Israel's God, or idolatry. These cover only five of the Ten Commandments:

a fornication	a' adultery	a" licentiousness
b theft	b' coveting	b" envy
c murder	c' wickedness	c" slander

and pride and foolishness

Matthew 15:19 has a list of six (or seven or five) evil thoughts, but these are the last five of a listing, just like in the antitheses in the Sermon on the Mount: (1) murder, (2) adultery, fornication, (3) theft, (4) false witness, (5) slander. Romans 1:29–32, in turn, is a disguised version. The same is true of lists in 1 Corinthians 6:9–10: "Do you not know that the unrighteous will not inherit the kingdom of God? Do not be deceived; neither the immoral, nor idolaters, nor adulterers, nor sexual perverts, nor thieves, nor the greedy, nor drunkards, nor revilers, nor robbers will inherit the kingdom of God." Note also 1 Timothy 1:9–10: "The law is not laid down for the just but for the lawless and disobedient, for the ungodly and sinners, for the unholy and profane, for murderers of fathers and murderers of mothers, for manslayers, immoral persons, sodomites, kidnapers, liars, perjurers, and whatever else is contrary to sound doctrine."

Thus during the time of the emergence of the Jesus group and the post-Jesus groups, the Ten Commandments, the only commandments given to all Israel directly from God, were not to be recited verbatim. They were appropriated in such a way that envy was one of the prohibitions. And the words of the Ten Commandments, written down and placed on doorposts and put in little leather boxes worn during prayer (phylacteries), could protect a person from the evil eye.

Summary

Envy is an emotion that makes a person feel aggrieved at the good fortune of another person, normally of the same social ranking. Good fortune meant honor, and honor sought expression through mediating goods. Envy sought expression in concrete actions that would reduce the envied person to a state of disgrace and misfortune. Envy differs from jealousy or zeal as well as from hate. It was of central concern in the ancient Mediterranean since all goods were considered limited, and the person expressing honor as well as the honor itself detracted from others. It took away something invariably at some other person's expense. Envious people demonstrated their envy by ostracism, gossip, negative challenges, litigation, or homicide. The most common indicator of envy was the evil eye. To avoid envy and the evil eye, people used a number of objects and gestures. They likewise concealed or denied their good fortune, offered conciliatory bribes and practiced true sharing. During the time of Jesus, envy was regularly counted among the prohibitions given by the God of Israel in the Ten Commandments. Table 3 summarizes the main features presented in this chapter.

Table 3: Envy in U.S. Experience and Ancient Mediterranean Experience

U.S. Experience	Ancient Mediterranean Experience
Envy occurs between single persons, replicating individualistic culture.	Envy occurs between groups, replicating collectivistic culture.
Envy is not confined to persons in the same economic status since individuals aspire to ever higher statuses.	Envy is confined to status equals, determined by genealogy, gender, and geography since individuals remain in the same status for life.
The person envied is seen as fortunate and elated in his/her new possession or relationship.	The person envied is seen as rising above the social level to which he or she is entitled by birth and ethnicity.
The person who envies begrudges his or her rival's good fortune but can find other fields in which to find good fortune and happiness.	The person who envies begrudges his or her rival's good fortune because it marks a deprivation of good for the envier and his/her group.
Honor and shame are internalized and introspective experiences.	Honor and shame are externalized, social experiences.
Shame is the rejection of an individual's personhood.	Shame is the rejection of one's group's claim to honor.
Shame provokes feelings of unworthiness, even suicide, in the individual.	Shame provokes plans of retaliation and vengeance in the group.
Honor is an internalized feeling of social success.	Honor is an externalized expression of social success.

U.S. Experience	Ancient Mediterranean Experience
People need goods and awards to gauge their success in an achievement-oriented society.	People need goods and awards to proclaim their honor-standing, that is, their social glory in a contentment-oriented society.
Since people need goods to express meaning or to communicate, individualistic societies with individuals expected to express individualistic opinions require a far larger amount of goods than collectivistic societies.	Since people need goods to express meaning or to communicate, collectivistic societies with central personages expected to express group opinions require far fewer goods than individualistic societies.
All goods exist in endless, unlimited quantity and are usually always in abundant supply.	All goods exist in finite, limited quantity and are always in short supply.
An economy of superabundance: a short supply of goods indicates monopolistic practices and market control.	A subsistence economy: a short supply of goods indicates the normal condition of human society.
Social and economic improvement are beneficial to individuals and society as a whole.	Social and economic improvement is always at the expense of others.
Social and economic improvement are perceived as outcome of hard work and initiative.	Social and economic improvement are perceived as a threat to the well-being of one's in-group (family, neighborhood).
Economic stagnation points to social dysfunction.	Economic stagnation points to community harmony and stability.
Envy is an internal state, best analyzed by introspection and psychological methods.	Envy is an internal state with a corresponding external manifestation—the evil eye.
No awareness, much less concern, for the evil eye.	Much awareness and great concern for the evil eye.

References and Suggested Readings

Elliott, John H. "The Fear of the Leer: The Evil Eye from the Bible to Li'l Abner" *Forum* 4, no. 4 (1988):42–71.

_____. "Paul, Galatians and the Evil Eye." *Currents in Theology and Mission* 7 (1990): 262–273.

_____. "The Evil Eye in the First Testament: The Ecology and Culture of a Pervasive Belief." In *The Bible and the Politics of Exegesis: Essays in Honor of Norman K. Gottwald on His Sixty-Fifth Birthday*, ed. David Jobling, Peggy L. Day, and Gerald T. Sheppard, 147–159. Cleveland: Pilgrim Press, 1991.

_____. "Matthew 20:1–15: A Parable of Invidious Comparison and Evil Eye Accusation." *Biblical Theology Bulletin* 22 (1992):52–65.

_____. "The Evil Eye and the Sermon on the Mount: Contours of a Pervasive Belief in Social Scientific Perspective." *Biblical Interpretation* 2 (1994):51–84.

Forbes, Christopher. "Comparison, Self-Praise, and Irony: Paul's Boasting and the Conventions of Hellenistic Rhetoric." *New Testament Studies* 32 (1986):1–30.

Foster, George M. "The Anatomy of Envy: A Study in Symbolic Behavior." *Current Anthropology* 13 (1972):165–202.

Ghosh, Amitav. "The Relations of Envy in an Egyptian Village." *Ethnology* 32 (1983): 211–223.

Hagedorn, Anselm C., and Jerome H. Neyrey. "'It Was Out of Envy That They Handed Jesus Over' (Mark 15:10): The Anatomy of Envy and the Gospel of Mark." *Journal for the Study of the New Testament* 69 (1998):15–56.

Malina, Bruce J. "Limited Good and the Social World of Early Christianity." *Biblical Theology Bulletin* 8 (1979):162–176.

Pilch, John J. "Secrecy in the Mediterranean World: An Anthropological Perspective." *Biblical Theology Bulletin* 24 (1994):151–157.

Walcott, Peter. *Envy and the Greeks: A Study of Human Behavior*. Warminster, Eng.: Ares & Phillips, 1978.

5

Kinship and Marriage

Fusing Families Together

Up to this point, we have come to know quite a bit about the group of foreigners whom we observe when we read the New Testament. We can see that their main concerns were lodged within perceptions controlled by honor and shame, in a sort of conflict-ridden arena of life. They participated in that arena as group-oriented and collectivistic personalities who saw the world as thoroughly limited and controlled by persons of various sorts. Their efforts were directed at maintaining their inherited status by means of dyadic contractual relationships. The question we turn to now concerns how they received their inherited status. Obviously, inheritance belongs within the field of family and kinship. What was first-century kinship like? What was the family like, and what did the marriage that constituted the family mean?

In order to answer these sorts of questions, we must once again turn to abstract chunking and model making, to similarities at a higher level of abstraction in order to see how we and they are similar. At the same time, we will have to dip down into the concrete in order to learn how similarities are expressed quite differently at the level of specific cultural norms and the behavior deriving from those norms.

Kinship

Social norms, as we have seen, present the "oughts" of a group. These are the cultural cues guiding people to perceive and evaluate the persons, things, and events of their experience. *Kinship* refers to patterns of such social norms that regulate human relationships directly based on the experiences of birth and the birth cycle—from the womb, through developmental stages, to death. Kinship norms basically fill human biological interactions and outcomes with meaning and value. In other words, kinship norms symbolize human biological interactions and the ongoing results of such interactions. At bottom, kinship norms are rooted in the social perception that human relationships can be and actually are established among persons by their being

134

born of certain parents or by the possibility of births resulting from the union of two (or more) human beings. *Marriage* refers to such a union of two (or more) human beings insofar as it relates to kinship; hence marriage is a subset of kinship norms.

The social area covering actual or potential births can be divided into four categories: (1) the selection of marriage partners; (2) the marriage bond—the relatively enduring, socially sanctioned sexual and social union of one or more men with one or more women; (3) the immediate conjugal family of husband(s), wife (wives), and children; that is, the nuclear family, the family of procreation, and the conjugal family bond; (4) the extended kinship relationship beyond the immediate conjugal family, that is, the extended family, the family of orientation, and the broader kinship bond. These social categories cover the area of kinship norms and are a form of boundary marking. For kinship norms make lines between and among people, delineating between "us" and "them" in a regular yet often kaleidoscopic way. Kinship norms indicate as well as regulate and prescribe how closely related one must be in order to be one conjugal family, one extended family, one people. They also point out and control how *other* one must be in order to be a spouse: other sex? other status? other family? other lineage? other ethnic group? They likewise imply a time factor, indicating how long bonds of marriage, family, and extended family stay in force. For example, how long do you expect to be your parents' son or daughter? Does your marriage imply a break in the son/daughter bond, or will that bond continue? What of the brother/sister bond; how long is that to last? How long will your parents stay husband and wife? Does this relationship survive death or not? How long must you stay with a partner before others in your group consider you married? Does having a child bear on the issue of marriage? Why isn't a chance sexual affair the same as a long-term relationship?

Kinship norms, in sum, deal with the selection of marriage partners as well as with the quality and duration of the marriage bond (husband and wife), the conjugal family bond (parents, children = brothers, sisters), and the extended family bond (relatives beyond the immediate conjugal family). The selection of marriage partners, again at a high level of abstraction, derives from how a given culture deals with potentially disruptive conflicts within a kinship group. Internal conflicts, such as those caused by the distribution of inheritance and wealth, must be kept within some restricted range. Furthermore, positive cooperation or solidarity has to be maintained at some minimal level so that the group might survive in a meaningful, human way. The expression of solidarity or positive cooperation can take the form of (1) prohibiting marriages within the kinship unit. This is called *exogamy*, the requirement that a spouse must come from outside the kinship unit. Exogamy, openness to outside groups, symbols universalism, since it links various solidarity groups on a broader scale (this is the practice in the United States). Further, positive cooperation can take the form of (2) prohibiting marriages outside the kinship group. This is called *endogamy*, the requirement that a spouse must come from within the kinship unit. Endogamy, closedness to outside groups, symbols particularism, since it results in a society of relatively small, closed segments (this was the preference in the Mediterranean world of the first century).

Finally, the quality of the marriage bond derives from a combination of social self-image, gender roles (what is required of males and females solely on the basis of their gender); the conjugal family system (the norms that prescribe and ascribe obligations and rights to family members in terms of birth order, gender, age); and the kinship system in general (the rights and obligations of related conjugal families). If this all sounds a bit complicated, that is because it really is. As a matter of fact, our own kinship system in the United States still eludes complete systematic analysis. What this means is that even though you might think that the kinship relations that you learned from childhood and that have become integral to your personality and language are completely "natural" because you take them for granted, they might not be that simple. First of all, kinship systems prove to be quite complicated when subject to analysis, and second, even the United States middle-class system, which most of us know, is simply not all that common in the world's cultures. It is highly unlikely that a "father" in first-century Israelite society would be the same as the "father" of Freud's central Europe or our contemporary American society.

Main Structural Features
of the Kinship System Compared

Since kinship is so complicated, perhaps the easiest way to grasp the differences between our kinship norms and those of first-century Israelite (and often Mediterranean) society is to run through our norms while contrasting them with those of our group of foreigners. We are still at a high level of abstraction, and this means that at the concrete level, not all the features listed will be perfectly and completely realized. Norms are ideal "oughts" that often get watered down in the living. Yet they continually support living and serve to gauge success or failure, compliance or noncompliance. If you wonder why you should go through all this sort of "dumb" analysis, you might look at the goal of this inquiry: How can we be fair to the group of foreigners we observe when we read the New Testament? What did they mean and feel about being father, mother, husband, wife, brother, sister? What did marriage mean to them? What did divorce entail? And what was Jesus driving at when he stated his well-known prohibition of divorce? None of these sorts of questions can be answered adequately without knowledge of kinship norms that are much like the hidden mass of an iceberg supporting the tiny, visible tip that comes through in the foregoing questions. Perhaps patience in plowing through kinship norms will yield a rewarding response to these dimensions of the New Testament.

As any Bible reader knows, the Bible is replete with kinship norms, some explicit, but most implicit. These norms change over time, from the period of Abraham, the immigrant to Canaan, through the conquest of the Canaanite elite by Joshua, to the Israelite postexilic period and the time of Jesus. In what follows, I shall present the features of the American kinship system followed by corresponding features of postexilic Israel of the first century A.D. We can consider preexilic biblical kinship features afterwards.

1. Prohibited intermarriage has as its function to prevent potentially disruptive conflicts within the kinship group. Such prohibited intermarriage is normally referred to as the *incest taboo*. In the United States, our norms prohibit sexual relations, hence marriage, with father, mother, child, grandparent, uncle, aunt, niece, or nephew, with twenty-nine States prohibiting first-cousin intermarriage. These are said to be "blood" relatives—a highly symbolic term intimating an abiding and enduring relationship.

In New Testament times, it seems the list of prohibited sexual partners from Leviticus 18:6–18 and 20:11–21 were in vogue. These rules originally looked to the obligations in the area of sexual behavior of the first-born head of the group in the prime of life. They are family laws to be observed by and enforced by the head of the household in a polygamous setting. By the first century, they were understood as a list of prohibited marriage partners. If you read them patiently, you will see that they include father, mother, children, grandparents, uncles, and aunts, much like our prohibitions, aside from nieces, nephews, and cousins—these were not prohibited. However, the list also includes a series of in-laws by our reckoning, beginning with stepmothers, sisters-in-law, daughters-in-law, aunts-in-law, and those corresponding male in-laws from the female's point of view. Further, a sister-in-law of a childless marriage was to be married by a surviving brother to raise an heir for the deceased brother; this is called *levirate* (from Latin *levir*, meaning brother-in-law) marriage. The question I might raise here is, Were such in-laws related by law or by blood? Note that for Paul, in 1 Corinthians 5:1 ff., a male is forbidden to marry his stepmother on his father's death. This would indicate that somehow she was related by blood. Further, according to Mark 6:18, a brother was not allowed to marry his divorced sister-in-law, again indicating some sort of abiding blood relationship.

2. In the United States, marriage is monogamous, with no obligatory patterns for marrying within the kinship group, outside incest limits. Rather, marriage is generally exogamous, outside the kinship group.

In first-century Judaism among the non-elite masses, marriage was usually monogamous, much as it was among Greeks and Romans. However, in the Mediterranean world, including the house of Israel, there was a marked preference for keeping daughters as close to the nuclear, conjugal family as the prohibitions of incest permitted. Further, while cross-cousin marriage between the offspring of either parent's siblings was eagerly sought, marriage with cousins from the father's side of the family was always preferred. This option for cross-cousin marriage—it was not an ironclad rule—is called *Mediterranean endogamy*.

3. Americans make no discrimination between paternal and maternal relatives for marriage purposes when they do consider marriage within the kin group. In the Mediterranean world, the paternal line is almost always favored as the preference in Mediterranean endogamy indicates.

4. In the United States, the family name descends through the male line but there is little other emphasis on the male line of descent. The descent system tends to be bilineal, or, more strictly, multilineal. These first four features indicate that in our system the ancestral lines can fan out indefinitely from any given individual, with many lines of heredity that can be emphasized for any given purpose. Thus the system of intramarriage and kinship is highly dispersed.

In the first-century Mediterranean, nearly the entire emphasis is on the male line of descent. Jesus' genealogies in Matthew 1:2–16 and Luke 3:23–38 indicate this. The descent system is patrilineal, with ancestral lines focused on the father and his lineage. Thus the system of intermarriage and kinship is highly concentrated.

5. The American system emphasizes the immediate conjugal family to the exclusion of in-laws, who are to be accorded equal treatment by the family of procreation. The conjugal family (our nuclear family) is a small, compact group of two generations (parents and their children) brought together by ties of diffuse loyalty and functioning to care for the young until they reach maturity and can repeat for themselves the process of family rearing. The age marking the end of the maturing period, the period of adolescence, now runs to about thirty; at this time persons ought be settled down and married. In this system, there are no intricate economic, political, or religious ties based on kinship, no ancestor worship, and no formal connection with remoter kin.

In the first-century Mediterranean world, the tightest unit of diffuse loyalty is the descent group of brothers and sisters whose spouses enter the kin group as strangers and remain always somewhat so. The affection we expect as a mark of the husband and wife relationship is normally a mark of brother-sister and mother-son relationships. The kin group frequently shares economic, political, and religious ties, with an awareness of and formal connection with remoter kin. This last point is illustrated by attitudes such as "We have Abraham as our father" (Luke 3:8); the genealogies; and Paul's awareness of his being "of the people of Israel, of the tribe of Benjamin, a Hebrew born of Hebrews; as to the law a Pharisee" (Phil. 3:5). In this system, close relatives could legally conceal each others' offenses from the outside and worked to protect family honor (thus Jesus' family comes to remove him from an embarrassing situation in Mark 3:20–31).

6. The immediate family of father, mother, and children is usually the effective American social, residence, and consumption unit. By social consensus, the independent and autonomous conjugal unit is regarded as desirable, right, and proper. If other relatives have to live in the household, it is considered unfortunate. American parents are not to interfere with the families of their children except in extraordinary cases.

In the Mediterranean world, the household might include father, mother, the first-born son and his family, along with other unmarried children. These would live in close proximity, perhaps even sharing the same courtyard with other married sons and their families. This sort of family tends to be the effective social, residence, consumption, and production unit. Each conjugal family should be autonomous, yet the honor of the broader kin group is a concern of all, and all readily interact. This is desirable, right, and proper by social consensus. Parents readily interfere in the families of their children. Relatives (along with subjects like slaves, hired laborers, and the like) in the household, especially parents, are positively regarded. Note that Simon Peter's mother-in-law lives in his house, a house in which both Simon and Andrew reside (presumably with their families, see Mark 1:29–31; Matt. 8:14–17; Luke 4:38–41; 1 Cor. 9:5, regarding Peter's wife). Further, the Jesus movement organization is eventually headed by "James, the Lord's brother" in Jerusalem after the Ascension (Gal. 1:19; see also Acts 12:17; 15:13). Jesus' relatives likewise take part in the spreading the movement, along with their wives (1 Cor. 9:5). Note that Matthew, Mark, and Luke have no mention of Mary, the mother of Jesus, at the crucifixion scene; however, after the Resurrection, Mary and Jesus' brothers are in Jerusalem (Acts 1:14), undoubtedly having come to claim his corpse, as family members should.

7. In the United States, the conjugal family group is typically a consuming rather than a producing unit, especially in urban centers where the vast majority now live.

The ruralized, preindustrial Mediterranean world is marked by families that are producing units. However, men's and women's work are sharply segregated (for example, note that the parable on anxiety in Matt. 6:25–31 has birds compared with men's work, while the lilies of the field are compared with women's work). As producing unit, the family was the focus of the activities of each family member, and potentially disruptive extrafamilial associations were taken care of by the head of the family. Similarly, membership in the craftsmen's guilds of the preindustrial city was normally based on kinship, just as membership in the elite classes derived from birth. A typical example of the family as producing unit at work is the scene of Zebedee, his sons James and John, along with hired hands in Mark 1:19–20.

8. Because the nuclear, conjugal family is the unit, and the kinship system is multilineal, American society places relatively little emphasis on family tradition and continuity. The fact that examples of "old society" (e.g., Boston, Charleston) are considered odd and humorous, along with the fact that the search for "roots" is a recent popular effort, only indicate that these aspects are not integral and solid parts of actual family life. At most, Americans accept limited continuity, as, for example, in name-giving.

First-century Judaism, of course, put great stress on family tradition and continuity, the traditions of "the house of Israel." From postexilic times (read Ezra and Nehemiah) at least, genealogies, pure blood or "holy seed," and the central symbolic importance of the twelve tribes are basic. Furthermore, highly important social roles such as the priesthood, requirements for admittance to the Temple, and proper marriage depended on genealogical purity. Hence emphasis on tradition and continuity was of great concern. The Passover celebration itself underscored this central concern. We shall return to it in detail later.

9. Americans enjoy a comparatively free choice of mates: free enterprise, the open market, and free competition are applied to marriage selection. This is possible because of the autonomy of the marriage unit; the married couple does not have to fit into an established, broader kinship group. This is American individualism applied to marriage selection. Kin have no right to interfere, and the choice is purely individualistic. Such behavior is further bolstered by American geographical and occupational mobility, deemphasis of kinship, and the general discontinuity of generations.

In the first-century world, we find group-oriented, collectivistic personalities along with females always embedded in some male. The choice of mates is highly limited, normally arranged by parents because the marriage pair have to fit into an established kinship group with important and complex repercussions on many other individuals. The new couple will reside within or very near one or both of the in-law families. They will maintain intimate associations with a continuous and extended kinship group. From this perspective, marriage is both a sort of treaty between groups and a personal, dyadic contract between collectivistic personalities oriented toward two disparate groups. Further, these newly married, collectivistic personalities are in a complex and delicate state of mutual interdependence that tends to greatly limit personal emotional feeling—or at least its direct expression in action. Any considerable range of spontaneous affection would greatly impinge on the entitlements, obligations, and interests of too many others, causing disequilibrium in the system as a whole. This need to limit spontaneous affection (e.g., to mother and son, brothers and sisters) is a basic feature of those arranged marriages found in kinship systems where the newly married couple is incorporated into a larger kin group.

10. In the United States, the system of residence is neolocal; that is, the newly married couple, even before the birth of their first child, resides independently of either family of origin. They thus live independently of the restraints that might come from living in the same house as, or in the immediate vicinity of, their kin group.

The first-century world favored a patrilocal rule of residence. This means that the new wife would normally move in with her husband's family until such time as the new couple could have its own residence, which in turn would be near his father's house. In this way, again, the new nuclear family has to be incorporated into the solidaristic, father-centered kin group. Once more, since the wider kin group preponderates, marriage tends to be an arranged union serving group interests, and the needs of the dyadic personality itself are strongly oriented to the group. An indication of this feature is found in the omission of any mention of a son-in-law in such sayings as that of Jesus in Matthew 10:35: "For I have come to set a man against his father, a daughter against her mother, and a daughter-in-law against her mother-in-law" (see Luke 12:53). There is no mention of a son-in-law, since it was the new wife who moved into her husband's house, not the husband into the wife's family. The daughter mentioned in the saying would probably be the unmarried daughter, since she is still around to conflict with her mother. This arrangement is equally implied in passages such as Ezekiel 44:25 ("They shall not defile themselves by going near to a dead person; however, for father or mother, for son or daughter, for brother or unmarried sister they may defile themselves") and Micah 7:6 ("For the son treats the father with contempt, the daughter rises up against her mother, the daughter-in-law against her mother-in-law; a man's enemies are members of his own house").

11. American social arrangements are marked by high geographic and social mobility. This sort of mobility results in open rather than closed social networks, with a resulting reduction of support for and constraint on marriage

partners. Such arrangements bolster American individualism and affect mate choice, gender-role segregation, child rearing, and many other aspects of family structure and process.

The first-century Mediterranean world was marked by geographical and social immobility that resulted in the heightened support and constraint of a closed social network. Such an arrangement bolsters the perception of limited good and collectivistic personality. It further affects the total character of the kinship system. When each party comes to the marriage with a close-knit circle of relatives and friends who have long lived in association with them and who realistically expect to do so in the future, the marriage has to fit into social networks already firmly established. Previous relations of kinship and friendship involve strong emotional ties, reciprocal relations of support and exchange, and interlocking agreements and expectations relative to social norms and their outcomes. The obvious path of least resistance and least disruption is for the new marriage to be negotiated, and for husband and wife to maintain the segregated, although perhaps somewhat overlapping, circles of associates that they had before marriage. Bonds of affection, then, normally reside in previous settings; thus the new wife would feel close to her brothers and sisters, with her mother mourning her loss to another household, while the new husband would feel close to his brothers and sisters, maintaining close affection for his mother in whose house the new pair will take up residence. The father in each case remains an authority figure mainly concerned with his family's honor and proper maintenance.

12. The United States shows a marked tendency for adult children to disperse from the parental household even before marriage, which takes place at a rather late age. This dispersion has reached extraordinary breadth, directly tied to vertical mobility between classes. Children need not remain in the social class of their parents, and often do not.

In the first-century Mediterranean world, adult male children normally remained within or close by the parental household, while females were married out. Usually the first-born male inherited his father's house; hence he remained in the household, with his married brothers living nearby. Males followed the occupation of their fathers and remained in the same inherited social status. In the parental household, the father was primarily responsible for those aspects of life that related the family to the larger social environment.

13. Finally, in the United States there is an effective norm against discussing marital or family problems with relatives or friends—a result of the social isolation of the nuclear family. Instead of family and friends, such problems are normally brought to experts such as the clergy, marriage counselors, physicians, and the like.

In the first-century world, marital problems were discussed with brothers and sisters, not with parents or friends. In the book of Sirach, there is a suggestive list of things to be ashamed of and not ashamed of (41:17–42:8), and the list is headed with this advice: "Be ashamed of immorality [literally: lewdness, sexual matters] before your father or mother." But given the foregoing features of the first-century Mediterranean kinship system, the expectations engendered in the collectivistic personalities involved would not generate our sorts of marital problems. For social life is so organized that men and women move at ease in two exclusive circles that might touch but never overlap, even on domestic occasions. These circles coincide with the gender and moral division of labor mentioned in chapter 1 on honor and shame.

Marriage

In the first-century Mediterranean world and earlier, marriage symboled the fusion of the honor of two extended families and was undertaken with a view to political and/or economic concerns—even when it might be defensively confined to fellow ethnics, as in first-century Israelite practice. As a process, Mediterranean marriage is the disembedding of the prospective wife from her family by means of a ritual positive challenge (i.e., gifts and/or services to her father) by the father of the prospective groom, along with her father's response. Should the father be unavailable, then responsible male members of the family, such as older brothers, paternal uncles, or the prospective groom himself, take part in the transaction. During this initial phase, the prospective spouses are set apart for each other; they are betrothed, "hallowed," or "sanctified" (which is what "set apart" means in Hebrew/Aramaic). The responsible males draw up a marriage contract, and eventually the bride's father must surrender his daughter to the groom, who takes a wife by bringing her into his house. The parable of the ten maidens in Matthew 25:1–12 pictures the bridegroom coming home, obviously with his bride (not mentioned in many English translations but appearing in some ancient documents). With the ritual movement of the bride into the bridegroom's house, the marriage process is complete. The wife-taking always results in the embedding of the female in the honor of her husband. She, in turn, symbols the shame of the new family—its sensitivity to public opinion and for its own self-image.

These stages of the marriage process seem to be alluded to by Paul in 1 Corinthians 7:29–31 in somewhat of a reverse order: "Let those who have wives live as though they had none [= the married couple], and those who mourn as though they were not mourning [= bride's family losing their daughter/sister], and those who rejoice as though they were not rejoicing [=

groom's family and their gain], and those who buy as though they had no goods [= groom's family who must pay bridewealth at betrothal], and those who deal with the world as though they had no dealings with it [= bride's family dealing at betrothal for suitable bridewealth]" (I follow J. Duncan M. Derrett in this explanation).

The bride's family looks for a groom who will be a good provider, a kind father, and a respected citizen. The bride does not look to him for companionship or comfort. Instead, as in all societies that exalt bonds between males and masculine lines of rights, the new wife will not be integrated into her husband's family but will remain for the most part of her life on the periphery of his family. As a rule, she is like a "stranger" in the house, a sort of long-lost relative of unknown quality. Just as life in the Mediterranean world is so organized that men and women move in exclusive circles that might touch but never overlap, so marriage is simply one phase of contact between male and female circles, with no overlapping expected. When does the wife shed the stranger's role? First of all, when she is the mother of a son; the birth of a son assures her security and status recognition in her husband's family. The son grows up to be his mother's ally and advocate of her interests, not only against his father, but against his own wife. In case of conflict in the household, daughters-in-law do not stand a chance. Thus the wife's most important relationship in the family is that with her son. Daughters are welcome but burdensome, since they can plague a father's honor. Sirach notes, "A daughter keeps her father secretly wakeful, and worry over her robs him of sleep; when she is young, lest she do not marry, or if married, lest she be hated; while a virgin, lest she be defiled or become pregnant in her father's house; or having a husband, lest she prove unfaithful, or though married, lest she be barren. Keep strict watch over a headstrong daughter, lest she make you a laughing stock to your enemies, a byword in the city and notorious among the people and put you to shame before the great multitude" (Sir. 42:9–11).

Further, a female is not a stranger when she is a sister, especially with brothers. Brother and sister share the most intense cross-gender relationship in this sort of cultural arrangement, so much so that the brother readily gets highly incensed when an unauthorized male approaches either his wife or his sister. Should a woman misbehave sexually, the father will hold his daughter responsible, while the brother will seek out the other party and attempt revenge. The last point is illustrated in the Bible most clearly in 2 Samuel 13:1–29, and somewhat in Genesis 34:1–31, although this last passage indicates that Jacob was not angered over his daughter Dinah's behavior, just at her brothers' actions. We shall consider these passages shortly. Here we will only note that the husband-wife relationship does not supercede the intense relationship between brother and sister. Thus, should the brother reside near his sister, and his sister and her husband quarrel and separate, this would be a matter of little more than inconvenience and mild regret to her and her brothers and sisters. Consequently, stability of marriage would be highest when the wife is decisively separated from her kin group of origin and is socially incorporated (by means of a son) into the kin group of her husband.

Finally, the new wife would not be a stranger if she married a parallel cousin, a sort of surrogate brother. This is as close as she might marry in her kin group, given first-century incest taboos, although some males did marry nieces, as complaints from Qumran indicate. However, while the last category would not be that prevalent, cross-cousin marriage would be quite common. (In contemporary Islamic countries, cross-cousin marriages account for forty percent of actual marriages). Yet the most frequent situation for new wives is as strangers in their husbands' houses.

Given the foregoing definition of marriage, divorce would be the reversal of the process described above. Hence divorce means the process of disembedding the female from the honor of the male, along with a sort of redistribution and return of the honor of the families concerned. Now, the extent to which the wife becomes embedded in her husband upon marriage as well as the extent of the disembedding effected by divorce would depend on the type of marriage strategies and marriage norms involved. In the Bible there are three major sets of marriage strategies, and to gain a better understanding of what the New Testament says about marriage and divorce, it might serve us well to consider the Old Testament background to the New Testament discussion.

Marriage Strategies in the Bible

From beginning to end, the books of the Bible reveal people much concerned with honor and shame, interacting in an agonistic way. Marriage, too, is part of the agonistic give and take of challenge and response that we have previously considered. With this sort of social setting for interaction, it would follow that, like other challenge-response strategies, marriage strategies might be of three types. Thus in a challenge situation I might readily give in to you for my benefit (conciliatory); I might attempt to struggle with you to gain some sort of supremacy (aggressive); or I might just ignore you and stick to my group entirely (defensive). Each strategy would entail a range of styles or permissible expressions, yet the focus would be either conciliation, aggression, or defense. When it comes to marriage strategies, it does in fact seem that the broad periods of the history of Israel were characterized by distinctive strategies, with conciliation typical of the patriarchal immigrant period, aggression typical of the Israelite preexilic period, and defense typical of the Israelite postexilic period. Mediterranean endogamy, the preference for keeping daughters close to the nuclear family, seems constantly to have been the ideal. Let us briefly consider the evidence.

The Patriarchal Immigrant Period

The legendary story of Abraham's immigration into the land of Canaan marks the beginning of the patriarchal period. In this period, Canaan (later Palestine) was fully populated. Abraham was not a nomad moving about trackless wastes. Rather he immigrated into a region controlled by monarchic cities and their kings. While we obviously lack a wide range of data for this period, it is not too difficult to see that Abraham and his "offspring" enshrined the endogamous ideal. Abraham married his half-sister (Gen. 20:12); Nahor married his brother's daughter, his niece (Gen. 11:29); Isaac married his father's brother's son's daughter, his first cousin's daughter (Gen. 24:15); Esau, among others, married his father's brother's daughter, his paternal parallel cousin (Gen. 28:9); Jacob married his mother's brother's daughters, his maternal parallel cousins (Gen. 29:10); Amram, Moses' father, married his father's sister, his paternal aunt (Exod. 6:20; Num. 26:57–59).

From these legends recorded in the Bible, we find that the patriarchs took a marriage strategy that was conciliatory—and by marriage strategy I specifically mean behavior based on the perception of how the female is embedded in the male's honor. As unstable immigrants, the patriarchs readily give their women in exchange for political protection and/or economic advantage after marriage, although preferring to retain them for themselves in marriage if possible. They are willing to offer their wives and married daughters to higher-status, local city-dwellers for political and economic ends. This was the strategy of Abraham with the Pharaoh (Gen. 12:10–20); of Lot with his daughters, even in the presence of their husbands (Gen. 19:12–16, 31–38); of Abraham and Abimelech (Gen. 20:2–18, and note especially v. 13 for Abraham's habitual immigrant attitude: "And when God caused me to wander from my father's house, I said to her, 'This is the kindness you must do me: at every place to which we come, say of me, He is my brother.'"); of Jacob with his daughter Dinah (Gen. 34:1 ff., and note Jacob's curse on Simeon and Levi for avenging their sister in Gen. 49:5–7). Thus sexual hospitality, specifically to one of higher social standing and for the controlling male's benefit, was the social norm. Sacred prostitution, a form of sexual hospitality in temples, could also be found in this period. The disembedded female, notably widows in our evidence, could readily dishonor males by proving too aggressive (thus the daughters of Lot in Gen. 19:31–38; the daughter-in-law of

Judah in Gen. 38). Incest with one's father's wife or concubine dishonors the father and hence is a grave insult symboling revolt against paternal authority (for Reuben, see Gen. 35:21–22; Gen. 49:3–4).

Typical of the period are plural wives (i.e., a legal, first-rank wife along with concubines or legal second-rank wives), as well as marriage with widows, foreigners, slaves, and the like (see Gen. 16:1–4; 25:1–6 for Abraham; Gen. 24:67 for Isaac; Gen. 20:34; 28:9 for Esau; Gen. 29:21; 30:12 for Jacob). Inheritance is patrilineal, and residence after marriage is normally patrilocal.

We might characterize the patriarchal period as symboled by kinship ties, a sacred or holy kinship group chosen by God and consisting of the patriarch and his "seed." The first-century author Seneca tells us what the ancients believed the "seed" to be: "In the semen there is contained the entire record of the man to be, and the not-yet-born infant has the laws governing a beard and grey hair. The features of the entire body and its successive phases are there, in a tiny and hidden form" (*Naturales Quaestiones* 3, 29, 3 LCL). In antiquity, human "seed," which only males have, is much like Russian nesting dolls or Chinese boxes, each containing the whole of forthcoming posterity. The patriarch heads this family, with worship centered in the kin group and with norms governing social interaction deriving from family custom.

The Israelite Period

The story of Shechem (Genesis 34) foreshadows a new set of kinship norms that characterize the marriage strategy of the Israelite period and that are codified in the early laws of Israel. In the story, Simeon and Levi, unlike their father Jacob, display an aggressive marriage strategy. They would deny their women to higher-ranking outsiders and even attempt to take the outsiders' women. In other words, their wives and sisters are perceived as embedded in their honor to such an extent that they feel compelled to defend that honor even in face of encroachment by higher-standing persons. Sexual hospitality is a thing of the past.

With this sort of behavior and its expression in subsequent law codes, the purity or shame of women becomes attached to male honor in such a way that it cannot be even temporarily disembedded. Once this happens, marriage strategy loses the potential for reciprocity that it has in the conciliatory mode. Now marriage strategy emerges exclusively as an agonistic value, a conflict in which the winners are those who keep their daughters, sisters, and wives and take the women of other groups in addition, giving only their patronage, their power, and their protection in exchange.

In the new ideology, males are now clearly vulnerable to varying degrees through their wives, daughters, and sisters. Aggressive strategy demands that fathers attempt to choose as mates for their daughters those who are closest and best known and who somehow already share in the collective honor of the patriline. The fathers of the patriarchal period, on the other hand, were more concerned about their sons than their daughters. In the aggressive perspective, daughters should marry relatives as close to home as incest laws allow. Sons, on the other hand, should marry nonrelatives but bring the spouse into the patrilocal community. In this way the honorable, aggressive head of the house gains sons-in-law, retains sons and daughters, and gains daughters-in-law along with a range of offspring. Given this sort of preference, marriage ends up being a competitive, agonistic affair of power in which there are winners and losers of women, more powerful and less powerful patrons and clients, and social statuses among which a certain mobility of family statuses takes place. This is simply an expression of the agonistic quality of social relations typical of sedentary Mediterranean communities from antiquity.

For the winners the result of such strategy is an increase in numbers, hence political power, along with the ability to acquire more women in exchange for patronage while avoiding the risks to honor by giving one's daughter away. Thus the competition for women in marriage negotiations is a competition for power. Provided that sons born of such unions can be kept faithful to the patriline, those heads of families with the most women expand fastest and attain a position of domination. This, of course, presupposes polygamy, with the corresponding problem of how much trust a father can have in his out-group wives and their sons.

Consider the biblical documents from the preexilic period. The importance of many wives in the struggle for power is noted by Gideon (Judg. 8:30), and subsequently for the kings of Israel, notably David (1 Sam. 25:39–43; 27:3; 2 Sam. 3:2–5), and notoriously Solomon (1 Kings 11:1 ff.). The problem of the degree of trust one can have in foreign wives and their like is signaled in the story of Abimelech's return to his matriline (Judges 9) as well as in the various stratagems of the king's sons, beginning with Absalom (2 Sam. 13:30). Numerous out-group wives mean trouble, or so the authors of the book of Kings think (of Solomon, 1 Kings 11:1–3; of Rehoboam, 1 Kings 14:21–24; of Asa, 1 Kings 15:11–14; 22:46).

The ideology of conquest and consolidation in the Israelite period envisions a land in which the Israelites will gain wives and daughters but give away no sons (e.g., Exod. 34:14–16, later tempered by Deut. 7:1–6; Josh. 23:11–13). The legislation of the period, both the early material in Exodus and Numbers and the later formulation in Deuteronomy, looks to solidifying as well as controlling those aspects of the aggressive strategy that might disturb the public order sanctioned by God and the king. Sexual hospitality, both public and private (i.e., the offering of one's daughter, sister, or wife), is now perceived as an affront against the male in whom the female is embedded (Deut. 23:17–18). The married female is now so fully embedded in the male that any dealing with the wife is invariably perceived as an affront to male honor; it now becomes inconceivable for an honorable man to offer his wife in hospitality to another (Exod. 20:14, 17; Deut. 5:18, 21; 2 Sam. 3:6–11). Adultery, of course, symbols grave trespass into the space of a fellow honorable male, a clear negative challenge requiring vengeance as a response.

The limits of incest are spelled out (Deut. 22:30 [In Hebrew texts 23:1]; 27:20–23; yet in 1 Chron. 2:24, Caleb is said to marry his step-mother), and incest still serves as an outraging symbol of revolt against one's patron-father (2 Sam. 16:20–22: Absalom and David's concubines; 1 Kings 2:13–17: Adonijah and Solomon's concubine). Concubines might be available from war (Deut. 21:10–17; see Num. 31:18) and through debt-bondage from one's fellow Israelite (Exod. 21:7–11). However, eloping with an unmarried and unbetrothed girl—the passage is often interpreted as rape and seduction—does not make the girl one's own, but rather the girl's father alone has the right to determine the girl's future (Exod. 22:16–17; Deut. 22:23–27). The father has the right because sexual dealings with his daughters are an affront to his honor and would lead her brothers to avenge her.

Since marriage transactions entail the mutual honor of the families concerned, such dealings are to be carried out fairly and without deception to prevent vengeance and feuding. The regulation on the tokens of virginity in Deuteronomy 22:13–21 point to this. However, the tokens of virginity—the female's blood from the ruptured maidenhead shed on first intercourse—have somewhat deeper symbolic implications. Just as the maidenhead symbols shame, so in the process of first intercourse a young man's first wife becomes the bearer of the man's and the subsequent families' positive shame—their sensitivity to honor. Further, the blood on both conjugal partners symbols that their marriage is a type of blood relationship—the husband "cleaves to his wife, and they become one flesh" (Gen. 2:24). Thus the emphasis on blood in the marriage process indicates that marriage is not simply a sort of legal contract, but essentially a blood relationship in which the stranger wife becomes a member of the husband's patriline. This blood relationship subsequently entails certain contractual obligations between the families and the marriage partners as well. In the aggressive strategy, the husband retains the right to disembed his wife from his honor should she dishonor him. This is the right to divorce in Deuteronomy 24:1.

This right to divorce in the Deuteronomic legislation is probably a compromise solution in favor of peace between families and public order. The reason I say this is that in situations that dishonor the male and involve blood relatives, the normal solution is to kill the one who causes dishonor (thus the wicked son in Deut. 21:18–21; the wicked daughter in Deut. 22:20–21). In the case of the duly married dishonoring wife, however, divorce is the available compromise solution. The certificate of divorce of Deuteronomy 24:1 indicates that the previous male cedes his rights over the female, hence that he will not be dishonored if the female marries again. However, he cannot take her back after a subsequent marriage because such behavior is tantamount to sexual hospitality. Sexual hospitality is prohibited in the aggressive strategy; any return to conciliatory strategy is "an abomination before the Lord" (Deut. 24:4). Finally, to prevent embedded females from dishonoring the male by entering into formal contractual obligations, the male has the right to rescind them (Num. 30:2 ff.). Only males have the prerogative of entering formal contractual arrangements. Yet widows and unmarried divorcees—unembedded, previously married females—can act as males in this regard, hence their ambiguous social status. The parameters for vengeance that might arise from aggressive strategies are also spelled out (Num. 35:16–28).

The laws of Israel from this period come from the political institution symboled by the palace-temple (in Hebrew, the same word stands for both palace and temple, normally built adjacent to each other). The political institution would seek to impose its laws by force, while custom would work to contravene the law. That customs from the conciliatory phase were still present is evidenced by the complaints of the prophets against sacred prostitution, for example, Hosea 4:14–19 and Jeremiah 5:7–9; 7:16 ff. (the queen of heaven in this last passage is probably the virgin to whom Job [31:1] does not lift his eyes). For a fuller picture, see the exilic reminiscences of Ezekiel 16:22.

We might characterize the Israelite period as symboled in the holy land, the land set apart by God for God's people, a land ultimately under God's control. Authority over this land lies in the hands of a leader/king. Political worship is disengaged from traditional domestic religion and situated first in various local political shrines, then in a centralized political shrine under the control of priestly families. The norms found in the customs of the elite become codified in law—the law of Moses, which is the law of God.

The Postexilic Period

Judaism gets its name from the Israelite kingdom of Judah, called by Greeks and Romans "Judea." It was common in the Graeco-Roman period to categorize people (and animals) by place of origin, so a "Judean" was a person from Judea. Judaism, in turn, referred to the behavior and customs of persons living in Judea. The Israelite tradition came to be focused on Judea and the Jerusalem Temple found in Judea when Judean elites returned to their preexilic homeland. The experience of the period of exile and subsequent return mark a change in the central symbols of Israel, hence in marriage strategy as well. The elite accounts of the return in the books of Ezra and Nehemiah indicate that not a few of the returning exiles, in order to fit into the prevailing society of Judea as they found it, divorced their wives and married into local non-Israelite families. Such behavior on the part of both the families owning the land and the returnees was a mutual conciliatory gesture. The book of Malachi sets the tone for this period in the area of marriage strategy, with its insistence that what God desires is "Godly offspring. . . . For I hate divorce, says the LORD the God of Israel, and covering one's garment with violence" (Mal. 2:13–16). In the circumstances addressed by Malachi, what God hates is the divorce of members of the house of Israel married to each other. There is silence about the divorce of Israelite and non-Israelite.

Be that as it may, the reforms of Ezra and Nehemiah require the divorce of all wives (and their children) acquired by the returning exiles from native non-Israelite families, along with marriage to fellow Israelites only. Thus, due to the priestly reform of postexilic Israel and its interpretation of fidelity to the covenant, the marriage strategy worked out in Ezra-Nehemiah leads to a defensive strategy: Females born within the covenant are to be kept, and entanglement with out-group women is to be resolutely avoided (read Nehemiah 9–10 and Ezra 9–10; a resident of the Israelite colony in Alexandria, one Demetrius, "proved" that even Moses' wife, Zipporah, was actually an offspring of Abraham, cited by Eusebius, *Praeparatio Evangelica* 9.29.1–3).

This defensive strategy would lead the newly formed, closed Judean community to monogamy (unlike the aggressive posture adopted in the earlier Israelite period and in later Islam). Further, the prohibition on divorce as proclaimed by Malachi is antipolygamy in its effects, whether polygamy be successive or simultaneous. It is this defensive marriage strategy coupled with the perception that embeds female sexual purity in male honor that lies at the bottom of the sexual behavior found in the Priestly writings of the Old Testament. These gradually are developed by "tradition" into the norms of first-century Israel. The laws from the previous strategy, as well as the customs of the patriarchal stories, have to be reshaped to fit the new strategy. The earlier creation story of Genesis 2:4ff. is prefaced by a Priestly creation story in which God's first command to the Earthling (this is what "Adam" means in Hebrew) is to increase and multiply (Gen. 1:28), which is, of course, in line with the defensive marriage strategy set out in the rest of the Priestly writings.

The holiness code of the Priestly tradition is a purity code (see next chapter), a set of explicitly formulated social lines that are to mark off clearly "us" (Israelites) from "them" (the rest of humankind). This set of boundaries is replicated in temple structure, in sacrifice procedures, and, for our purposes here, in sexual behavior. The general principle is that everything is forbidden unless it fits within its designated social space. Legislation specifies designated social spaces. To begin with, early Israelite customs on forbidden sexual relations are restated as incest lines of prohibited degrees of marriage in Leviticus 18:6–18; 20:11–12, 14, 20. Adultery is not only an outrage to male honor but also an abomination (Lev. 18:20; 20:10). Sexual hospitality (Lev. 19:9), keeping Israelite women as slave-wives (Lev. 25:44–46), males acting as females in sexual encounters (Lev. 18:22; 20:13), priestly marriages with once-embedded or shamed women (Lev. 21:7, 13–14; see Ezek. 44:22)—all these are not simply affronts to male honor but equally abominations before the Lord. Male honor is symboled in the male sexual organs, and both the priest (Lev. 21:20) and the nonpriest (as in the previous period, Deut. 23:1) must have their sexual organs intact to be full members of the community.

Since holy seed or holy offspring are paramount symbols, genealogies tracing holy seed come to have emphatic symbolic importance (read the genealogies in Ezra and Nehemiah; also in the books of Judith and Tobit). Sexual bodily effluvia render a person unclean (Lev. 15:16–18, 32 for the Israelite male; Lev. 22:4 for the priest; Lev. 15:19–30 for the female; the new defensiveness is clearly articulated in the rules about sexual relations during menstruation in Lev. 15:24; 18:19; 20:18). "Homosexuality" dishonors the male (one partner plays a female role) and confuses defensive boundaries— and it is an abomination to the Lord (Lev. 18:22; 20:13). Bestiality applies to both the sons as well as the daughters of Israel (Lev. 18:23; 20:15–16). Finally, while sexual hospitality or sacred prostitution is dishonoring and forbidden (Lev. 19:29), sexual intercourse with a slave woman is frowned on as defiling (Lev. 19:20) and requires a guilt offering. So much for the law.

In the customs of the period, the sages warn against adultery because of the vengeance that will surely come from the outraged husband (Prov. 6:25–35). The women most likely to be unfaithful are those whose husbands do not stay at home: "For my husband is not at home; he has gone on a long journey; he took a bag of money with him; at full moon he will come home" (Prov. 7:19–20; see 9:13–18). This passage implies, again, that the trader not only offends against the common sense of limited good but has not enough honor to keep his wife properly cordoned off.

Perhaps the most information about the customs of defensive strategy is to be found in the book of Sirach, who wrote about 150 B.C. in Jerusalem. This is city-elite information, the sort of ideal norms toward which the non-elites aspire. To begin with, Sirach tells us that fathers arrange marriages (7:25; see 4 Esdras 9:47 for a mother who arranges the marriage, perhaps in default of a father). In the Hebrew and Syriac manuscripts of Sirach, the father is told, "Do you have sons? Correct them, and choose wives for them while they are young" (7:23). This points to the practice of early arranged marriages in which the father engages the girl for his son and vice versa before either of them are of marriage age, which is puberty. Children owe their lives to their parents, a debt that they can never adequately repay (Sir. 7:28). In his advice to married men in 9:1–9, Sirach offers counsel on attitudes toward various classes of women. The married man ought to avoid married women because of penalties that might be exacted—presumably by their brothers and father (9.5)—and because married women can ensnare a man in the vengeance of their husbands (9:8–9). Prostitutes lead to a loss of inheritance, either because any offspring remains "fatherless," or because the man's father would be shamed by his sons' actions (9:6).

Sirach views the wife as embedded in her husband, since divorce means to "cut her off from your flesh" (Sir. 25:26); this is further indication that marriage is considered a sort of blood relationship, resulting in "one flesh," much as children are "one flesh" with their parents. Daughters marry out; they live in their husbands' families although even there a daughter can still shame her father (22:3–6, note v. 3: "the birth of a daughter is a loss"). Sirach 25:16–26:27 discusses the range of wifely behavior, from shameful to honorable, including rival wives. An important cultural value is alluded to by Sirach in 25:21, where the ideal wife is one who is beautiful and wealthy (note that Judith is such an ideal female, yet a widow who does not remarry: Judith 8:1–8; also Sarah, the future wife of Tobit, is such: Tobit 6:11–12). However, by means of marriage, the wealth of the female should pass to the male, for "there is wrath and impudence and great disgrace when a wife supports her husband" (Sir. 25:22). The story of the younger Tobit indicates his proper social placement, since Sarah belongs to his patriline and her wealth belongs to him should he marry her (Tobit 6:11).

As mentioned previously, the father is all too vulnerable through his daughters (Sir. 26:10–12 and especially 42:9–11). Hence the cultural imperative to marry them off as soon as possible, which means shortly after the onset of menstruation. Because they are embedded in the male, women can all too easily shame their fathers and husbands. Thus, "better is the wickedness of a man than a woman who does good; and it is a woman who brings shame and disgrace" (Sir. 42:14; note 40:19: Even in defensive strategy, where offspring are all important, a blameless wife is better than children and the honor that comes from giving public endowments).

This defensive marriage strategy stands as the basic perspective and chief mode of perception for the discussions of marital and sexual behavior in the Qumran writings as well as the reactions of Jesus recorded rather differently in Matthew, Mark, and Luke. In the nonlegal documents of the period, such as Sirach, Tobit, and Judith, a person's intentions, his heart, counts in sexual encounters. The focus of this intention in marriage is on offspring, on holy seed, this being the sole valid motivating factor for sexual encounters. Any other motives are shameful. Thus Tobit's sexual union with Sarah on their wedding night is motivated not by her wealth and beauty, but by holy seed (the former being called immorality or immoral motives, the latter truth— Tobit 8:7). Likewise, in Israelite tradition, a man's getting married because of the beauty or wealth of the bride is equivalent to immorality; the offspring of such marriages are almost tantamount to bastards, the symbolic opposite of holy seed. Given this emphasis on defensive strategy and holy seed, imputations of doubtful lineage are among the gravest insults in the culture, sure to get prompt attention. For example, John the Baptist's calling the Pharisees and Sadducees of Jerusalem a "brood of vipers" (Matt. 3:7; Luke 3:7; Jesus uses the term according to Matt. 12:34; 23:33) means nothing less than "snake bastards," a doubly offensive term. Similarly, Jesus calls his contemporaries an "adulterous generation" (Mark 8:38; Matt. 12:39; 16:4), literally "a generation of bastards," the offspring of adulterous unions. These are powerful insults in a culture where purity of lineage is a central concern. Jesus' parable on divorce, with remarriage called adultery, likewise implies bastard offspring in such a union (Mark 10:11; Matt. 5:32; 19:18; Luke 16:18). Jesus' teaching on divorce will be considered later, in the "Study Questions for Hypothesis Testing" section at the end of this book.

Now, we might characterize the postexilic Israelite period as focused on the symbol of holy offspring. These holy offspring form a holy people, headed by priests, with worship in the central Temple in the central preindustrial city of Israel. Norms for the period derive from Priestly law that cover the behavior of priest and nonpriest alike.

When we turn to the New Testament and the typical marriage strategies developed in post-Jesus communities, we find that they are in most respects continuations of the defensive strategy of Israel. For these early communities, the Bible means Israel's sacred scripture, the Old Testament. With this in mind, consider the churches of Paul and the churches after Paul as mirrored in the New Testament. I present them as prolongations of the defensive strategy, hence the name "Pauline interval."

The Pauline Interval

With Paul and the early post-Jesus communities that nurtured him, a new twist on the defensive marriage strategy develops. The Pauline period does not cover any lengthy time span but is an interval between Paul and the post-

Pauline churches. The basis for Paul's strategy is his conviction that all people can have access to God in Christ regardless of gender roles, ethnicity, or social status (read Gal. 3:27–28; see also Rom. 10:12; 1 Cor. 12:13; Col. 3:11, which is probably a baptismal formula). Since in the community in which Paul was socialized (he called himself "a Hebrew" by birth and "a Pharisee" by Torah practice), norms about sexual behavior, ethnicity, and social status all derived from the prevailing understanding of the Torah, the Old Testament, and since Paul rejects this Torah as normative for post-Jesus groups, he thus rejects Torah laws about sexual behavior, ethnicity, and social status for post-Jesus group members. In fact, what he does is to reject "law" and to revert to "custom." Let me explain this point for a moment.

For analyzing Paul, it is important to understand the difference between law and custom. Relationships between human beings are patterned and controlled by more or less obvious rules of behavior, by "oughts." Such rules of behavior or "oughts" are called norms. Now, both law and custom have this in common—they are bodies or sets or collections of norms. The difference between law and custom is sanction, that is, who puts the teeth into the norms when you do not follow them, who enforces the norm. Custom is sanctioned by the same social institutions that the norms themselves create, while law is sanctioned by some other institutions, specifically some form of political institution. If this is too abstract, consider the following example. Why do you treat your parents like parents, and why do they treat you like their child? The norms and oughts of parent behavior and affection toward their children, as well as the norms and oughts of children's behavior and affection toward their parents, make up an aspect of what is called the family. The family, in this aspect of parent-child relationship, consists of such reciprocal norms of behavior. The norms create the institution.

Now, what if the state or national government passes a directive that says parents and children must treat each other properly and with affection. What the government is doing is taking a custom from family behavior, from the family institution, and doubly institutionalizing it by having government power enforce and sanction what was previously custom. Law is always a custom that has been doubly institutionalized—custom from the sphere of family, economics, religion, or education, all of which consist of norms that are customary. People follow rules in their family interactions, in their economic dealings, in their religious approaches to God and fellow humans, and in their teaching each other the traditions of our society. And they follow those rules even before they find out that the government in question might take certain aspects of their behavior in these areas and make those customary norms binding on all in the group with the teeth that government can provide.

Furthermore, social institutions can become so complex that they formalize certain norms and outfit themselves with little quasi-political bodies called administrations that in turn raise what was previously custom to law. Administrations then act as a type of enforcing agency for the laws thus doubly institutionalized. So, for example, universities and colleges have administrations that make laws that consist of previous customary behavior. These laws work in the university like national laws work in the nation and are often further sanctioned by the national government; thus, they are institutionalized three times. The same holds for religious bodies. They, too, when complex enough, set up administrations that give a political cast to previous custom, thus doubly institutionalizing religious norms and making them laws.

Now, when I say that Paul rejects law and reverts to custom, what I mean is that he no longer recognizes the political institution of Second Temple Israel consisting of the priestly elite of Jerusalem, the Sanhedrin, and their formalized norms, the Torah as they understand it. He thus rejects the Israelite priestly system and its sanctions in favor of norms and sanctions deriving from the interacting partners within the group. In this case, the interacting partners are the collectivistic persons interacting within the community called the church. The customs Paul envisions as binding post-Jesus group members in their reciprocal interactions derive from the activity of God's power, the Spirit, within those communities. This I would call a charismatic strategy. Recall what was said about the Spirit and collectivistic personality above.

However, Paul also insists that his fellow post-Jesus group members not confuse societal realities (the laws of the Greek, Roman, and Israelite jurisdictions) with the open access to God and the "oughts" flowing from this access as symboled in Christ. Rather, post-Jesus group custom and societal law now stand in dialectical opposition. This means that they mutually influence each other in Paul's period of spontaneous expectation of the return of Jesus as Messiah with power. On the one hand, openness to God and neighbor is necessary and can be fully expressed in post-Jesus group gatherings, but in line with the customs thus far developed in post-Jesus groups (thus 1 Cor. 11:2–16; note v. 16: "we recognize no other practice, nor do the churches of God"). On the other hand, the opinion of outsiders (societal reality, prevailing law) is to be taken into account. The presumption is that post-Jesus group custom is to be at least as good as the best in surrounding cultures (e.g., 1 Cor. 5:1). Hence post-Jesus group members need only do what is honorable in Christ, regardless of the law. "Whatever is true, whatever is honorable, whatever is just, whatever is pure, whatever is lovely, whatever is gracious, if there is any excellence, if there is anything worthy of praise, think about these things. What you have learned and received and heard and seen in me, do; and the God of peace will be with you" (Phil. 4:8–9).

In the light of the prevailing cultural context, I would call Paul's marriage strategy a charismatic defensive strategy. It is charismatic insofar as it derives from post-Jesus group custom, and it is defensive insofar as the norms for sexual encounter have to at least match the best in Israelite and "civilized" (the meaning of "Greek") legal tradition, which was defensive.

The prevalent symbol of the Pauline interval is the holy group (the church of the saints) headed by charismatic leaders, with worship centered in the prayer and activity of the group. Its norms derive from its customs. Within the framework of these symbols, Paul is still concerned about holy seed (1 Cor. 7:13–14), a point he refers to as he deals with Jesus' parable about divorce, now taken as group norm (1 Cor. 7:10, 11). First Corinthians 7 deals mainly with the problem posed by the Corinthians as to whether sexual relations are allowed to post-Jesus group members. The chapter is not really about marriage and the relationship of husband and wife in marriage. Paul's advice, though, is that post-Jesus group members ought to stay in the marriages they had when they became group members, but if the unbelieving partner causes difficulty, peace is a greater value than preserving the marriage (1 Cor. 7:15). However, as regards new marriages and remarriages, these should take place "in the Lord" (1 Cor. 7:39; 2 Cor. 6:14–7:1), presumably with fellow group members. This feature marks a centripetal direction of social interaction within the holy group, a form of defensive strategy in which those in the group intermarry without divorce. This strategy is further developed in the subsequent period.

The Post-Pauline Period

The post-Pauline development of post-Jesus group traditions discernible in the New Testament marks a consolidation of the charismatic customs developed previously. Post-Jesus group custom moves on the way to becoming post-Jesus group law, with sanctions deriving from the governing body (administration) of the group. Now, due to the general obligations of membership in a post-Jesus group and fidelity to the new covenant demanded by them, women born within the new covenant or entering the group in an unmarried state are to be kept, and marital entanglements with outsiders are to be avoided. This strategy is a defensive marriage strategy, but it now takes place in Christ and is hence a form of post-Jesus group defensive strategy. And predictably, the new post-Jesus group norms are much like the old defensive rules of Second Temple Israel, but are now outfitted with post-Jesus group motivation. We find such rules in Ephesians 5:22 ff.; Colossians 3:18 ff.; 1 Peter 2:11–3:12; 1 Timothy 2:8–15; 4:1–5; 5:3–16.

This post-Pauline period is likewise the time in which the Gospels were written down. Matthew, Mark, and Luke, as previously mentioned, each present a tradition in which Jesus' parable on divorce is shaped into a type of post-Jesus group norm, further underscoring post-Jesus group defensive marriage strategy. About A.D. 106, Ignatius, bishop of Antioch, urges that marriages of group members take place before the local bishop, a procedure that is within the same strategy.

What characterizes the post-Pauline development of Resurrected Jesus traditions is the symbol of holy church, an association of collectivistic personalities who are to keep the association holy. The association is headed by duly chosen officers, with worship gradually localized. Developing custom now takes on the quality of law, administered by duly chosen officers.

The main structural features of the kinship system described at the beginning of this chapter for the Mediterranean world would apply to both the defensive strategy of Second Temple Israel and the defensive strategy of post-Pauline groups. For the New Testament reader, it should be useful to know that these kinship features were the ones shared both by Jesus' audience and by the early post-Jesus churches that collected the New Testament writings.

Summary

The models presented in this chapter include a set of features of the kinship system and a set of marriage strategies. Kinship and its major generating institution, marriage, deal with the meanings and values embodied by persons who are involved in the birth of a child and the process begun by birth. This process, from the perspective of kinship, covers the developing webwork of human relations—by blood and in law—rooted in the culturally interpreted fact of birth. Birth, of course, is the effect of the sexual union of a male and a female human being who share some sort of previous relationship. When this relationship is one that agrees with the kinship norms of a society, it is called marriage. Kinship and marriage are sets of social norms that can be analyzed into a range of features.

Distinctive features of kinship norms in first-century Israelite society include incest taboos, monogamy, a sort of endogamy, emphasis on the male line of descent, patrilocal marriage, a somewhat extended family living arrangement, the family as unit of production, emphasis on family traditions, arranged marriages, geographic and social immobility, ties of affection between brothers and sisters and mother and children rather than between husband and wife, and the wife as a blood relation who often remained a stranger in the house.

In the first-century Mediterranean world, marriage meant the fusion of the honor of two extended families, undertaken with a view to political and/or economic considerations. Marriage is a process of disembedding the female from her family and embedding her in her husband—and his family. Females are always perceived as embedded in some male unless they find themselves in the anomalous situation of being a widow or divorcee without kin.

The first-century house of Israel followed a marriage strategy that might be called defensive, while the Bible evidences two other forms of strategy as well, the conciliatory and the aggressive. The patriarchal period reveals a conciliatory marriage strategy marked by endogamy and sexual hospitality toward persons of higher social rank, with a view to the economic and political benefit of the male. The Israelite period is marked by an aggressive marriage strategy in which power comes from the possession of females and their offspring, with a resulting emphasis on polygamy, wife-taking from other groups, and the refusal of daughters to outsiders if possible. The Second Temple Israelite period, the period of the ministry of John the Baptist and Jesus, is characterized by a defensive strategy in which the marriage partners should both be under the covenant, with the avoidance of foreigners altogether. During the interval of expectation of the return of the Jesus as Messiah with power evidenced in Paul's writings, the defensive strategy of the house of Israel is maintained but interpreted in the light of developing post-Jesus group custom. In the post-Pauline writings, these developing post-Jesus group customs become law for at least the Pauline tradition of the Resurrected Jesus movement organization, and a distinctive defensive marriage strategy gets under way. The main features of each of these periods are set out in Figure 4.

Figure 4. *Marriage Strategies in the Bible*

Marriage and Kinship	Conciliatory	Aggressive	Defensive	Charismatic Defensive	Christian Defensive
Main Symbol:	Holy Family	Holy Land	Holy Seed	Holy Churches	Holy Church
Period:	Patriarchal	Israelite	Judean	Pauline	Post-Pauline
Head:	Patriarch	Leader/King	Priest	Charismatic Leaders	Church Officers (Bishop)
Norms:	Custom	Law	Law	Custom	Law
Worship:	Family	Temple/Palace	Temple Group Activity	Group Activity	Church Group Activity

From the Pauline perspective (read Galatians 3–4), we can further describe these periods as:

	Conciliatory	Aggressive	Defensive	Charismatic Defensive	Christian Defensive
	Promise	Law	Law	Fulfilled Promise	New Law
	Abrahamic Covenant	Sinai Covenant	Ezra Covenant	New Covenant	New Covenant

Old Jerusalem in Israel   **New Jerusalem in Christ**

References and Suggested Readings

Bohannan, Paul. "The Differing Realms of the Law." In *The Social Organization of Law*, ed. Donald Black and Maureen Mileski, 306–317. New York: Academic Press, 1973.

Bradley, Keith R. *Discovering the Roman Family: Studies in Roman Social History.* Oxford: Oxford University Press, 1991.

Derrett, J. Duncan M. "The Disposal of Virgins." *Studies in the New Testament* Vol. 1, Leiden: E. J. Brill, 1977, 185–192.

Diamond, Stanley. "The Rule of Law Versus the Order of Custom." In *The Social Organization of Law*, ed. Donald Black and Maureen Mileski, 318–341. New York: Academic Press, 1973.

Fitzmyer, Joseph A. "The Matthean Divorce Text and Some New Palestinian Evidence." *Theological Studies* 37 (1976):197–226.

Guijarro, Santiago. "The Family in First-Century Galilee." In *Constructing Early Christian Families: Family as Social Reality and Metaphor*, ed. Halvor Moxnes, 42–65. London and New York: Routledge & Kegan Paul, 1997.

Halvor Moxnes, ed. *Constructing Early Christian Families: Family as Social Reality and Metaphor*. London and New York: Routledge & Kegan Paul, 1997.

Hanson, K.C. "The Herodians and Mediterranean Kinship: Part I: Genealogy and Descent." *Biblical Theology Bulletin* 19 (1989):75–84.

_____. "The Herodians and Mediterranean Kinship: Part II: Marriage and Divorce." *Biblical Theology Bulletin* 19 (1989):142–151.

_____. "The Herodians and Mediterranean Kinship: Part III: Economics," *Biblical Theology Bulletin* 20 (1990):10–21.

_____. "BTB Reader's Guide to Kinship." *Biblical Theology Bulletin* 24 (1994): 183–194.

Jacobs-Malina, Diane. *Beyond Patriarchy: Images of Family in Jesus.* Mahwah, N.J.: Paulist Press, 1993.

Malina, Bruce J. "Mary and Jesus: Mediterranean Mother and Son." In *The Social World of Jesus and the Gospels*, 97–120. London: Routledge & Kegan Paul, 1996.

Peristiany, J. G. ed. *Mediterranean Family Structure.* Cambridge: Cambridge University Press, 1976.

Pitt-Rivers, Julian. *The Fate of Shechem or the Politics of Sex: Essays in the Anthropology of the Mediterranean.* Cambridge: Cambridge University Press, 1977, 126–171.

Quesnell, Quentin. "'Made Themselves Eunuchs for the Kingdom of Heaven' (Mt. 19,12)," in *Catholic Biblical Quarterly* 30 (1968):335–358.

Todd, Emmanuel. *The Explanation of Ideology: Family Structures and Social Systems.* Oxford: Basil Blackwell, 1985.

Williams, Robin M., Jr. *American Society: A Sociological Interpretation.* 3d ed. New York: Knopf, 1970, 47–98.

6

Clean and Unclean

Understanding Rules of Purity

With this chapter we take a further look at that group of foreigners who people the New Testament, this time considering their concern about and interest in persons and things that are clean or unclean. Certainly this was a central concern in the Second Temple Israelite period. Jesus directed a parable to this concern, as most New Testament readers know: "Hear me, all of you, and understand: there is nothing outside a man which by going into him can defile him; but the things which come out of a man are what defile him" (Mark 7:14–16). Further, Jesus seems to have observed some of these purity rules himself, as witnessed by the fact that after he touches a leper (in Mark 1:40–45), and the leper tells people about it, "Jesus could no longer openly enter a town," since he was unclean because of this contact. As for Peter, Luke informs us that in response to God in a vision experience, Peter avows, "I have never eaten anything that is common or unclean" (Acts 10:14). He subsequently interprets the vision to mean "I should not call any human being common or unclean"—so the vision was not about food at all (Acts 10:28; read the whole passage, 10:1–48). Finally, post-Jesus groups seem to have been bothered by "questions of food and drink or with regard to a festival or a new moon or a sabbath" (Col. 2:16), as well as particular observances of "days and months, and seasons, and years" (Gal. 4:10). These sorts of indications point to purity rules. What are purity rules? What do they mean? Why are they of central concern in first-century Israel? What was the attitude toward them harbored by post-Jesus group members? To understand these questions, perhaps the best place to begin is with the common human experience called *the sacred*.

Sacred and Profane

Let me start with a series of examples. Imagine that you are in your favorite department store to buy a new pair of jeans. All of a sudden a little girl walks in, browsing and licking a full ice cream cone. To your surprise the little girl proceeds to the tables with the jeans on them and carefully puts her ice cream cone along the seams of the piled clothing, streaking several piles of the expensive pants in this way. What is your reaction when you see this? How do you feel? What will you do? You might laugh, tell the child to stop it, look for her mother, tell a salesperson, or some such thing. But what if you walk into the store, pick up your jeans, pay the salesperson for an expensive pair, and while you are waiting for a receipt and a bag, the little girl runs up and smashes her ice cream cone on your new purchase? Now that the jeans are yours—well fitting and paid for—what is your reaction? The feeling you have for what you have set apart for yourself is a feeling of the sacred; the jeans on the table in the store, not set apart for anyone yet, are profane.

Or imagine that you are reading and all of a sudden hear someone in your vicinity yelling for help. What is your reaction? You might get up, attempt to scare off an intruder, call a security guard or the police. But what if the person being assaulted and screaming for help is your mother, father, sister, or brother? What is your reaction then? How do you feel? The feeling you have for those persons somehow set apart and special to you, your parents, brothers, and sisters, for example, is a feeling of the sacred. Other human beings normally do not get you so emotionally involved when they are in dire straits. After all, you see them on the TV news every day; those others are profane as far as you are concerned.

Or imagine that you see a person dumping some garbage in the middle of the street where you live. What is your reaction? How do you feel about it, even if you are not especially ecology-minded? Now, imagine that the person with the garbage walks into the building in which you live and up to your room and proceeds to dump the garbage on your bed. How do you feel about that? The feeling you have for your space—your room and your bed—and its being invaded in that way is a feeling of the sacred. What is outside your house, outside your room, what belongs to the public (meaning, in our culture, to no one in particular) is profane and requires a different set of feeling cues.

Finally, imagine that you have worked hard the whole year and are looking forward to a forthcoming vacation to ski or swim, or do whatever your favorite vacation pastime happens to be. Then vacation time comes, and you find that your boss or your teachers have assigned you all sorts of work, leaving you no vacation time. What is the difference between work time and vacation time? How do you feel about vacation time? How does the feeling differ from your feeling about work time? Our lives are punctuated by breaks in the regular flow of normal time—by vacations for longer stretches of work time, by weekends for shorter stretches. Vacation time, like the weekend, is time set apart, special to you and your purposes; it is sacred time. Work time, regular time like ordinary clock time, is profane.

What I want to illustrate by means of these examples is that even in our individualistic, so-called secularized world, we still share in the basic human experience called *the sacred*. The sacred is that which is set apart to or for some person. It includes persons, places, things, and times that are symboled or filled with some sort of set-apartness that we and others recognize. The sacred is what is mine as opposed to what is yours or theirs, what is ours as opposed to what is yours or theirs. (In our culture, it might be no one's, since we believe in all goods being limitless, but in the first-century world, there is nothing that is no one's—all goods are limited and distributed). Some common synonyms for the sacred include *holy*, *saint*, and *sacral.* We feel jealous about our sacred persons, places, and things (as noted in chapter 4).

The opposite of the sacred is *the profane*, the unholy, the non-sacred. The profane is that which is not set apart to or for some person in any exclusive way, that which might be everybody's and nobody's in particular to varying degrees. Thus the words *sacred* and *profane* describe a human relationship of varying degrees of exclusivity relative to some person or thing (and I include time and space under "thing"). For example, to say that human life is sacred is to point out that human life is set apart and exclusive among the forms of life we might encounter, and therefore that it should be treated differently from animal life. Again, to say that sex is sacred means that human sexual encounters are set apart and exclusive among the various forms of sexual encounters we might know, and therefore that human sexual encounters are unlike and not to be treated as animal copulations. These examples derive from a comparison of the human with the animal domain and indicate belief in the exclusivity of the human. To profane human life and behavior is to treat them just like animal life and behavior.

You have undoubtedly noted that marked-off set-apartness can take place in different dimensions: between mine and yours, between ours and theirs, and between the human and the nonhuman. Obviously, other lines can be drawn, and perhaps the set of lines we are most used to are those that mark off the area of persons, things, and events set apart by or for or to God. We often refer to this area as *the* sacred, *the* holy, *the* sacral. We speak of God's holy people—a group of people set apart by or for God or God's service; God's holy name—God's person symboled by some specific name and belonging to a category that is fully unlike and not to be treated as any human name or person. We also talk of sacrifice, a word that literally means to make (*-fice*) sacred or holy (*sacri-*), hence, to set apart to or for God, the nation, the family, or some other person. The word *sancti-fy* means much the same thing.

The perception of the sacred, of the set-apart, clearly implies some sort of social lines marking off one side from the other, animal from human, mine from yours, ours from theirs, God's from ours. You might recall that in the discussion of honor and shame, I began with the observation that human meaning building is a process of socially contriving lines in the shapeless stuff of the human environment, thus producing definition, socially shared meaning. Human groups draw lines through and around time (the social times of childhood, adulthood, old age) and space (the social spaces called your house and your neighbor's, or called the United States and Mexico). They also mark off persons with social roles and statuses, things with norms of ownership, and God as a unique being controlling the whole human scene.

Human beings the world over are born into systems of lines that mark off, delimit, and define nearly all significant human experiences. Not only do people define and delimit, but they also invest the marked off areas (persons, things, places, events) with feeling, with value. Line drawing of this sort enables us to define our various experiences so as to situate ourselves and others and everything and everyone that we might come into contact with, as well as to evaluate and feel about those experiences on the basis of where they are located within the lines. Thus the set of social lines we learn through enculturation provides all of us with a sort of socially shared map that helps and compels us to situate persons, things, places, and events. Line making normally results in a special social emphasis on the boundaries, since clear boundaries mean clear definition, meaning, and feeling, while blurred boundaries lead to ambiguous perceptions and reactions.

Purity: Clean and Unclean

Consequently, social lines are quite necessary for us to perceive set-apartness. Set-apartness relative to persons and the sorts of exclusive relationships between persons and other persons, places, things, and events refer to the experience of the holy, the sacred. However, not all human experiences deal with exclusiveness in relationships. There are things and places and persons that we define, situate, and locate, but with which we have no sort of relationship of exclusiveness. We do not invest ourselves in everything and everybody in the same way as we invest ourselves in our possessions; our parents, spouses, children, or brothers and sisters; our special times and places; our God. Yet we do in fact use a set of lines to define, situate, and locate others, even those whom we might never see in a lifetime on this planet—for example, people, places, and things in other parts of our state, country, and world. Now, purity is specifically about the general cultural map of social time and space, about arrangements within the space thus defined, and especially about the boundaries separating the inside from the outside. The unclean or impure is something that does not fit the space in which it is found, that belongs elsewhere, that causes confusion in the arrangement of the generally accepted social map because it overruns boundaries, and the like. The sacred and profane, then, would be subsets of purity rules dealing with differences in exclusivity (sacred) and nonexclusivity (profane). Purity rules in general deal with places and times for everything and everyone, with everyone and everything in its proper place and time. Yet if the arrangements presented in purity rules are exclusive to our group and no other, we might readily consider them sacred purity rules.

Purity rules are much concerned with dirt. Garden dirt in the backyard is in its proper place. When the same dirt gets into the house, the house is considered "dirty, defiled, unclean, impure." Dirt is a way of speaking of something out of place. Dirt is a sort of metaphor for matter (and sometimes persons) out of place. It is matter out of place that makes your room dirty. And of course, there are degrees of dirt. For example, college students usually clean their rooms for the upcoming visit of parents, yet when a mother sees the room she invariably says, "This is clean?" She finds dirt where the student purified and cleansed. Clean and dirty, then, are matters of degree. But please note one thing here. Wherever people perceive dirt, we can presume that some conception of an ideal order exists. Dirt presumes a system, a set of line markings or definitions. Otherwise one would never know that anything was dirty, unclean, or out of place to begin with. Further, dirt presumes that persons, places, and things do get out of place, since dirt is matter out of place. In this connection, our society calls people out of place (negatively) "deviants."

Once persons, places, or things get put in their proper places, put in order, the result is a restoration of the clean and pure. The process of restoring things and people to their places can be called purifying or cleansing. Conversely, the process of putting things and people out of place can be called dirtying or defiling. Now both defilement and purification presuppose some movement across a symbolic line that marks off the clean from the unclean. Such line crossing is a sort of transition from the clean to the unclean state, or vice versa. And this transition is across a boundary. As we have previously noted, boundaries are often ambiguous, often a source of anxiety and conflict as well as of satisfaction and fulfillment. For example, graduating from college is a transition, a line crossing. Some students are happy about the crossing; others feel anxious and unsure. In either case, graduating students go through a social transition, a line crossing. For the present, please note that between clean and unclean there must be a line.

Anomalies and Abominations

While every culture patterns reality by means of such line making, no culture thoroughly exhausts all the dimensions of human being and human experience, just as no human language makes use of all the sounds human speech organs are capable of producing. Cultures are selective, limited, and limiting. So every culture eventually has to confront experiences that defy its cues, that do not measure up to its assumptions and classifications. Our culture, for example, cues us to perceive other human beings as individualistic personalities, while our first-century foreigners were cued to perceive others as group-oriented collectivistic personalities. What happens when one culture is confronted with the other's prevalent personality type?

Our culture cues us to perceive the functioning of human organisms in terms of biological "laws" and to adjust malfunctions of such organisms by means of technological manipulations: when your appendix gets infected, you have someone cut you open and cut it out. Our first-century foreigners were cued to perceive the functioning of human beings in terms of personal causality in significant circumstances, so illness was healed by various interpersonal and nontechnological means—for example, an exorcism along with an application of olive oil or the laying on of the hands of a healer. First-century folks would truly have been impressed by the miracle of modern medicine, just as we tend to disbelieve or wonder about the miracles of their quite usual wonder workers.

What I am driving at is that cultures have to deal with realities that do not fit their cues, and every culture eventually faces a greater or lesser number of such realities. These experiences that do not fit socially shared patterns or norms are called *anomalies* (the word literally means something irregular). If we are enculturated to react with strong negative feelings toward certain anomalies, to view them as triggers of disgust or hate, we would call this class of anomalies *abominations*. For example, we learn that it is proper to get rid of excess matter in the nose by blowing it out into a handkerchief or tissue, then carrying it around with us until we can dispose of it. We find it disgusting if a person bends over and blows the nose without benefit of tissue, directly onto the pavement. This latter type of behavior is an abomination in our culture, perhaps more abominable than killing someone who is trying to steal our TV set.

Be that as it may, cultures do not ignore the anomalies that specific cultural cues dredge up but cannot fit into their patterns. The reason for this is that if anomalies are ignored, people who embody the culture will lose confidence in the cultural cues. For example, our culture cues us to believe all goods are limitless, and this same culture recurrently forces us to face a job shortage, a case of something not being limitless. We must now fit this limit within our shared belief in limitlessness. If we can—for example, by the development of new jobs—then the system will go well because the limit has been removed and obliterated. But if we cannot fit the anomaly into our system, then we will be forced to adopt living arrangements that are limited—

and there goes capitalism and the American way. Similarly, in the first century, members of the "house of Israel" believed they were the chosen people of their ancestral God, living in this God's land, and worshiping that ancestral God of power who was capable of everything. What an anomaly it must have been to have the land occupied by the Persians and Greeks, and then ruled by Romans and their traditional gods. The longer the domination, the more urgent became the problem of reconciling the power and abilities of the God of Israel in the face of the anomalous unbelievers and their gods' power. A similar anomaly faced European Jewry, God's chosen people, when annihilated by a group with an equally "chosen people" ideology, Nazi Germany. Unless such a major anomaly were reconciled, the cultural system would run down or be radically changed. So every culture must have some ways for dealing with anomalies or abominations that fall between the cracks of its boundaries or lie outside its classification system.

There are at least five ways of facing up to anomalies. First, elites or opinion leaders can settle for one interpretation of life, thus reducing ambiguity and eliminating anomalies from attention. For example, we can settle for a belief in a mechanistic, technological view of reality, and thus anything supernatural would be classified as superstition, hallucination, error, insanity, or heresy. Post-Jesus groups got rid of dissenting interpretations of the experience of Jesus by settling on a canon or collection of normative writings—our New Testament. This collection sustains a single range of interpretation of Jesus, with all other interpretations considered erroneous, heretical. Second Temple Israelites settled for one range of interpretation of marriage relations, with all others ranked unclean or abominations.

Second, any anomaly might be controlled physically. For example, people in our society who commit murder are generally physically removed from our midst. Criminal Roman elites were exiled or banished, thus physically removed from their society. Israel's Torah directed that certain classes of people be removed to the peripheries of towns and cities, such as those afflicted with certain types of skin disease (notably psoriasis, which our translations give as "leprosy"; actual leprosy, or Hansen's disease, was rare or nonexistent in the Middle East during biblical times).

Third, society might impose strict and clearly spelled-out rules for avoiding anomalous persons, things, and behavior. Such rules affirm and strengthen what is socially unacceptable and indirectly underscore what is acceptable. For example, our belief that smoking causes cancer is being worked out in rules for avoiding smoke, and hence smokers are confined to certain places, even though we believe in individualism to such an extent that a minor female or a married female needs no one's consent to have an abortion. The smoke avoidance rules affirm what is socially unacceptable and indirectly underlines what is acceptable. Roman citizens were forbidden to marry slaves, thus maintaining boundaries between statuses and their ascribed honor and indirectly highlighting the rank of citizen. Israel's food prohibitions imply a list of foods that are to be positively favored.

Fourth, the anomalous person, thing, or event can be labeled as a public hazard, thus putting the anomaly beyond discussion and furthering conformity. For example, nuclear plants that might break down are subsequently officially labeled a public hazard. Such a label makes discussion of the benefits of nuclear energy beside the point and aids in forming opinion against nuclear energy. By labelling the ideology of Judeans, both Ben Zakaiists and post-Jesus groups, as "atheist," that is, lacking belief in the traditional gods of the Romans, Roman leaders put any discussion of exclusivistic Israelite Yahwism outside the realm of possibility and thus furthered conformity in rejecting it. By labeling Jesus' healing activity as the work of Beelzebul, Jesus' opponents try to make it highly unlikely that anyone would take him seriously, thus helping generate conformity in rejecting him.

Fifth, anomalies can be used in ritual to enrich meaning or call attention to other levels of existence. Thus violence—an anomaly in our law-and-order society—can be used in our national ritual of football. It can also be used to remind us of the violence we must do to ourselves to lead a good life, or how hard we must compete to make it in the economic "rat race." Jesus drives out a demon named "Legion" (an allusion to the Roman occupying forces) and sends the multiple demon into a herd of swine (a perpetually unclean, abominable creature in elite Israelite perception), thus calling attention to the relationship of the demon to the Roman presence as to the abominable. Undoubtedly you can think of more examples that might fit these categories. A whole series of them might be found in ordinary college bull sessions about science and religion, science here meaning technology, as it ordinarily does among college students and not a few of their teachers. Religions imported into the United States (such as the various types of Israelite religion in Christian and later Jewish forms, as well as Islamic religions) provide a host of anomalies that do not fit the technological paradigm, while technology provides a large number of anomalies that cannot fit religions of other cultures.

Be that as it may, purity rules deal with system and order, with definitions of general boundaries and of exclusivity, with the anomalies that simply defy classification or that are positively abominations. Every culture has such purity rules, for every culture has a classification system. Yet cultures adopt different emphases, perspectives, or horizons in developing their classification systems. Our culture is poised on an individualistic horizon of limitless good attained by the individual's mastery of the social and natural environment, hence by means of social and physical technology, like ten rules to manipulate another to get him or her on a date, or five rules to follow to get better gas mileage. From this horizon, we get a set of rules, of classifications, that differs notably from the first-century Mediterranean, which was pivoted on group-rooted, collectivistic personality and the perspective of limited good to be maintained by interpersonal competence in line with honor and shame.

Furthermore, since purity rules present a sort of grid that covers all aspects of society, such rules are equally concerned with maintaining the wholeness or completeness of the social body. The pure social body is much like a perfect container with no overflow or oozing in or out, a complete body. From this perspective, purity rules are very concerned with the outer borders of the society and strive to maintain society's integrity or wholeness. For example, note our interest in illegal aliens, passports, visas, health certificates for immigrants, and the like. As I mentioned previously, purity rules have a place for everything and everyone, with everything and everyone in its place—and with anomalies properly excluded. And just as society as a whole is a social body defined by purity rules, so also is the individual. The individual in a given society is a personal body defined by purity rules that replicate the societal rules and fit the individual into the social body. In other words, the individual human being can be considered a sort of portable road map of the terrain and features that mark and define the larger social world. Thus the individual, too, will be concerned about wholeness and completeness, about being a perfect entity with no overflow or oozing in or out, hence with individual completeness. For example, note our zeal in curbing offensive odors in the individual with mouthwashes, deodorants, scented soaps, and the like, that keep odors from the borders of others and within our own. Finally, since God-talk, or theology, necessarily consists in comparisons drawn from human experience, God, too, will be described in terms of the concerns of society and of the individual in the society. God will be described as complete, whole, perfect, and this perfection will be discernible in God's relationship to God's people and God's world.

The common perception is that observance of purity rules brings prosperity both to the society and to the individuals in that society, while infringement brings danger. In our society, the main purity rules concern the symbol called money, with health running a close second. Money is a quantitative line marker serving as norm for social status; it enables the pursuit of individualistic happiness within those statuses that we consider significant. Health is individualistic, technological health (the body as a sort of mechanical organism is viewed technologically). Health marks the ability of the individual to compete with others, hence to function productively within society as a whole and within an individual's own status in particular. You might note that the only forms of segregation and discrimination permitted in the United States (hence, the only overt boundary markers) are those deriving from money and health. You can live wherever you want, eat and buy whatever you want, regardless of who you are, provided that you have the money. If you lack the money, you are in effect segregated from those who have it, hence you are in a lower class. Similarly, you are considered a possible productive member of society when you are physically and emotionally capable of acting as an individual, individualistically. Adults who are physically or emotionally dependent on others are generally considered unclean, unable to respect societal lines. On the other hand, those who are a threat to the money or health of the moneyed or healthy are abominations, deviants. Deviants get excluded from ordinary social intercourse, while normal folks who find themselves in an unclean state by means of crossing boundaries into areas where they ought not be (e.g., breaking a parking law, infringing on your neighbors' rights to privacy) have to be purified and cleansed, normally with money (fines, fees, and so on).

In the limited-good perspective of our first-century foreigners, the main task in life was not symboled by achievement in terms of money but rather by the maintenance of one's inherited position in society. This brought prosperity and insured the most harmonious relationship possible in terms of time, place, interpersonal relationships with one's fellows, and relationships with God. This kind of prosperity was the task of the group-oriented, collectivistic persons as well as of their society as a whole. The purity rules of the society were intended to foster prosperity by maintaining fitting, harmonious relationships. Thus perfection—the wholeness marked off by purity rules—characterizes God, the people in general, and the individual. This perfection gets spelled out in replicating patterns (recall that replication means the same rules in different areas), perhaps most apparent in the categories of persons and their interaction in marriage, in temple worship, as well as in the fellowship of the meal. Before we consider Jesus' reaction to Israel's purity laws, it is obviously necessary to have some idea of what those rules were and how they outfitted society with meaning.

General Israelite Perspectives

For any first-century Israelite, whether Judean, Galilean, Perean, or émigré, there would be little doubt concerning the center of the inhabited earth. Due to God's will, Israelite orientation was focused on the central place of the land of Israel, Jerusalem. And even more sharply, the central focus of Jerusalem was the Temple of the God of Israel. Traditional Israelite ideology was pivoted on the awareness of the holiness of the God of Israel. Holiness is social exclusivity, and the God of Israel demanded such exclusivity from the people who were chosen to be exclusively God's—or so went Israel's story line.

In terms of Israel's ideology, then, what was sacred to God had to do with what was exclusive to God, while the profane or nonexclusive to God consisted of all creation categorized in terms of a system that would allow everything and everyone a certain meaning-endowing, sense-making situation or place. This was the purity system of Israel, providing a place for everyone/thing, and expecting everyone/thing in its place. Israelites believed that this purity system derived directly from the God of Israel who created all that exists. In the very act of creation, Israel's God set up the system of categories into which all created beings properly fit (Gen. 1–2:4a). Thus Israel's purity laws were in fact natural laws directly established by the creator (this was the prevailing, Priestly view; however in Genesis 2, Adam sets up the initial categories, a feature noted in the Pharisee and later Ben Zakaiist tradition). For its own welfare and prosperity, it was up to Israel, as a people sacred and exclusive to God, to live in purity. And it was notably up to the sacred attendants of God, Israel's priestly tribe, as God's divinely chosen retainers, to see to the observance of purity rules, both for themselves and the people at large. To approach the sacred, one had to be sacred and pure. To approach the sanctuary in general, one had to be pure. This idea lies behind Israelite classification of persons and animals, as we shall see.

As for morality, if Israelites are to be exclusive as their God is exclusive, they too will have to behave in a manner befitting their exclusivity over against the rest of humankind. This exclusivity includes living according to the categories established by Israel's God in the created world. It is these categories that serve as the matrix for Israelite definitions of what is in place (pure, clean) and what is out of place (impure, unclean). With purity a condition for access to the exclusive, only the clean can approach the God of Israel with any hope of success in the interaction.

Thus the orientational map of Israel consists of two major category sets: the sacred and profane (exclusive and nonexclusive) and the pure/clean and impure/unclean (in proper place/out of place). These category sets cut through the five major classifications typical of all societies: self, others, animate and inanimate creatures, time, space. Temple arrangements point to the application of these category sets to space and to selves/groups permitted in this space.

Some categories of behavior, however, fall outside Israel's God-given purity system. They are simply anomalous. Those who perform such actions must be punished. The actions are irrevocable, and therefore the guilty person simply cannot make up or atone for them. Such crimes prohibited by

God and expressed in Israel's conventions and customs are full of danger for the community. Hence there are permanently applicable, divine sanctions for such deeds, to be applied in one of two ways: either by God himself or by the Israelite community.

The *sanctions applied by God* are those in which a person is "cut off" (*karet*). These are penalties for persons defiling the sacred and thus violating the distinctions between sacred and profane, the foundational category for the whole system of meaning. Since God is exclusive (sacred) like the realms God marks off as exclusive, so too Israel is an exclusive people and must observe the boundaries of the sacred (Lev. 11:44, 45; 19:2; 20:7, 26). Violators are therefore expected to incur the penalty of being "cut off"; in other words, their deeds are expected to result in calamity to their entire lineage through the direct intervention of God ("automatically") and without any societal action. This belief in automatic retribution protects the realm of the sacred by deterring acts that would encroach on the realm of the sacred.

However, crimes whose sanction is the death penalty to be applied by society fall outside the boundaries of behavior controlled by "cut off" penalties. The behaviors requiring the death penalty are transgressions of the Ten Commandments. The first set of transgressions include crimes that dishonor the God of Israel to such an extent that the requirement for satisfaction of honor is irreversible and irrevocable. The offender must be put to death. This includes infractions of Sabbath observance. Then come crimes against parents, and finally crimes that dishonor a man and his family honor requiring vengeance and resulting in feuding. As Josephus observes, "Now the greatest part of offenses with us are capital, as if anyone be guilty of adultery; if anyone force a virgin; if anyone be so impudent as to attempt sodomy with a male; or if, upon another's making an attempt upon him, he submits to be so used. There is also a law for slaves of the like nature that can never be avoided" (*Against Apion* 2.215).

Consider the Torah prohibition of men lying with men as with a woman (Lev. 18:22). This prohibition is found in the passage running from Leviticus 18 to 20, a subset of crimes judged to be typical of non-Israelite behavior. In Israel such crimes deserve the death penalty to be applied by Israelite society as explicitly commanded in the Torah: "You shall not do as they do in the land of Egypt, where you dwelt, and you shall not do as they do in the land of Canaan, to which I am bringing you" (Lev. 18:3). Hence these are behaviors typical of the non-Israelites that Israel knew. In his letter to the Romans, Paul found that these behaviors were typical of the non-Israelites that he knew as well. The listing of behaviors in Leviticus 18 is outfitted with penalties in the parallel Leviticus 20; actions requiring the death penalty, should they be found in Israel, include the following: offering children to Molech

(Lev. 20:2), cursing father or mother (Lev. 20:9), adultery (Lev. 20:10), incest with mother/mother-in-law (Lev. 20:11) or daughter-in-law (20:12), a man lying with a man as with a woman (Lev. 20:13), man or woman lying with a beast (Lev. 20:15–16, and the earlier Exod. 22:19: "Whoever lies with a beast shall be put to death"), and acting as medium or wizard (Lev. 20:27). Such acts are said to pollute the land of Israel and the pollution of the land cannot be rectified by ritual purification.

It seems that when Paul speaks of things "according to nature" (*kata physin*) and "contrary to nature (*para physin*)," as in his letter to the Romans, he adopts a Hellenistic Judean appropriation of traditional Israelite categories: (a) *according to nature* = according to the conventions (*nomos*) and customs (*ethe*) of Israel, that is, holy and pure behavior as well as clean and unclean behaviors that can be "naturally" purified; (b) *against nature* = prohibitions in the conventions and customs of Israel sanctioned by a communal death penalty or direct divine punishment. These categories can be diagrammed as follows:

Israelite according to nature:

Exclusive (holy, sacred)

Nonexclusive (profane) { In place (clean, pure)

{ Out of place (unclean, impure)

Israelite contrary to nature

No place (anomalous) { To be eradicated (death penalty)

{ To be left to God (divine penalty)

In this regard, it is important to note that for Paul, the presence of non-Israelites in his post-Jesus groups is something "contrary to nature" (Rom 11:24). The few non-Israelites in the Roman Jesus groups "have been cut from what is by nature a wild olive tree, and grafted, contrary to nature, into a cultivated olive tree" (Rom 11:24). This "cultivated olive tree" is the group consisting of Israelite followers of Jesus.

Classification of Persons in Israel

For Jesus and Paul, Israel's categories of pure and sacred persons were something obvious. After our discussion of kinship and marriage in first-century Israelite ideology, we know that the defensive marriage strategy of Second Temple Israel required marriage partners to come from within the house of Israel. However, as we might expect from a limited-good society, this Israelite community was highly stratified into categories of persons who received their place by birth. Genealogical purity, the lines defining one's inherited status within the defensive community, was certainly a major concern of the elites, and perhaps of the non-elites as well. In Ezra 2:2–58 and Nehemiah 7:7–60, we find a simple classification of the population in terms of degrees of purity deriving from proximity to the Jerusalem Temple, the political-religious focus of Israel. The Temple was a large area of courts and buildings with the central pivotal locus being the sanctuary, the Holy of Holies. From the viewpoint of the kinship system and the defensive approach to life, since the whole genealogical community is perceived as God-given, its genealogical purity lines are considered to be God's will for God's people. God's promises of life in the age to come hold for the people, the offspring of Abraham, to the degree of their God-appointed purity. The period after the rise of post-Jesus groups saw the formulation of Ben Zakaiism and the rabbinic traditions that marked the formation of Israelite non-Temple domestic religion in the third century A.D. These traditions, some of which probably mirror the situation during New Testament times, report that the genealogical categories of persons one might find in Second Temple Israel— from an Israelite perspective—included the following (cited from Joachim Jeremias, *Jerusalem in the Time of Jesus*, p. 271 ff. and conflated):

a   1. Priests

b   2. Levites

c   3. Full-blooded Israelites ("laymen")

d $\left\{\begin{array}{l} \text{4. Illegal children of priests} \\ \text{5. Proselytes or Gentile converts to Judaism} \\ \text{6. Proselytes who once were slaves, hence proselyte} \\ \text{\ \ \ freedmen} \end{array}\right.$

e $\left\{\begin{array}{l} \text{7. Bastards (those born of incestuous or adulterous unions)} \\ \text{8. The "fatherless" (those born of prostitutes)} \\ \text{9. Foundlings} \\ \text{10. Eunuchs made so by men} \end{array}\right.$

f $\left\{\begin{array}{l} \text{11. Eunuchs born that way} \\ \text{12. Those of deformed sexual features} \\ \text{13. Hermaphrodites} \end{array}\right.$

x   14. Persons of all other ethnic groups (= "Gentiles")

What is the basis of this set of categories? You will remember that in the defensive marriage strategy, it is imperative to intermarry solely with those belonging to the Israelite community—and within one's social status, if possible. Hence potential marriage partners must be members of the house of Israel by birth or by ritual birth (converts, called "proselytes") and occupy a given social status. Further, the defensive strategy calls for holy seed, hence offspring exclusive to God because born of parents respecting God's rules for God's holy people. Thus the persons marrying must be capable of having children, thereby transmitting their own inherited status—inheritance of status follows the father. Therefore, the criteria for fitting into the purity lines of this group include membership in the house of Israel and capacity to procreate. Further, this defensive community possessed a fundamental, overt status structure based on birth: priest, Levite, and full Israelite. Thus membership in Israel likewise implied inherited status.

The marriage rules, that is, purity rules applied to marriage, were obviously the work of the preindustrial city elites. They went as follows:

1. True Israel consisted specifically of priests, Levites, and other full-blooded Israelites (categories a, b, c). These persons were genealogically clean, with proper pedigrees. They could all freely intermarry.

2. Proselytes and proselyte freedmen were ranked separately, since they might be said to bear a slight genealogical doubt. Along with them were included the illegal children of priests. These latter were not illegitimate, but rather children of priests who married prohibited women such as widows, divorcees, or seduced women (see Lev. 21:7). Technically, a priest must always marry a female of true Israelite pedigree, "unused" or untouched by any other male; otherwise, his offspring are ranked with proselytes. Persons in this category (d) did in fact belong to Israel and could marry Levites and full Israelites, but never priests. Hence they were clean for some Israelites, unclean for others.

3. Category (e): Bastards, the fatherless, foundlings, and eunuchs had a grave genealogical impediment about them: they were simply not whole and complete. They could not properly trace their ancestry, might derive from highly disreputable ancestors, and in the case of the eunuch, could no longer transmit covenant status. These persons do not possess *both* covenant membership by birth and the capability of transmitting the status of proper covenant membership. They might possess one feature or the other, but not both. These could intermarry or even marry proselytes, but they were forbidden to marry priests, Levites, full Israelites, and the illegal children of priests—the group functionally forming "true Israel" and intimately bound up with the Temple.

4. Category (f): Eunuchs from birth, those of deformed sexual features, and hermaphrodites could not marry at all. They were incapable of sexual relations, hence incapable of transmitting Israelite status.

5. Category (x): Persons of all other ethnic groups (= Gentiles) were an abomination, simply off the purity scale altogether.

If we view these inherited statuses and the permissible defensive marriage interactions in terms of a Venn diagram, the picture would look as follows:

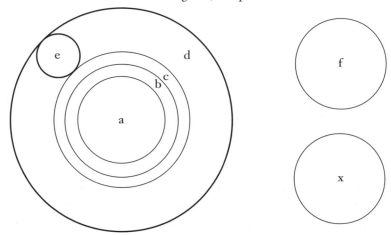

The categories derive from proximity to the Temple (and its holy place)—priest, Levite, Israelite—along with two qualities: being a member of the Israelite community by birth or ritual birth and the capacity to transmit one's status within the Israelite community:

x: abomination: off the purity scale entirely, hence necessarily unclean
f: always unclean for marriage since they cannot fit the criteria for inclusion on the purity scale
d: Israel, including those by ritual birth (proselytes). Some in this category are capable of marrying into "true" Israel at the Levite and Israelite level, but not at the priest level, hence they are clean for some, unclean for others in the inner circles.
c: those who are Israelite by birth, "true" Israel, but among these there is a special category (b)
b: Levites: these persons are fit for Temple service, but lack the qualities to fit them into category (a)
a: priests: fit both for the Temple and for the altar (holy place)
e: those of (d) who either fit dubiously in Israel or have a questionable inherited status to transmit or cannot transmit it any longer.

These categories of persons in first-century Israelite society represent an abstract conception of the purity lines of Second Temple Israel, a symbolic statement of who is in the social body of Israel. Entrance into the house of Israel is by birth, and circumcision marks the rite of entry. It should come as no surprise if we find that the classification of clean and unclean animals—what in the realm of animals is allowed to enter the individual body of the

Israelite or the worshiping body at the Temple—closely fits these categories of persons. This would be another instance of replication: the same rules in another dimension.

Classification of Clean and Unclean Animals

In fact, much as the holy land is holy because it is exclusive to the God of Israel, so is all Israel along with Israel's domestic animals. This parallel between Israel and its domestic beasts can be seen in the fact that the first-born, "the first to open the womb among the people of Israel, both of man and of beast," is the Lord's (Exod. 13:2; 22:29b–30; Lev. 27:26–27; Num. 3:13; 8:17–18; 18:15), as well as in the fact that temple sacrifices are to come only "from the herd or from the flock" (Lev. 1:2), that is, from domestic animals. Domestic animals are to observe the Sabbath, just as their owners and masters do (Exod. 20:8–11; Deut. 5:12–15; for the Sabbath year, Lev. 25:6–7). Finally, just as Israel is to avoid marriage with other ethnic groups—as though other ethnic groups formed another species—so too the cross-breeding of domestic animals of different species is forbidden (Lev. 19:19).

By replication, the categories that divide one class of Israelites from another in the marriage purity rules will divide their animals. However, there are nondomestic animals in the land as well, and these too must be patterned to make sense of the total environment. This is precisely where the categories of clean and unclean in Leviticus 11 fit in. These categories cover all the animals of the environment: water, air, and land creatures. The replication of marriage purity rules mainly looks to land creatures, as we shall see. At present, consider Leviticus 11.

The categories of Leviticus 11 cover all the animals of the environment, with only the domestic variety fit for the Temple. The animals are divided, first of all, according to their habitats: water, air, or land. The anomalous are rejected immediately; they are an abomination because they fall outside the categories—for example, amphibians that live between two spheres and in both (Lev. 11:10). Then specific criteria for each category are spelled out: proper land animals are "whatever parts the hoof and is cloven-footed and chews the cud" (Lev. 11:3). The proper water animal is "everything in the waters that has fins and scales" (Lev. 11:9). Finally, proper air animals are those that do not eat blood and carrion, can fly or hop with their wings and two legs (like the locust: Lev. 11:13–22).

Anomalies in these categories include any creatures having the defining features of members of another category, like land animals that swarm like fish or insects (Lev. 11:29 ff.), winged creatures that go on all fours like land animals (the insects, Lev. 11:20), or creatures lacking in the main defining features (e.g., crabs and eels are water creatures lacking fins and scales). However, creeping, crawling, and/or swarming and teeming creatures lack criteria for allocation into any one class, since there are animals in all three areas that behave this way. Thus "every swarming thing that swarms upon the earth is an abomination; . . . Whatever goes on its belly, and whatever goes on all fours, or whatever has many feet, all the swarming things that swarm upon the earth, you shall not eat; for they are an abomination" (Lev. 11:41–42). Now for purposes of comparison with the previous classification of persons, consider the following Venn diagram of land creatures (taken from Mary T. Douglas):

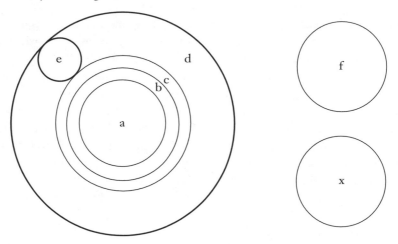

These categories, like those for persons, derive from proximity to the Temple (and the altar) along with two qualities: domestication and cud-chewing, parted-hoofed features.

- x: abomination: any land animal that swarms is off the purity scale entirely, hence, necessarily unclean
- f: always unclean for table use, since they cannot fit the criteria for inclusion on the purity scale. These have neither cloven hoofs nor chew the cud, are not domesticated, and they would include predators and carrion-eaters such as lions, bears, foxes, and dogs (which were not pets in the ancient Near East).
- d: animals of the land of Israel that are domesticated or not domesticated, but have cloven hoofs or chew the cud or both. These can be clean or unclean for table use.
- c: those animals that have parted hoofs and chew the cud are clean and fit for table use (Lev. 11:3; Deut. 14:4–6 for nondomesticated). Among these there is a special category (b)

b: unblemished clean animals of domestic herds and flocks; these are fit for the altar (Lev. 22:20 for the general rule), unless an added requirement is demanded (e.g., Lev. 1:3, 10; 4:3, 23, 28; 5:15, 18).

a: unblemished clean animals of domestic herds and flocks fit for the altar with added requirement of age (e.g., a year old—Lev. 9:3; 23:18) or quality (e.g., all first-born are to be given to the priest [Num. 18:15]).

e: those of (d) that do not *both* have cloven hoofs and chew the cud, i.e., do one or the other but not both, even when domesticated (Lev. 11:4–7). The pig is listed here quite neutrally but in the second century B.C. becomes an especially unclean animal because of its use as sacred animal by outsiders, notably from the Maccabean period on (see 1 Macc. 1:41–64 and 2 Macc. 6:4–5).

Thus, as Mary Douglas has pointed out, we find a parallel set of purity lines marking off Israel and its animals. These might be summarized as follows:

Israelites: Their animals:

c

b

a

c

b

a

c: all who are under the covenant, clean and unclean—but never abominable

b: fit for Temple worship or sacrifice: only the clean without blemish

a: consecrated to the Temple: first-born without blemish, of men and beasts (read Lev. 21:17–23; 27:26–27; Exod. 13:2, 11–16; 22: 29–30).

Relative to category (b) above, those fit for Temple worship or sacrifice, our previous classification of persons dealt only with their clean or unclean state relative to birth. Birth marks only the beginning of a process in which persons have further occasion to be blemished or rendered unclean, hence unfit for social intercourse with their fellows in various degrees, running in concentric circles from the central hub, the Temple. For example, Leviticus 12–15 lists those who are unclean and must withdraw from social relations with their fellows. These include persons suffering from skin disorders or unusual, abnormal bodily flows such as menstruation, seminal emission, suppuration. In these instances the personal boundaries of the individual prove to be porous; the individual is not whole. The same holds for contact with a cadaver. Further, a blemished priest or Israelite was not allowed to offer sacrifice. What might constitute a blemish is duly noted in the following prescription: "For no one who has a blemish shall draw near, a man blind or lame, or one who has a mutilated face or a limb too long, or a man who has an injured foot or an injured hand, or a hunchback, or a dwarf, or a man with a defect in his sight or an itching disease or scabs or crushed testicles" (Lev. 21:18–20). In these cases, the persons described are likewise not whole. The unclean and the blemished simply cannot symbol wholeness and perfection, and hence they cannot replicate the ideal: the perfect individual in the perfect society under the perfect God.

Now that we have some idea of how persons fit into their proper places, and how animals replicate persons and fit into their proper places, we will turn to the processes by which persons and their animals symbolically interact with God. One process is called *sanctification* or sanctifying. To sanctify is to set apart for God, to make holy to and for God. Another process is a specific form of sanctifying called *sacrifice*. Underlying both processes is the human way of making someone or something sacred to another.

Sanctifying and Sacrifice

At the beginning of this chapter, I set out a number of examples pointing to how we experience the sacred in terms of what we consider exclusively set aside for ourselves. Recall the jeans in the first example. How did the jeans get set apart to or for you? The process, which we might call buying or purchasing, has three abstract steps to it. At the beginning the jeans are rooted in their normal merchandising position, the property of some impersonal corporation such as the manufacturing company or the department store. As you start making your selection, you set some jeans apart from this normal state as you try them on, consider their qualities, and the like. And as your interest in a particular pair grows, you consider them as possibly yours, as not exactly the same as all the rest on the tables or racks, and you would be offended if another customer came and took them from your hands—even though they are not yet yours. The jeans as a possible purchase, as potentially yours, are in a middle phase, separated from the merchandiser's pile, but not yet yours. This is a sort of boundary or marginal state. To help you through the marginal state, you get yourself a ceremonial leader, a salesperson, who runs through a ceremony or rite by means of which the marginal jeans are passed on to a new status: they become yours, set apart to or for you. They become sanctified to or for you. This little rite of sanctification, then, consists of three phases that might be depicted as follows:

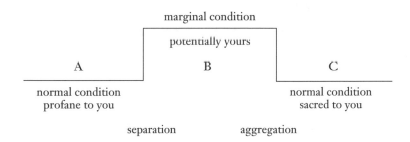

This sort of process can be discerned in our dealings with many things. However, it also underlies the significant social changes that persons undergo. For example, a person's movement into the marginal condition called college is toward a new sort of sacred state, a profession or life career. Students begin this movement from a normal condition of being qualified for nothing in particular. Similarly, getting married is a sort of process from the normal condition of being unmarried through a marginal condition of decision, planning, and rite, to a new normal condition of being married. In the first phase, potential mates are profane to each other; in the second phase they become potentially sacred to each other and eventually go through some sort of ritual that realizes the mutual setting apart. The result is the new normal state of being holy to or for each other, being married. Note that both throughout college and in getting married, there are ritual leaders, socially acknowledged, who bring a person through the marginal condition.

This description is temporal since it looks at the process in terms of time. However, we can also depict the process from the viewpoint of space. Relative to things, you already own a number of things in a spatial sphere that we might call your sacred area (your house, your room, your closet). Then there is obviously an enormous amount of things outside your sacred area that are not yours, that are profane to you. Finally, there is the overlapping area where you interact with the profane and acquire new items that become sacred to and for you, a sort of spatial marginal area (the area around a cash register or in a layaway room, for example). Spatially, the arrangement would look as follows:

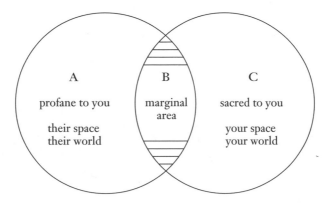

The way you set apart or sanctify things is by moving them from their world (or nobody's world in our limitless-good culture) to your world. Your world, including the persons and things in that world, are sacred to you. You shaped and acquired your world because your parents introduced you into your world (which was their world with you as outsider) from the marginal area of birth. At this marginal area, they could either accept or reject you, and in this sense there is little difference between being born to or adopted by a given set of parents: in either case parents have to choose to accept their child.

Now, take the time to apply these two models of space and time to the relationship of human beings to God. From the viewpoint of time, what is the process of setting apart to God like? From the viewpoint of space, how do the areas of God and humankind intersect? In first-century Israel, the space of God was symboled by the political-religious edifice, the Temple, which replicated both the entire holy land and the whole world, like a set of Chinese boxes or Russian dolls within each other. The process of setting persons and things apart to or for God is called *sanctification*, "holy-ing," or hallowing (as in "hallowed be thy name"); the process of interacting with God by means of persons and things thus set apart is called *worship*. The purity rules of our first-century foreigners point to the categories of persons and things and their proper condition and location for taking part in this interaction between God and humankind—in the Temple, in the holy land, and in the world at large. Such rules also replicate in the division of time throughout the year, which covers Temple time, time in the holy land in terms of a week punctuated by Sabbath rest, and the broader annual time, punctuated by special feast days. Temple time, Sabbath time, and feast-day time are all marginal times, transition times, times when you can ignore your watch, much as you do when you are at a party that you really enjoy or when you are in love or on a fantastic vacation. Watch time makes little sense in those circumstances, much as focusing on everyday routine matters makes little sense at parties, on dates, or on vacations. Such times are holy times and require a different set of focuses.

To get back to our foreigners, consider the spatial arrangement, the holy spatial lines, of the Jerusalem Temple in the first century. The Temple, much like later Christian church buildings and shrines the world over, consisted of three general areas: A) a place where properly prepared persons can assemble; C) a place marking God's space, the sanctuary proper, such as the altar area in some Christian churches; D) an intermediate space where interaction can take place. Of course these general areas can be and are subdivided, but for starters, take the overall view. The areas would thus correspond to the circles of space that is yours and not yours, depicted above. However, for greater exactness, I will surround both circles with a line that embraces persons not belonging to God's people, hence not fazed by the interaction:

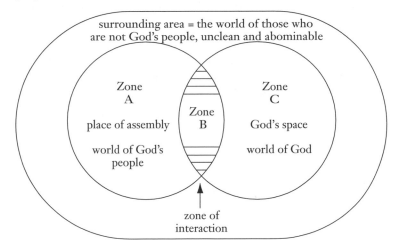

The Temple arrangement replicates that of the holy land in which it is situated. The Temple is found in Jerusalem, on one of the three hills called the Temple Mount in the first century. Now, just as the holy land is God's land relative to the world created by God, so Jerusalem is God's city (Matt. 4:5; 27:53) relative to the holy land, and the Temple Mount is God's special mountain relative to the city of Jerusalem. Finally, the sanctuary building (Matt. 24:15; 1 Cor. 3:17) in the Temple area is God's space relative to the Temple area in general. Again, we have a set of Chinese boxes or Russian dolls that divide up space to fill it with meaning by reference to a center. In each case the problem area, the area of anxiety and concern as well as of joy and emotional highs, is the area of interaction, the margin or borderline. Judean émigrés coming from abroad are happy to see the holy land; on pilgrimage they are happy to see Jerusalem on the horizon; as worshipers they are overjoyed to see the Temple Mount; and as sacrificers they are emotionally elated when in the place of assembly they see the altar and the sanctuary behind it. On the way to Jerusalem, hitting the margins causes emotional response. For unclean persons, persons not allowed at the margins, a sort of reverse experience might be expected. And in the face of a conquering horde of alien invaders, anxiety would mount as margin after margin, limit after limit was crossed over in a march of desecration, of defilement, of reducing everything to the profane. This is how margins, definitions, and limits of purity work in human experience, ours as well as theirs (and I might note, incidentally, that they work on the individual body just as they do on the social body).

As we know, Israel believed that its margins, its purity lines, were God-given and God-willed. Relative to the Temple area, we might depict the space vertically as follows (passages describing Solomon's Temple are Exodus 25–27—even though it is said to take place in the wilderness—and Ezekiel 40–43—this future Temple is based on recollections of Solomon's temple; for Herod's first-century Temple, known as the Second Temple, based on biblical regulations and later practice, see Joachim Jeremias, *Jerusalem in the Time of Jesus*, pp. 79–82 for rabbinic sources:

Symbolic space category	O.T. category	1st century
mixed nature: clean, unclean, and abominations	outside the camp	outside the holy land
mixed culture: clean or unclean, but no abominations	inside the camp	in the holy land replicated by Jerusalem, the holy city
zone A: space of God's people: assembly space	court of tent	Temple mount and courts of a. Gentiles (strangers and sojourners in the land) b. (Israelite) women c. Israelites
threshold of God's space zone B: space of interaction final limits of man's space	altar and laver table and seven-branched candlestick curtain before the sanctuary	
zone C: God's space	tent with ark holy of holies	porch holy place holy of holies

In this arrangement, the Holy of Holies marks the center of the Temple Mount, which marks the center of Jerusalem, which marks the center of the holy land, which marks the center of the world. At the center of centers, God's holy people have the opportunity to interact with God under the ritual direction of God's priests aided by their Levites.

God's greatest gift to the chosen people is life. Life in the ruralized, preindustrial societies of the first-century Mediterranean was quite precarious. People were all too aware of the uncertainty of life. And they were sure that life comes from God alone, hence ultimately belongs to God alone. One of the major forms of interaction with God in the Jerusalem Temple focused on life. to celebrate life or restore life. This life-focused interaction is sacrifice. Sacrifice is a ritual process in which God is offered some form of inducement, rendered humanly irretrievable, with a view to some life-effect for the offerer(s).

As a ritual, sacrifice involves setting apart some living entity—animal, vegetable (and often with mineral)—making it irretrievable to the sacrificer then offering it to God. Rendering the living entity irretrievable transforms it into an irrecoverable form: killing, baking, pouring out, burning salt, incense. The living entity becomes a victim—a technical term of sacrifice. Then the victim is ingested by the one(s) offering and by God, or by God alone (as in whole burnt offerings). The central elements of life in living beings belong to the deity alone, (even if at times utilized by worshipers, e.g., in Israel: fat and blood; cf. Jesus' flesh/body and blood; in Greece: fat and bone). The effect sought in sacrifice is a life-effect: the maintenance or restoration of life, ascribed solely to the deity. Life-maintenance sacrifices celebrate life in festivity. Life-restoration sacrifices revitalize after accidental deviance, or after stepping outside the human realm, as when a mother steps into the realm of prehuman in order to conceive a child, or a husband or son steps into the realm of dead in order to bury a relative.

We already know that we are dealing with group-embedded and group-oriented personalities who sought out patrons from higher social strata to help them in maintaining their assigned and inherited social status. In this perspective, the God of Israel occupies the highest conceivable social status and alone can help people maintain life. This God invites those people set apart to interact in life-focused rituals. God, however, does not need their sacrifices; rather, they need to sacrifice to God. Why? First of all, to celebrate life-giving benefits of God's patronage, which include God's power as well as the joy of God's presence, then to restore life-threatening relations ascribed to offenses against God. Sacrifices to God are analogous to gifts given to higher-class patrons. What patrons want of their clients is recognition of honor, submission, a following. Sacrifice to God symbols a gift of a client to a patron, an expression of asymmetrical but reciprocal relationship with a view to power, protection, and the joy of bathing in the presence of the patron of patrons. In Temple sacrifice the offered object—some prescribed and clean victim—stands for the offerer, who likewise must be clean and unblemished.

The object is taken by the ritual leader of the intermediate or marginal zone, the priest, who acts as a bridge between the donor's space and the space of God, space that symbols their worlds. By means of this bridge and the activity in the marginal zone, the benefits of the patron pass to the donor, who may be an individual, a group, or the nation at large. In this way sacrifice symbols an interaction between a distinctive people and God across the marginal or transitional zone. In life-restoring sacrifices, the victim is totally burned on the altar. In life-affirming sacrifices, after it passes to the marginal zone most of the food offered in sacrifice is eaten by the offerers, their entourage, and the Temple personnel. The transformation of the portions burned at the altar symbolizes passage of the donor to God. The fellowship of the Temple meal clearly symbols the fellowship of a benign patron with his clients. The purpose of it all is clearly "religious" in the first-century sense of the word, that is, a recognition of the preeminence of God above all social statuses, the admission that God is the one who controls all—hence a broad symbol of honor, submission, and obedience of the donor to God, along with God's acceptance of the donor as client.

Thus sacrifice is always about life directed to the person in control of human life. The fact that humans cannot spontaneously, technologically, or mechanically produce life makes life itself the prime natural symbol of gift—life always comes from another. That ultimate source of life from which all life derives is another description of God to whom sacrifice is directed. Since sacrifice is about a life-effect, it is always directed to the one responsible for life as human adults experience it. Either the maintenance of life or the restoration of life is what sacrificers are concerned with.

For just as an offense against one's fellows that might result in lethal feuding requires reconciliation, so there was a range of purification and reconciliation sacrifices directed to God to keep life-threat away and to reestablish life-supportive relations. These sacrifices marked reconciliation and a new social start; they are often called *expiatory sacrifices*. And just as a person attempts to initiate relations with another human being by offering a gift of sorts, so too such "feeling-out" gifts to assure the goodwill of a deity may be offered to deities; these are called *propitiatory sacrifices*. There is a type of propitiatory sacrifice that insures protection against some life-threat inflicted by another (an apotropaic sacrifice) either in pure protection or with something inflicted on another.

In sum, sacrifice is always about life; its purpose is to have some life-effect. Sacrifice takes place at those junctures of social processes when life needs to be affirmed or restored. Sacrifice is a ritual transaction that affirms or celebrates the life of a kin group or polity, or that marks the restoration of life of a person or group deserving to forfeit life. In antiquity, as in many non-Western societies today, the mediating material in this social process is some living being (animal or vegetable) that is killed, then ingested partially or totally by the transacting partner considered responsible for life, that is, God. The living being is transformed, rendered irrecoverable and irretrievable by the one sacrificing: human or animal is killed; flour is baked; wine is poured out. Then God receives a portion: a part in the case of life affirmation, to be shared with the sacrificing circle; or the whole in the case of life restoration, standing for the person or entity that should in fact have been killed.

The foregoing models of clean and unclean persons on the basis of birth, of clean and unclean animals somewhat replicating personal categories, of sacred and profane space, and of procedures to cross boundaries all seem to have been in vogue among concerned Israelite elites and non-elites during the lifetime of Jesus. Such purity rules formed the implicit and explicit lines by means of which persons and things were situated in Second Temple Israel.

However, not long after the death and resurrection of Jesus, a notable group of Jesus followers rejected those purity arrangements for members of (the abominable) other ethnic groups who accepted Jesus as Messiah to come with power. According to Israelite ideology, however, God's Messiah would come to God's own people to transform Israelite society with its God-given purity arrangement. To accept Jesus as Messiah without Israel's purity arrangements clearly meant to spurn God's will and to reject the order ordained by God for patron-client interaction. And with the destruction of the Jerusalem Temple in A.D. 70—after which most of our Gospel documents were written—the sacred center of centers ceases to mark off sacred space as previously, thus vindicating those Jesus followers, such as Paul and his followers, who considered Israelite purity rules as optional for Israelites "in Christ" even before A.D. 70.

Purity Arrangements in Post-Jesus Groups

If we stick to the earliest traditions in the Gospels, we find it to be quite certain that Jesus proclaimed the kingdom of God and healed people. His healing frequently looked to persons who, in terms of purity rules, were blemished, hence either incapable of social relations with the rest of the holy people of Israel (such as lepers, Mark 1:40–45; Luke 17:11–19; the woman with a hemorrhage, Mark 5:25–34) or barred from the Temple and sacrifice because of some sort of permanent impediment or lack of wholeness (such as those possessed, the paralyzed, the lame, the blind). These healings are frequently linked with the role and function of sacred time, notably the Sabbath (e.g., Mark 1:21–27; 3:1–6; Matt. 12:1–14). By healing on a Sabbath, Jesus provokes debate about the meaning of the Sabbath—hence about the meaning of purity rules applied to time. This, of course, would imply questions of the meaning of purity rules applied to space and persons as well, since such rules replicate each other, and an alteration in one set requires alterations in the others.

In these debates, Jesus accepts the system of lines set out in the purity rules of Israelite tradition, much as he assumes the defensive marriage strategy typical of postexilic Israel. But what he seems to question is the general social purpose of these rules and the way they are interpreted in line with this purpose. Their purpose is not to lop off ever greater portions of God's people from access to God, symboled by the clean and the sacred of the purity rules (thus constricting or diminishing zone A in the figures previously presented). Rather, they are to facilitate access to God. The purity rules are to make this access easier, not close it off. Another way to say this is "The sabbath was made for human beings, not human beings for the sabbath" (Mark 2:27).

Furthermore, just as God really has no need of sacrifices, so too God does not need purity rules to confine and hedge God in from the dishonor and outrage of human beings. God is perfect because God is open to all Israelites, both the good and the bad. Relative to God's distinctive people in God's holy land, "he makes his sun rise on the evil and on the good, and sends rain on the just and on the unjust" (Matt. 5:45). Since God is open to all the covenanted people of Israel, to do God's will is to be open to one's fellow Israelites, whether good or bad, just as God is open to them. God's will, then, is the welfare of this people. Hence any interpretation of the purity rules should be in the direction of the welfare of Israel, not in the direction of simply maintaining the system in some mechanical way—at the level of hands and feet only. The purpose, the heart, must enter the picture. For example, "Moses said, 'Honor your father and your mother'; and, 'He who speaks evil of father or mother, let him surely die'; but you say, 'If a man tells his father or his mother, What you would have gained from me is Corban' (that is, given to God)—then you no longer permit him to do anything for his father or mother" (Mark 7:10–12; also Matt. 15:4–6, where God rather than Moses commands respect for parents). Jesus' contention is that this sort of interpretation, with parents' rights being irreversibly overruled by a person's decision for God and the Temple, indicates lopsided priorities. The same holds for priorities in Temple sacrifice: "So if you are offering your gift at the altar, and there remember that your brother [fellow Israelite] has something against you, leave your gift there before the altar and go; first be reconciled to your brother, and then come and offer your gift" (Matt. 5:23–24). Consequently, if purity rules are to facilitate access to God, and if the God to whom one wants access has human welfare as the main priority in the divine will for the chosen people, it follows that proper interpretation of purity rules must derive from giving primary consideration to relationship with one's fellows. This is what righteousness is about. For righteousness means proper interpersonal relationships with all those in one's society, between God and covenanted human beings and between human beings and their fellow beings. In the righteousness symboled by Jesus, proper relationships between God and human beings—which are extremely necessary, as the purity rules indicate—require prior proper interhuman relationships. Otherwise, the God-human relationship remains at the level of the hands and feet, of activity alone, without the substance of the whole person. This sort of action, without the heart in it, is called *formalism*. Thus, in the interpretation of the parable on clean and unclean (Mark 7:14–23), "what comes out of a person is what defiles a person." And note that the evil intentions generated by the heart refer to interpersonal relationships that do harm to one's fellows: "For from within, out of the heart of a person, come evil thoughts, fornication, theft, murder, adultery, coveting, wickedness, deceit, licentiousness, envy, slander, pride, foolishness."

Thus, while Jesus shares his opponents' view of the symbolic value of the purity rules of Israel's scriptures, his activity and teaching point to a new vision of priorities based on Jesus' own perception of God and God's will. The purity rules, while important, do not have precedence but are secondary to some other central concern. The emphasis ought not to be on how Israel should approach God but on how God, in fact, approaches Israel. The purpose of interaction with God (in zone B in the previous figures) is to replicate and reveal how God acts toward God's people (openness to all, openhanded and openhearted), not to replicate and support how Israel has acted toward God in the past (selective defensiveness developed in traditioning the past). In his activity, Jesus focused on those in Israel who for some reason or other could not fit into the assembly of God's people (zone A in the previous figures). He thus insisted on a similar focus as priority for proper relationship with God. Such an interpretation, of course, tends to displace the Old Testament as God's priestly Torah, God's instruction sanctioned as law by the ruling elites of the day, in favor of taking the Old Testament as God's people's Torah, God's instruction as clarified by God's ongoing, present activity among and for the chosen people.

What results is the embedding of the purity rules of the Torah within the Torah as a whole instead of fitting the Torah as a whole into the purity rules, as the concerned elites and non-elites would insist (and as normative Talmudic Judaism would do when it emerges as the Jewish religion in the fifth century A.D.). Thus interaction with God takes place on the basis of Torah—including Temple sacrifice and purity rules as subsets of the Torah—and not on the basis of God's space confined to the Jerusalem Temple and mediated by priests alone. This would look as follows:

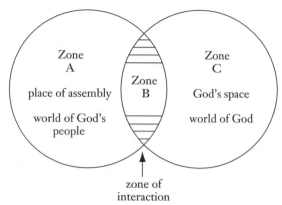

God's space is wherever God chooses to reveal, wherever people strive to obey and honor God in line with God's Torah. The place of assembly is wherever God's people gather to obey and honor God. Such an approach would look quaint to the urban elites of Jesus' day. It rather smacks of the prophetism of old with its emphasis on compassion and on practical attachment to one's neighbor as to oneself as highest ranking priorities, with sacrifice running second (Matt. 9:13; Mark 12:33; Hos. 6:6; Mic. 6:6–8). Certainly some of the non-elites of Jesus' day and age bought into these priorities, notably the scribes of the Pharisee group. With the fall of Jerusalem and the demise and exile of the city elites, these scribes under the aegis of Johannan Ben Zakkai did in fact implement a program (often called "rabbinism") somewhat similar to that envisioned by Jesus. The Ben Zakkaists developed a viable Israelite domestic religion to take the place of Israel's former political religion. And Ben Zakkaists did so largely through interaction with post-Jesus groups. Nearly a generation earlier, these post-Jesus groups developed their own, Jesus-inspired version of a viable Israelite domestic religion in place of the Temple's political religion.

For at an earlier period, in the A.D. thirties, Jesus' followers launched a program of their own. For these followers the resurrection of Jesus meant that Jesus indeed was right in his assessment of the Torah and its implications, since God himself indicated his approval of Jesus by raising him from the dead. If Jesus is right and God's will is human welfare coupled with purity rules that should symbol ready access to God, then it is no longer "in Israel" that people should seek this access, but "in Christ." And significantly, Jesus of Nazareth is this Christ, soon to come with the power that befits the Christ.

He himself is indication of God's ongoing activity; hence he supercedes the Torah as law indicating what pleases God. Instead of a Torah-centric being in Israel, early post-Jesus groups developed a Christocentric being "in Christ" (Christ occupying zone B).

The first problems facing post-Jesus groups seem to have dealt with how, in fact, persons get "in Christ." Must one first be "in Israel" or not? So long as post-Jesus group members belonged to the house of Israel, that was not a problem, of course. But what of the other ethnic groups? What if some Romans wanted to join a post-Jesus group? Must they accept the beliefs of Jesus if they came to believe in Jesus? "Some believers who belonged to the party of the Pharisees rose up, and said, 'It is necessary to circumcise them, and to charge them to keep the law of Moses'" (Acts 15:5). To this approach the Jerusalem community offered a compromise. Members of other ethnic groups who wanted to live "in Christ" and interact with the Israelite members of this community need only follow the customs proper to resident aliens in Israel. Thus the so-called "apostolic decree" of Acts 15 directs, "For it has seemed good to the Holy Spirit and to us to lay upon you [members of other ethnic groups who want to be a post-Jesus group member] no greater burden than these necessary things; that you abstain from what has been sacrificed to idols [see Lev. 17:8–9] and from blood [see Lev. 17:10–12] and from what is strangled [see Lev. 17:13–16] and from unchastity [Lev. 18:1–23]. If you keep yourselves from these, you will do well. Farewell" (Acts 15:28–29). What this decree required was a minimum set of purity rules to be observed by non-Israelite group members so that they might interact "in Christ" with Israelite group members. The apostolic administrative board in Jerusalem, rather than the Jerusalem elites of Israel, now sanctioned this sort of interpretation of Torah.

However, people like Paul believed that the purity rules of Israel—raised to the rank of law and sanctioned by administrative authority—were no longer binding "in Christ." As we have seen in the section on marriage strategy, Paul reverts to custom. Post-Jesus group purity rules will henceforth derive from the interaction of group members "in Christ" rather than from previous biblical injunctions. These interactions became the new norms for situating persons and things in their proper places. Paul never cites any Torah norm apart from the Ten Commandments (see chapter 4) as law, as legally binding. The reason for this is more clearly expressed in traditions postdating Paul. There we learn that God himself gave the Ten Commandments to Israel, the authentic, first Torah. But since Israel turned to idolatrously worshiping the Golden Calf at the time, God gave another set of laws, this time through Moses, to remedy Israel's sin, hence another, "second" Torah. The third-century document called the *Didaskalia* speaks of the "Second Legislation" (in Hebrew: *Mishnah*) as follows: "For the first Law is that which the Lord God spoke before the people had made the calf and served idols, which consists of the Ten Words and the Judgements. But after they had served idols, He justly laid upon them the bonds, as they were worthy. But do not therefore lay them upon yourself; for our Savior came for no other cause but to fulfil the Law, and to set us loose from the bonds of the Second Legislation" (Connolly, p. 14; for the same argument, see the second-century author Irenaeus, *Adversus Haereses*, IV, 25, 3; IV, 26, 1; IV, 28).

For Paul, the purpose of this post–Ten Commandments "second Torah" was to train Israel in obedience to God: "Therefore the law was our disciplinarian until Christ came" (Gal. 3:24). Thus Paul never considered anything previously sacred in Israel as binding in sacred fashion for God's newly called people in Christ. For when Paul talks of access to God, of what is sacred to God, he and his communities never adopt and adapt anything considered to be sacred, holy, or sacral to God by their contemporaries, both "set-apart" Judeans and "civilized" Greeks. As we have seen above, such sacred, holy, or sacral items include the Temple, the organization of the people (the worshiping community), sacrifice, sacred personnel, and sacred times and seasons. How do Paul and the post-Pauline tradition after him speak about these areas?

1. *Temple:* For post-Jesus group members of the Pauline tradition, the Jerusalem Temple was no longer a specific, designated area of sacred space. Rather, the temple, or more specifically, the sanctuary itself, was the gathering of group members who formed the body of Christ filled with the Spirit. They together were the "temple of the Holy Spirit" (1 Cor. 6:19; see 1 Cor. 3:16–17) or "the temple of the living God" (2 Cor. 6:16). Furthermore, it is always the holy group, never the individual, that is the temple of God and the body of Christ. After all, we are dealing with group-oriented, group-controlled collectivistic personalities.

2. *Organization of the People:* Purity lines now consisted only of a distinction between inside and outside, in-group and out-group. The lines deriving from social status, gender roles, and ethnicity were to be leveled, at least when post-Jesus group members gathered (Gal. 3:28; 1 Cor. 12:13; Col. 3:11), but not in such a way as to bring shame to the group (i.e., male and female, married and unmarried distinctions were observed). People were either "in Christ," or they were not. Openness to outsiders and concern for their opinion of the in-group was important. The symbolic passage from outside to inside was marked by the rite of baptism (much as circumcision marked entry into Israel, e.g., cf. Col. 2:11–12). Thus, as the author of Ephesians tells non-Israelite group members, "you are no longer strangers and sojourners [the resident aliens of Israel], but you are fellow citizens with the

saints and members of the household of God, built upon the foundation of the apostles and prophets, Christ Jesus himself being the cornerstone, in whom the whole structure is joined together and grows into a holy temple in the Lord; in whom you also are built into it for a dwelling place of God in the Spirit" (Eph. 2:19–22; read also 1 Pet. 2:4–10).

3. *Sacrifice:* For post-Jesus group members, sacrifice to God assuring life-maintenance and life-restoration is no longer anything animal or vegetable. Thus the term "sacrifice" is used metaphorically. Metaphorical sacrifice includes prayer (a way of influencing the patron) and activity (a way of revealing the God you believe in, hence an honoring or glorifying of God). In other words, the "sacrifice" of group members consists in their common prayer or conduct (read Rom. 12:1; 15:16; Eph. 5:2, 5–20; Col. 3:16–17; 1 Thess. 5:19–21; James 1:27; 1 Pet. 1:17; 2:4–10). The idea of interpreting Jesus' death as a sacred sacrifice in terms of Israelite Temple ritual is rare in the New Testament, found mainly in the letter to the Hebrews (which you might read in this connection). Rather infrequently, Jesus' death is interpreted as something like the sacrifice of the Passover lamb (1 Cor. 5:7 and perhaps John 19:14).

4. *Personnel:* The various titles given to post-Jesus group leaders all derived from the non-sacred spheres of society in the eastern Mediterranean. This means that no group leader bore a "clerical" or "religious" sacred title. "Apostle" means authorized messenger; "bishop" means supervisor, overseer, superintendent, especially of fiscal matters; "presbyter" means elder, a senior member, a senior in the faith, perhaps; "deacon" means a master of ceremonies at a meal. Further, such personnel are appointed to tasks (in Latin "ordain" means to appoint to a job); they are not consecrated to a sacred post or set apart for the sacred like pagan and Israelite priests (e.g., Lev. 8:12; 21:8). Since the only lines in the post-Jesus group perspective were between inside and outside, all on the inside had ready access to God along with corresponding obligations toward God—although some had tasks to perform for the group's sake, within the group and perhaps toward outsiders, but not toward God.

5. *Times and Seasons:* If Jesus' death-resurrection ushers in the period in which the forthcoming (transformed society under God's rule, the age to come) is already present in the present, if Jesus' God-given task is a once-for-all affair (1 Cor. 5:7–8), then all times are now sacred for those on the inside. Hence there is no need to "observe days, and months, and seasons, and years" (Gal. 4:10).

Thus, while the early post-Jesus group members of the Pauline tradition (and there were others not of this tradition, as Acts 15 indicates) rejected what their contemporaries considered sacred, holy, or sacral to God, they did in fact consider their group to be like a temple, hence a holy, consecrated body of people. Their task relative to purity lines was twofold: (1) to keep this body free from what did not fit "in Christ" and (2) to interact at the margins of the body in such a way that it would please God, hence on the basis of the attitudes and actions rooted "in Christ." The Pauline inside/outside model overlays zones A and C of the previous model and places zone B at the margins of the whole, as follows:

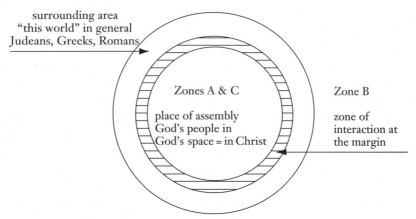

surrounding area
"this world" in general
Judeans, Greeks, Romans

Zones A & C

place of assembly
God's people in
God's space = in Christ

Zone B

zone of
interaction at
the margin

Or in terms of the previous vertical Temple model:

Outside: Space of this world of people often hostile to God in Christ	"This world" of Judeans, Greeks, and Romans based on law and political authority
Zone B: Zone of interaction God and the world	Activity in Christ which is the same as sacrifice
Inside—Zones A and C: Place of assembly and God's space overlap	The group of saints in Christ, holy churches, a temple, the body of Christ based on custom

Keeping the social body free of what did not fit "in Christ" was normally a matter of rejecting behavior that was not as good as the best in the cultural norms of the day (e.g., 1 Cor. 5:1 on expelling a community member who marries in a deviant way). It also required rejection of those who sought to compromise the new existence "in Christ" by separating zones A and C, that is, by urging requirements that more befitted previous existence "in Israel" than existence "in Christ" (e.g., Gal. 5:2–12). On the other hand, interaction with "this world," that is contemporary society, at the margins, the place where post-Jesus group "sacrifice" or sanctification was focused, had concern for neighbor, i.e., one's fellow group member, as top priority. In general, it required behavior that was honorable and proper in the Greco-Roman world (e.g., Rom. 13:1–7 on respect for the emperor, paying taxes, and the like). In

particular, it required interactions with the sacral world of various Mediterranean groups in such a way that concern for neighbor be maintained while
the inside of the body not be infected. As a general principle, so long as a person remained in the group, in the body, he or she was holy, consecrated to
God along with those embedded in that person. Thus the presumably minor
children of parents belonging to post-Jesus groups as well as unbelieving
partners married to group members along with their offspring, were holy (1
Cor. 7:14–15). This meant that group members could freely interact with
them without becoming unclean. Presumably, the holiness of the group was
more effective than the uncleanness outside of it; in fact, it was capable of
rendering it exclusive, holy. The same holds true for the holiness of a marriage partner belonging to the group in face of the uncleanness of a non-
Christian spouse. All this was due to the ready presence of God made
available by the holiness of Jesus Christ, in whom group members were made
holy.

Further, relative to food and times, Paul could say, "I know and am per-
suaded in the Lord Jesus that nothing is unclean in itself" (Rom. 14:14). The
reason for this is that a new set of purity rules takes the place of the old set,
and in the new set there is no room for the unclean. However, while everything and everyone in the body is clean, this by no means signifies that the
social body of post-Jesus group members and their actions are morally irrelevant. In other words, just because a group member did something "in Jesus's
name" did not make it good. And whatever a group member did was not
automatically good provided he or she had good intentions. The heart counts
highly, that is true, but so does the action. Both actions and motives count—
and this both for the social body and for the individual who replicates the
social body. Thus, while nothing is unclean for the post-Jesus group member, at the margins where one interacts with people who believe in another
model of clean and unclean, the perceptions of others must be taken into consideration and respected. This holds for interactions with both "the set-
apart" and "the civilized," that is, with "Judeans and Greeks" (1 Cor.
10:17–19) as well as with one's fellow group members. Paul's advice for
behavior at the margins of the group is "Give no offense to Judeans or to
Greeks or to the church of God" (1 Cor. 10:32). However, the most frequent
problems Paul alludes to deal with offenses against one's fellow group members of Israelite background at the individual level, the personal level that
replicates the social level. Here, as at the social level, neighbor has priority.
Hence, "if your brother [fellow group member] is being injured by what you
eat, you are no longer walking in love. Do not let what you eat cause the ruin
of one for whom Christ died. . . . it is right not to eat meat or drink wine or
do anything that makes your brother stumble" (Rom. 14:15, 21; see also

1 Cor. 8:7–13). And if some group member of Israelite background still resonated with symbolic times, that too need not be a problem provided that "he who observes the day, observes it in honor of the Lord" (Rom. 14:6). In sum, group attachment revealed in care and concern for one's fellow group member has priority (1 Corinthians 13, where "love" means group attachment, hence care and concern for fellow group members).

Much of the practical advice in Paul and the other New Testament letters is about making the margins of the group sharper and clearer. Emphasis is on firming up the focus of the group toward the center of the social body. The customs developed and shared in these early post-Jesus, Mediterranean communities would eventually lead to more complex purity structures. And when post-Jesus groups become embedded in the political framework of Constantine's empire and later (fourth century A.D.), their purity structures turn out not too different in arrangement from those of first-century, city-elite Israel.

Summary

This chapter deals with purity rules, with the way social groups mark off persons and things, time and space. Purity rules enable us to situate the elements of our environment, including ourselves, in some orderly way. This order facilitates our making sense of our experiences of persons, things, time, and space. Purity rules point out what or who is in or out of place, in or out of phase. A subset of purity rules deals with the sacred and the non-sacred, with relations of exclusivity, with the person, things, times, and spaces with which we personally resonate, and those beyond our immediate concern. Just as we have sacred and profane, so by analogy does God. Postexilic Israel portrayed God's sacredness in terms of categories of persons through marriage, in terms of space in Temple worship, and in terms of persons and things in sacrifice. Since Jesus was seen as Israel's Messiah soon to come, the post-Jesus movement organization, set under way by the death-resurrection of Jesus, had to come to terms with the purity rules of Israel. Further they were concerned with Israel's mode of set-apartness because purity rules, as Jesus' criticisms indicated, likewise symbol the model of God that one believes in. Post-Jesus group members, with their new model of God deriving from the experience of Jesus, reassessed all that was sacred to their contemporary cultures and began to establish new rules for the sacred based on their group as analogous to a temple, or holy space/people with immediate access to God in Christ.

References and Suggested Readings

Connolly, R. Hugh. *Didascalia Apostolorum: The Syriac Version Translated and Accompanied by the Verona Latin Fragments, with An Introduction and Notes.* Oxford: Clarendon Press, 1929. Reprint 1969.

Douglas, Mary T. *Purity and Danger: An Analysis of Concepts of Pollution and Taboo.* London: Routledge & Kegan Paul, 1966.

———. "Deciphering a Meal." *Daedalus* 101 (1972):61–81.

Eilberg-Schwartz, Howard. *The Savage in Judaism: An Anthropology of Israelite Religion and Ancient Judaism.* Bloomington, Ind.: Indiana University Press, 1990, esp. the chapter "Menstrual Blood, Semen, and Discharge: The Fluid Symbolism of the Human Body," 177–194.

Elliott, John H. "The Epistle of James in Rhetorical and Social Science Perspective: Holiness-Wholeness and Patterns of Replication." *Biblical Theology Bulletin* 23 (1993):71–81.

Esler, Philip F. *Galatians.* New Testament Readings. London and New York: Routledge & Kegan Paul, 1998.

Frymer-Kensky, Tikva. "Pollution, Purification, and Purgation in Biblical Israel." In *The Word Shall Go Forth: Essays in Honor of David Noel Freedman in Celebration of His Sixtieth Birthday,* ed. C. L. Meyers and M. O'Connor, 399–414. Winona Lake, Ind.: Eisenbrauns, 1983.

Hanson, K. C. "Blood and Purity in Leviticus and Revelation." *Listening: Journal of Religion and Culture* 28 (1993):215–230.

Jeremias, Joachim. *Jerusalem in the Times of Jesus: An Investigation into Economic and Social Conditions during the New Testament Period.* Philadelphia: Fortress Press, 1969.

Malina, Bruce J. "Mediterranean Sacrifice: Dimensions of Domestic and Political Religion." *Biblical Theology Bulletin* 26 (1996):26–44.

Neyrey, Jerome H. "The Idea of Purity in Mark's Gospel." *Semeia* 35 (1986):81–128.

———. *Paul in Other Words: A Cultural Reading of His Letters.* Louisville, Ky.: Westminster/John Knox Press, 1990.

———. "Ceremonies in Luke-Acts: The Case of Meals and Table-Fellowship." In *The Social World of Luke-Acts: Models for Interpretation,* 361–387. Peabody, Mass.: Hendrickson, 1991.

———. "The Symbolic Universe of Luke-Acts: 'They Turn the World Upside Down.'" In *The World of Luke-Acts: Models for Interpretation,* 271–304. Peabody, Mass.: Hendrickson, 1991.

———. "Clean/Unclean, Pure/Polluted, and Holy/Profane: The Idea and the System of Purity." In *The Social Sciences and New Testament Interpretation,* ed. Richard L. Rohrbaugh, 80–104. Peabody, Mass.: Hendrickson, 1996.

———. "Meals, Food, and Table Fellowship," In *The Social Sciences and New Testament Interpretation,* ed. Richard L. Rohrbaugh, 159–182. Peabody, Mass.: Hendrickson, 1996.

How Jesus Groups Evolved

Understanding Group Development

Every year sees the publication of many scholarly books on the life of Jesus, books usually ignored in the frequent TV shows about Jesus. What nearly all the scholarly books have in common is that they take rather seriously the perspective provided by the prologue to the Gospel of Luke:

> Inasmuch as many have undertaken to compile a narrative of the things which have been accomplished among us, just as they were delivered to us by those who from the beginning were eyewitnesses and ministers of the word, it seemed good to me also, having followed all things closely for some time past, to write an orderly account for you, most excellent Theophilus, that you may know the truth concerning the things of which you have been informed. (Luke 1:1–4)

What the prologue states, as you can see, is that the author of the Gospel of Luke used sources that were based on those who witnessed what Jesus said and did. In other words, we have an author, such as "Luke" (final level of the tradition, level 3), telling us what somebody else said (intermediate level of the tradition, level 2) that Jesus said and did (the career of Jesus, level 1). Now, if the author is writing around the year 80–90 and if Jesus' career dates back to the late 20s and the early 30s, then the time span between Jesus' career and the author's writing is about fifty years. The question then is, What perspective did the author adopt in telling the story of Jesus fifty years after the event? We know several things for certain. There were no early Jesus-group writings prior to Paul, around A.D. 50, again twenty years after the event. And from Paul's writings we see that apart from Jesus' death and resurrection, Paul himself was not interested in the story of Jesus.

Furthermore, consider our contemporary understanding of how memory works. Among psychologists, memory is no longer thought of as an archival system of specific memories, an ever-expanding library consisting of full and complete records of discrete episodes. Researchers suggest that memory is best thought of as a process involving bits and pieces of information that are continually interpreted and reconstructed during the course of remembering.

Furthermore, psychological research dealing with the life narratives of subjects points increasingly towards the inadequacy of the archaeological metaphor for modeling human memory. Remembering does not consist of the uncovering of a fixed deposit of memories. Remembering is not a process of uncovering objective facts and details of a life story, or what might be called historical truth. Rather, remembering is the production of an articulated narrative understanding of one's life story refashioned at various times. Hence it produces a sort of updated, edited narrative truth. If you doubt this, consider all the advice you get from older people about how things were "when I was your age." These are updated, edited versions of what life was like "when I was your age," not really the way things and people were.

Consequently, memories that are handed down are updated memories, edited memories. In this sense the traditions about Jesus are just like TV news shows. These shows always present interpreted news in a format that is essentially a show, an entertainment. Their concern is not with what really happened, but with the usefulness of what news editors think really happened presented in a way "good" for you the viewer in your time, social setting, and geographical location. If, for example, you want to see nearly sixty years of interpreted news having little to do with what was really happening, consider U.S. news reports about the state of Israel and its military oppression of Palestinians since the Catastrophe, the founding of the Zionist state. The perspective on U.S. TV news shows is always that of Israel and its U.S. supporters. The purpose of these news reports is to ensure continued U.S. material support for Israel, duly orchestrated by pro-Israel lobbies in Washington. The perspective repeatedly underscored over nearly sixty years is that Arabs in general and Muslims in particular are not trustworthy human beings (they are the quintessential terrorists). Hence whatever immoral and indecent action Israel takes in breaking international treaties, the Geneva Convention about military occupation and occupied lands, and the UN charter of human rights is perfectly permissible. The problem, of course, is that this is not news reporting but propaganda directed to U.S. taxpayers and government officials supported by "friends" of Israel.

With one very large difference, the same process was at work in early Jesus-group writings. The difference is that early Jesus-group writings were never intended for outsiders, that is for people who did not belong to Jesus-groups. All the Jesus-group documents we have are in-group documents, written for Jesus-group members alone. No one would write up papyrus documents costing, roughly speaking, ten thousand dollars and more to give them out on street corners so people might know the story of Jesus. Even if they did, the vast majority of people could not read anyway.

The ancient documents that present the story of Jesus were meant to be memory helps for people who knew the latest version of that story. The written document would remind readers of what they knew, in specific places and times as they recited the story to equally knowledgeable listeners. The New Testament documents are occasional writings. What they do is take the story of Jesus as remembered in a community and appropriate it in new circumstances. They intimate the relevance of that story for people hearing the story. As a result, in the Gospels we do indeed have memories of what Jesus said and did, but these are updated memories, facts made relevant, and presented in a way that would make sense in new circumstances. The story appropriates the traditions about Jesus in circumstances that saw the destruction of Jerusalem and the dispersal of the city's inhabitants. This same story was set down in various ways by final authors living in various post-Jesus communities spread around the Mediterranean. The task of scholars interested in sketching out the "historical Jesus" is to start with our Gospel documents, adopt some explicit criteria, and make some determination concerning what fits the available scenarios of the story of Jesus in the early 30s (level 1) while beginning with the situation of the author(s) who present(s) the final document (level 3), and perhaps take notice of what went on in between (level 2).

In this final chapter we shall consider two significant groups responsible for telling the story of Jesus. The first is the group that first heard the story of Jesus as set out in our Gospel documents. What would have been of interest to these post-Jesus group members who first listened to Matthew, Mark, Luke, or John in the second half of the first century A.D.? The second group is the group that Jesus gathered during his career. What would have been of interest to Jesus and his immediate following?

As we consider the cultural context of the ancient Mediterranean, we have been learning to understand the New Testament largely by considering the story of Jesus presented in the Gospels. Most scholars would agree that the earliest version of this story of Jesus consisted of the following certain elements: Jesus began his career with John the Baptist; Jesus recruited a faction; then Jesus was apprehended, crucified, and appeared to his followers. The sequence of events between Jesus' baptism and his apprehension by Jerusalem authorities is said to be uncertain. The thread of the narrative that runs from activity in Galilee, through a journey from Galilee to Jerusalem, as well as the incidents that follow one upon the other in the narrative, are judged to be rather unrelated anecdotes and descriptions of what Jesus said and did in various times and places. The only thing that holds them together is location: after his baptism by John, Jesus was in Galilee, recruited a faction, and undertook a final trip to Jerusalem, in Judea. Given this uncertain state of affairs, can we establish a sure framework within the margins marked by Jesus' baptism, his recruitment of followers, and his apprehension? In this chapter I invite you to consider a simple model of small group formation that is sociological, not anthropological. That means that irrespective of the culture involved, it seems that all human beings form groups in a similar, if not identical, way.

By *group* I mean any collection of persons who come together for some purpose. A group stands opposed to a *collectivity*, a random gathering of people. I believe it fair to say that Jesus and his initial following, as well as clusters of post-Jesus followers, formed groups that were essentially small, face-to-face groups. Whether these post-Jesus group members were aware of belonging to a wider social entity extending beyond their small group, for example, a larger "church," is not my question here. To help imagine what was going on both with Jesus and his faction as well as with post-Jesus groups and their founders, I present a model of the formation of small groups and their development that might fit the data preserved in the Gospel documents that postdate Jesus by nearly a generation. The model is structural-functionalist, with empirical validation.

We first look at why small groups are formed at all, including the group recruited by Jesus as well as the post-Jesus groups. Then we will consider a model of small group development that would characterize both Jesus' group and post-Jesus groups, too. Finally our focus will turn to general small-group interests, countergroups, and recruitment. The purpose of learning about how small groups work is to develop a model of significant scenarios for understanding what is being presented in the story of Jesus as we read it in the Gospels.

Why Small Groups At All

A social scientific approach to early Jesus groups, their formation and development, requires that the interpreter explicitly define the terms, models, and goals of investigation as clearly as possible. From the perspective of structure (and story), the New Testament presents the reader with two general types of Jesus groups: the group of followers contemporary with Jesus and groups of followers that postdate Jesus. The fact that it is these latter that are our main evidence for the original Jesus group would lead one to expect traces of post-Jesus group concerns in their updated and edited descriptions of the story of Jesus and the group that he recruited.

The study of the group contemporary with Jesus and groups that postdate Jesus is much like studying two trains moving in one direction at varying rates of speed while sitting in a third, passing train that moves in the opposite direction. I say this because of the temporal confusion inherent in the Gospel documents, a confusion that is generally acknowledged in biblical studies. It is well known that the groups founded by Paul and others antedate the composition of the Gospels. In other words, the story of Jesus' career and following mirrors a period before the foundation of early post-Jesus groups, yet that story was set down in various forms some time after the foundation of those post-Jesus groups. These stories often move like two trains passing each other in one direction. And we who are distanced from both Jesus and the post-Jesus groups that followed have to move to get a focus on the dimensions of either story. How can we be fair in discussing both without too much of a distortion from a mental Doppler effect? You will recall that the Doppler effect makes us see the wheels of a car or train rotating in one direction suddenly reverse their motion in the opposite direction, while the vehicle continues to move forward. There must be distortion, with later concerns put into the mouth of Jesus (e.g., Jesus speaking of a "church," dealing with divorce initiated by women, showing interest in the poor in spirit, or thirsting for righteousness). In the study of early post-Jesus groups this distortion is generally called "the interests of the community" that told the story. In biblical study in general, further distortion derives from the interests of interpreters and their modern audiences, looking for a Jesus relevant to twenty-first-century matters.

Be that as it may, Jesus' group as well as early post-Jesus groups were organized at all, putting it simply, because such groups were useful and meaningful for Jesus or Paul, for example, as well as for those who became members, and/or for bystanders. As a result of their experience with Jesus' group or some early post-Jesus group, individuals who had a stake in them became interested in the group's fate. This brings us to our first observation about why early post-Jesus groups existed at all.

All groups derive from some person who sees the need for change. In the New Testament, for example, both Jesus, in his context, as well as Paul in his saw the need for change. Change here means the desire for social satisfaction. The social satisfaction Jesus sought was a forthcoming theocracy ("the kingdom of heaven"). Paul envisioned Israel's redemption (restoration of ethnic honor) and salvation (cosmic rescue) as taking place "in Christ." A motive for change is a person's capacity to find satisfaction in some envisioned state of affairs and a disposition to seek that satisfaction. Jesus and the following he recruited obviously found satisfaction in their belief that the God of Israel was on the verge of launching such a new political arrangement. Paul's experience of the resurrected Jesus assured him of the new state of affairs that Jesus proclaimed.

On the other hand, not every instance of awareness of the need for change results in a group. Rather the person aware of the need for change must share this awareness with others. John the Baptist shared his awareness of God's intentions for Israel with those who came to him for baptism, including Jesus. For Jesus to follow John in this, he would have to compare existing situations, options, obstacles, and the like. Should he (and others) agree with the shared awareness after comparing alternatives, he would join John's group and declare its purposes to others. Hence at the bottom of every group is the sequence: aware—share—compare—declare.

The positive response of those whom Jesus recruited to assist him points to some societal trigger state. The trigger state arouses individuals to join a group and work to maintain it. A trigger state converts a social situation into motivational material, for example, some unjust act into striving for a just social order; a grievance against some authority into desire to eliminate the grievance. The trigger state behind Jesus' proclamation of theocracy seems to have been the fact that Israel's aristocratic landowners refused their role of patron for their fellow Israelites. Instead they collaborated with the monarchy and Roman authorities to amass the lands of smallholders, leaving them "poor" and "meek." In face of this tragic situation, the God of Israel would institute a new political order and thus "save" his people.

The Synoptic tradition indicates that Jesus shared the awareness of John the Baptist. Both proclaimed the need for "getting one's affairs in order" and the onset of a distinctive theocracy ("the kingdom of heaven is at hand, repent" [Mark 1:15]). The existence of the Jesus faction indicates that Jesus himself believed a specific situation should be changed and that one person acting alone could not create that change. Individuals joined the core group of Jesus' faction by invitation. Invitation was required in deference to the honor of those asked to join. And since they did in fact join, they too believed some specific situation should be changed and that Jesus acting alone could not bring about that change.

What of post-Jesus groups? It seems that the awareness of the need for change derived from "experiencing the Risen Lord." All traditions that mention the point trace the rise of post-Jesus groups to the experience of the Risen Lord (Matthew's edict 28:18–20; Luke's final vision of Jesus in Acts 1:6–11; Paul's personal insistence on having seen the Risen Lord in Gal. 1:16; 1 Cor. 15:8, and his knowledge of five-hundred plus group members who saw the Risen Lord also in 1 Cor. 15:3–6). For these persons, it was an experience of Jesus interpreted through a shared story of Jesus that led them to believe some specific situation should be changed. The situation here dealt with that divine, cosmic rescue called "salvation." The change sought here was something that would guarantee God's salvation. And the guarantee was accepting God's call to join the group rooted in Jesus as Israel's Messiah to come.

For a small group to emerge, however, there must be (1) conditions favorable for change, (2) along with a vision of a new situation (3) coupled with hope concerning the successful implementation of the new situation, (4) and all this in a social system that has problem-solving groups. These are facilitating circumstances for the creation of any group. Since groups emerged both with Jesus and with post-Jesus communities, obviously all four of these dimensions were present. Consider each in turn:

1. *Presence of conditions for change:* Conditions in the environment or in the behavior of influential persons (a) were unsatisfactory or (b) offered an opportunity for favorable change. The formation of any group is always rooted in some person's desire for change perceived as feasible due to the presence of conditions favorable for change. A potential organizer such as Jesus in Galilee obviously realized that a situation was not what it might be and that something ought to be done about it. In the Synoptic story, it was John the Baptist who presumably suggested this realization to Jesus (clearly articulated by Matt. 3:1–4:17, presumably thanks to Mark 1:1–14; Luke 3:1–5:11 unpacks it differently). On John's arrest, Jesus proceeds to recruit a faction to carry out the program suggested by John. This was a political program premised on the need for Israelites to get their lives in order in face of God's impending takeover of the country.

On the other hand, organizers of post-Jesus groups believed something ought to be done largely because of their experience of the Risen Jesus, and what this implied for the cosmic rescue of interested persons—first in Israel, then among foreigners. The strategy was not political, but one of social support, hence family-like groups "naturing" appropriate individuals through recruitment and nurturing through group attachment and assistance.

2. *Vision of new situation:* Some subsequent satisfactory state of affairs was conceived by organizers. A potential group organizer does not simply perceive something to be wrong, hence a potential need for change. Rather a group developer foresees how things could be improved and successfully transmits this vision to others. These better possibilities are often envisioned by one person or a few persons, and others are then invited to improve on the plan and to join its activities. Jesus' plan, rooted in John's proclamation and God's activity, was clearly in mind as he recruited a number of core associates, but we are given details of the plan only when he sets his faction into performing his own chosen task of proclaiming theocracy and healing fellow Israelites (Mark 6:7–13; Matt. 10:1–11; Luke 9:1–5). In turn, those who created post-Jesus groups believed not only that something was amiss with Israel and the cosmos, but also that something could readily be done to improve matters. Their assessment was rooted in the resurrection of Jesus. The New Testament documents portray these organizers as developing their vision of the new situation while they recruited group members as fictive kin, prior to formulating the group's charter, its creeds.

3. *Hope for success:* Organizers and group members believed their joint actions would succeed if they tried to achieve the proposed better state of affairs. Members join because they believe that they will achieve a satisfactory state of affairs. The organizers' efforts will be empty unless they trust that the group's activities will create the desired end and get adherents to believe the same. Group leaders are responsible for building confidence in the organization. Often, they can do this best by making it possible for members to build their own faith in the group's fate (e.g., "love the church," a collectivistic abstraction; e.g., 1 Corinthians 13). Jesus got his faction to successfully proclaim and heal along with him. Their successes pointed to the group's achievement potential (Mark 6:12–13). Paul's post-Jesus groups witnessed a range of alternate-states-of-consciousness experiences (e.g., speaking in tongues, various gifts of the Spirit) enforcing confidence in the achievement of the group's purposes of naturing and nurturing one another (1 Corinthians 12). Participants then developed confidence in their group by their active participation and success in realizing the group's objectives.

4. *Cultural context:* Conditions in their society encouraged persons to establish a group and to take part in its activities. Societies must offer their members the option of group formation if groups are to be formed. Societal conditions favoring group formation are called promoters. Persons are more likely to form a group if sources of influence foster such a move or, at the least, offer little resistance to it. Given the presence of the preceding three conditions, interest in creating and joining a group tended to be greatest if the social context were stimulating, that is, if people lived in a society where groups were common and valued. For Galilee and Judea of Jesus' day, the presence of Pharisee, Sadducee, Herodian, Essene, and other groups point to such an environment. The circumstances affecting the formation of the Jesus movement group would be quite similar to those affecting similar political action groups.

Similarly, the widespread formation of philosophical schools and clubs (*collegia*) in the Hellenistic world would account for a founder-friendly climate for post-Jesus group formation. Some of these circumstances include the following: frequent contact among potential members, similarity among members, personal preference for working with others rather than for working alone, more benefits available to members than otherwise, existing legal requirements for the creation of groups (e.g., Roman *societas*), and the way of life in a given place supportive of group activity. Conflict would occur in those societies where such circumstances did not exist. Thus the situation described by the early second-century Roman official, Pliny the Younger, was not triggered by a desire to "persecute" post-Jesus groups. Pliny wrote to the emperor about what to do with the post-Jesus groups in his jurisdiction. His problem, it seems, was based on Roman legal requirements that were hostile to the creation of enduring groups. Roman history indicates that not only post-Jesus groups were involved in that situation.

From the viewpoint of social psychology, groups develop when people in the society are willing (1) to join groups, (2) to tolerate ambiguity during the early days of a group's life, (3) to favor values in the culture that support a particular group, (4) to forgo interest in keeping things just as they are, and (5) to develop the knowledge and skill needed for being a member.

In contrast, persons who are aware of a need for change do not create a group (1) if they can not conceive of a better state of affairs (hence no vision), (2) if they do not think a group could attain such a state (hence no hope of success), (3) if people are not willing to join groups in their society, (4) if they have no skills in being group members, (5) if they have values opposed to those of potential members, or (6) have no tradition that fosters group formation (hence no cultural context). It was perhaps this lack of cultural preparedness that limited the spread of post-Jesus groups among the *pagani*, rural residents in a city surround.

Group organizers must declare a purpose for the body they organize. In order to establish a purpose, members must desire certain outcomes for their group as a whole or for participants as individuals, and they must be reasonably confident they can attain those ends. When a purpose is known, understood, and accepted by many participants, this purpose can evoke a word of honor guaranteeing commitment to group activity. People need to know the purpose of their group. The purpose provides a direction for activities, and members are uncomfortable if they do not have this guide. It tells members what they ought to do and what they can expect of colleagues. It offers a criterion for evaluating whether the efforts of members are as effective as they ought to be. It is a focus for the personal commitment a member might make to that unit. It may serve, after the fact, as a rationalization for actions members take before they have a precise aim for their efforts. It reduces participants' sense of aimlessness in their work for that unit.

For the Jesus faction, the purpose was to have Israelites get their lives in order in preparation for God's forthcoming takeover of the country. The goal was political since people did not experience a "separation of church and state." When religion is embedded in politics, then political concerns and religious concerns are scarcely perceived as different. For Pauline and other post-Jesus groups, the prevailing purpose was salvation, cosmic rescue from the present situation. Their organizations consisted of those called by the God of Israel to attain God's rescue by enduring, persevering, and waiting "in Christ." Their problem, given this purpose, was to inform people summoned by God about how to get "in Christ," and how to remain "in Christ." The goal is characteristic of fictive kin groups. When religion is embedded in kinship, then kinship concerns and religious concerns are scarcely perceived as different.

In sum, groups are organized when some person or persons are not satisfied with a situation, have enough social standing to define the undesirable state of affairs, envision a successful alternative, give others hope for success, in a culture that prepares people for group roles. The envisioned better state of affairs is the group's purpose or objective.

By way of appendix, consider the following scenario. Before the emperor Constantine, post-Jesus group religion, a type of fictive kinship religion, was not embedded in politics. The political religion after Constantine is usually called Christendom, and all forms of modern Christianity derive from it in one way or another. If it is a truism that an individual was more likely to join and remain a member of an early post-Jesus group that had a purpose, what happened with the advent of Christendom with Constantine? Post-Jesus group structures were now embedded in politics, with the norms of the political institution serving to channel the values of post-Jesus groups. Further, allegiance to a cosmic Christ entailed allegiance to the emperor and his representatives. Christianity now emerged as a political religion. As a single, empire-wide, imperial church, its presiding officer was the emperor, the Vicar of Christ on earth. Christian clergy became imperial officials with the task of urging faithful imperial subjects to live peaceably by obeying the emperor's dictates. Thus all faithful, imperial subjects could attain cosmic salvation in Christ. If salvation in Christ were now available to all, what sort of norms determine Christian behavior? Would the goals of a political religion that guaranteed salvation to all faithful, imperial subjects produce the levels of belief and morality experienced in the fictive-kinship religion of earlier post-Jesus groups? It would seem that in the emerging circumstances, some persons grew aware of problems in a generic, imperial, political Christendom. They envisioned their solutions to these problems in terms of ascetic holiness. They nourished the hope of implementing their solution if only because their social system did indeed have groups devoted to ascetic holiness even before the advent of Christendom. These ascetic holiness groups usher in post-Jesus groups' next major phase and mark a major shift in purpose, from salvation to ascetic holiness.

Stages of Small Group Development

The study of the internal workings of small groups looks to both changes over time in the group as a whole as well as changes in the relationship between the group members. These dimensions of group development have been articulated in a useful model developed by Tuckman and further corroborated by Moreland and Levine. Tuckman's model indicates that over time small groups develop through the following stages: forming, storming, norming, performing, and adjourning, with verifiably predictable behavior at each stage. Consider each of these.

Forming Jesus Groups

The forming stage is the period when the group is put together. Groups are formed either to accomplish some extragroup task or for intragroup social support. The faction recruited by Jesus was a group with an extragroup task to perform. The task activity of this group is articulated variously in the Synoptic tradition. At first it is vague: "fishers of men" (Mark 1:17; Matt. 4:19; Q 10:2 remembers a reference to "harvest," as does John 4:35; Rom. 1:13). In the so-called "mission" charge the vague project is expanded: to proclaim God's rule, theocracy, and to require Israelites to get their affairs in order to this end, and to heal those in need of healing. Mark indicates that group members were chosen with healing abilities (Mark 3:15 and 6:7 mention only that Jesus gave the Twelve authority over unclean spirits, yet when they return "they anointed with oil many that were sick and healed them" [6:13]). Matthew 10:6 and Luke 9:1, on the other hand, state that Jesus bestowed this healing ability on his recruits. During the forming stage, group members discuss the nature of their task and how it might be performed.

Post-Jesus groups, on the other hand, were not task oriented like the Jesus faction. Rather post-Jesus groups were social activity groups. During the forming stage, individuals are invited by a central personage to join the group, while others seek out this central personage with a view to group affiliation. The forming stage develops group dependence.

At this stage, members of both types of groups, that is the task-oriented and the social type, are anxious and uncertain about belonging to the group. They exhibit typically cautious behavior. Each member cautiously tries to ascertain whether the group will meet his or her needs. The behavior of group members toward each other is tentative; commitment to the group is low.

Storming in Jesus Groups

At the storming stage, group joiners jockey for position and ease into interpersonal stances. Members of task activity groups such as the Jesus faction resist the need to work closely with one another. Conflict among members emerges, with emotions getting free expression. In the Synoptics we have many remembrances of this phase: the dispute about who is greatest

(Mark 9:33–37; Mark 18:1–5; Luke 9:46–48); a general argument about precedence (Mark 10:41–44; Matt. 20:24–27; Luke 22:24–27); concern for sitting next to Jesus in the kingdom (Matt. 20:20–23—the mother asks; Mark 10:35–40—disciples ask; not in Luke); and the general concern about rewards (Mark 10:28–31; Matt. 19:27–30; Luke 18:28–30). Peter's rebuking Jesus after talk about suffering and death is an attempt to persuade Jesus to change goals to fit what the group is concerned about (Mark 8:32–33; Matt. 16:22–23; not in Luke).

Post-Jesus social activity groups likewise break out in conflict, with group members arguing with each other and heaping criticism on the leader. Paul's letters give eloquent witness to this state. Read, for example, 1 and 2 Corinthians or Galatians from this point of view.

In both types of groups, group members become more assertive, and each tries to change the group to satisfy personal needs. Resentment and hostilities erupt among group members with differing needs. Each member attempts to persuade the others to adopt group goals that will fulfill his or her needs. The behavior of group members toward one another is assertive, and their commitment to the group is higher than it was before.

Norming in Jesus Groups

The norming stage is marked by interpersonal conflict resolution in favor of mutually agreed on patterns of behavior. This phase is one of exchange in task activity groups such as the Jesus faction. Everyone in the group shares ideas about how to improve the group's level of performance. The task norms for the Jesus core group are listed in the so-called "mission" discourse (Matt. 10:5–16 and expanded with vv. 17–25; Mark 6:7–11; see 3:13–15; Luke 9:1–5).

In social activity groups such as Paul's post-Jesus fictive kin groups, on the other hand, it is a phase of cohesion. Group members begin to feel more positive about their membership in their particular group. In this regard, read Paul's letter to the Romans, who were members of post-Jesus groups that Paul himself did not found.

In both cases, norming involves group members in the attempt to resolve earlier conflicts, often by negotiating clearer guidelines for group behavior.

Performing in Jesus Groups

With the performing stage, group participants carry out the program for which the group was assembled. Performing marks the problem-solving stage of task activity groups. Members solve their performance problems and work together productively. From the evidence provided in the New Testament documents, it is clear that the Jesus faction moved into a performing stage (return from successful task performance: Mark 6:12–13; Luke 9:6; no report in Matthew). The sending of the seventy (-two) and their success (Luke 10:1–20) points to enlarged activity. This implies further recruitment or forming, with subsequent storming and norming to lead to greater performing. Thus, what the performing consisted of, by all accounts, was proclamation and healing. Healing took place in a context of political religion, hence readily threatened those in authority. The purpose of healing was to restore the ill person to his/her station in society. Jesus himself had healing abilities as did his core group members. They likewise knew how to enter altered states of consciousness (transfiguration). Jesus' own altered-state-of-consciousness experiences (at baptism, walking on the sea, transfiguration) made it easy for his core group and his fellow Galileans to consider him a holy man (shaman) and prophet.

Social activity groups, on the other hand, move into the performing stage by role-taking. Members take social roles that make the group more rewarding to all. They work together cooperatively to achieve mutual goals. There is little, if any, evidence for a performing stage in Pauline post-Jesus groups. The problems addressed in the Pauline corpus look to storming and norming. The same seems true of the several letters written in Paul's name that postdate the apostle. The desiderata listed in the Pastorals concerning group leadership still look like items desired and not yet realized.

Jesus Groups Adjourn

With adjourning, group members gradually disengage from task activities in a way that reflects their efforts to cope with the approaching end of the group. Of course, the event that precipitated the adjourning of the Jesus group was Jesus' crucifixion. The motive for Jesus' being put to death was reported as envy (Mark 15:10; Matt. 27:18)—a motive that perfectly fits the general Mediterranean culture area, with its perception of limited good and concern for honor. It seemed to be certainly the motive of the collectivistic persons who had Jesus put to death. As regards Jesus' core group, the post-crucifixion stories liberally attest to the adjourning phase. Jesus' prediction, "You will all fall away" (Mark 14:27; Matt. 26:31), notably Peter (Luke 22:31–34) points up how they all abandoned Jesus. The only ones present at Jesus' death, and this "at a distance," were a group of supporting women (Matt. 27:55–56; Mark 15:40–41; Luke 23:49; John 19:25, however, is quite distinctive).

But with the experience of the appearance of the Risen Jesus, a feedback loop enters the process of small-group development, with new forming, storming, norming, and subsequent performing. This process is described telescopically in the final sections of Matthew (28:16–20) and Luke (24:36–53) but at length in the first half of the book of Acts (Acts 1–15). The new norms point to a shift from political concerns to fictive kinship concerns.

The ritual of baptism commanded in Matthew and described in Acts points to such fictive kinship focus. The quality of these post-Jesus groups as fictive kin groups is further indicated by the main group ceremony, the common meal. Thus in the development of post-Jesus groups, the adjournment of the Jesus movement group signaled by the crucifixion of Jesus loops back to renewed storming, norming, and performing for former Jesus faction members, around whom post-Jesus fictive kin groups emerge. The trigger event for this loopback was their experience of Jesus after his death, an experience understood as the work of the God of Israel, now perceived and revealed as "He who raised Jesus from the dead" (Acts 3:15; Rom. 8:11).

I should like to note in conclusion the observation of Moreland and Levine, who state that most theories of group socialization implicitly assume that the group is in the performing stage of development. This, of course, is the situation in studies of early post-Jesus groups, whether of "wandering charismatics" or Pauline communities! Our New Testament documents come from storming and norming situations for the most part and are studied by scholars in performing (or adjourning) phases. Furthermore, the documents are used in churches that are into performing. Obviously inattention to this state of affairs can lead to some distortion due to the Doppler effect signaled previously.

Small Group Focuses

Groups always have a purpose that consists in the perception of some needed and meaningful change. The required or desired change may be seen to inhere in persons, in groups, or in society at large. Consequently small groups form to support and advance intrapersonal, interpersonal, extragroup, or intragroup change or a combination of these. Extragroup objectives are transitive objectives, directed toward changing nonmembers or even society at large. Groups with extragroup objectives are also called instrumental groups. Intragroup objectives are reflexive objectives, looking to change members of the group itself. Groups with intragroup objectives are often called expressive groups. The following diagram illustrates these options, with some examples:

	extragroup	intragroup
intrapersonal	conversion appeal based on healings	advice to individuals in the group
interpersonal	Jesus movement group organization	post-Jesus movement group organization

The group recruited by Jesus was an instrumental group, a faction with extragroup objectives. The Gospel tradition tells of the Jesus group with a mission to Israelite society as a whole, in Galilee as well as Perea and Judea. This point indicates that the Jesus group sought to change Israelite society. When the change envisioned by a group is societal, the change involved is a social movement. The group supporting and implementing the change is a social movement organization.

Social Movement Organization: Fictive Polity

A consideration of social movements and social movement organizations will indicate the main difference between the Jesus movement and the movement that succeeded him. According to McCarthy and Zald, "a social movement is a set of opinions and beliefs in a population representing preferences for changing some elements of the social structure or reward distribution, or both, of a society. Persons who embrace the opinions and beliefs of a social movement and guide their lives accordingly form a social movement group or organization."

The Jesus movement was a social movement; his group was a social movement organization. On the other hand the post-Jesus groups founded by those change agents called "apostles" were not social movement groups since their purpose was not to change "elements of the social structure or reward distribution, or both, of a society." Rather, post-Jesus groups looked to the cosmic rescue of the person, that is, the collectivistic selves of the first-century Mediterranean world. For this reason post-Jesus groups were associations most like ancient clubs and *collegia*, equally concerned with the social well-being of collective selves.

Countermovement Organizations: Pharisees and Others

To return to the Jesus group, it is fair to say that Jesus conceived and articulated a social movement in support of social change. The outcome was a Jesus movement organization. A social movement invariably stands along with a countermovement. McCarthy and Zald define a countermovement as "a set of opinions and beliefs in a population opposed to a social movement." And countermovement organizations are equally part of the Gospel scenario: Pharisees, Sadducees, Herodians, and the like.

Countermovements oppose change. They focus on stability and permanence. These are realized in organizations, in contrast to those we have been examining, whose members make a point of holding to the same purposes indefinitely. Perhaps the easiest way to insist on such permanence is to make eligibility for membership reside in birth. In that way, prospective members can be duly socialized to fit into permanency patterns. Thus Sadducees rooted in aristocratic families, Pharisees rooted in Abrahamic pedigree, and Herodians rooted in a monarchic family clearly aim at well-guarded permanence. Israelite officialdom is based on birth, with religion rooted initially in kinship as well as in the body politic by means of some properly pedigreed ruling kin group.

Such groups normally emphasize the value of stability and tend to establish procedures that protect against attempts to change objectives. The Sadducees insist on Torah and only applicable Torah. The Pharisees allow for a growing tradition that must necessarily fit some presumed practice of the ancients. The Herodians focus on a single set of properly rooted heirs. In all cases, we have established doctrine, ceremonies that ask participants to revere an unchanging set of beliefs, a society pledging faith to its (implicit) charter— all with staffs that lay plans that fit respective special systems of behavior. Each group's firmness of purpose is duly guarded by officials who train members not to doubt the aims of the organization and who punish persons who deviate from the set's objectives. Politically embedded religious bodies are particularly likely to police the behavior of members in this way.

These groups consisted largely of individuals who felt most comfortable with things as they were. They insisted on interpretations of Torah in terms that were familiar to them. As members of the house of Israel, they would press officials to keep societal goals as these have been in the past. With Roman control a number of monarchic or priestly agencies might have disappeared, but interested parties sought to make sure that their purposes were preserved. The initial objectives would be passed on to a body whose life is continuing. The disembodied purposes were thus transplanted and kept vital because Jerusalemite elites who benefitted from the government's activities toward those ends pressed their representatives to maintain support for these objectives. The agencies of embedded religion were not immortal, but their purposes appear to have been.

Some objectives in organizations remain unchanged and do not emerge as a source of concern because there is no way to tell whether the group is moving toward desired ends. Does Torah observance in Sadducee or Pharisee style actually please God? Does it produce righteousness among group members? Does scribal study of Torah further Pharisee or Sadducee purity? Do these groups actually help the house of Israel by their way of life? Questions like these were hard to answer, and members could only guess whether their goals were being satisfied. Participants most often estimated that the group's objectives were being satisfactorily fulfilled and ought not be changed. Thus even with the destruction of Jerusalem in A.D. 70, Israelite countermovements to the Jesus movement saw no real need for change—just adaptation to a new situation.

Elective Associations: Fictive Kin Groups

Groups are shaped, of course, in terms of the norms of the social institutions within which they are embedded. The Jesus movement group was a type of political action group, looking to societal change by God's intervention. Post-Jesus groups, on the other hand, were a type of fictive kin group shaped by norms of the prevailing kinship institution. Thus post-Jesus groups expected the "birth" of new members and their nurture until the group's ultimate goal of salvation was realized. The institutional quality of groups is normally replicated in the places where such groups gather and/or perform their major activities. Thus regular meeting in quasi-public places and buildings points to political action groups (Jesus faction members on the road, amid crowds, in the Temple); while meeting in people's houses points to fictive kin groups (post-Jesus groups mentioned in Acts and Paul). In modern society, home surrogates in a city (such as restaurants and bars = kitchen of a house = commensality; hotels = bedrooms = coition) point to commercialized fictive kinship; business surrogates (such as downtown streets in front of stores = goods for sale = commerce) point to economic relations; while out-of-bounds places (railroad sidings, bridge abutments, dumps, and the like) point to placeless persons.

Simply put, post-Jesus groups were fictive kin groups rather than social movement groups. The type of group that expresses the common values and solidarity of fictive kinship is what in the Mediterranean would be an elective association. Elective associations depend on a person's choices and result from contracts, quasi-contracts, or competition. Such choices, however, are almost invariably made due to social compulsion and necessity. At times such grouping are called "voluntary" groupings, even "voluntary associations." Yet Mediterraneans as a rule do not volunteer for anything outside of their natural grouping. If they had their "druthers," Mediterraneans would confine everything to "natural" (i.e., kin and extended kin) groupings. Contemporary

U.S. voluntary associations are groups seeking to promote the common interests of the membership, with membership being noncoercive. It would seem then that the groups founded by post-Jesus change agents like Paul and others were post-Jesus voluntary associations. To differentiate first-century associations from those of today, I have called the first-century version an elective association. It was an "elective group" as opposed to a natural group based on birth and geography. Yet given the press of social circumstances and the vagaries of life, at times persons found themselves under compulsion to join groups outside of their natural in-groups.

As pointed out in chapter 1, the persons involved in elective groupings have no sacred qualities as persons because of who they are in relationship to others. This sacred quality inheres in family and monarchy roles. In elective groupings, it is the posts, positions, or offices in such groupings that bear the qualities otherwise embodied by persons in natural groupings. While in-group opinion as well as general public opinion are at work in natural group-ings, in elective groupings public opinion is sovereign. Some such elective groupings in the first century would be trade guilds, municipalities (systems of villages), city-states with republican forms of government, elective burial organizations, and Palestinian parties such as the Pharisees, Sadducees, Essenes, and the like. Perhaps the early post-Jesus groups likewise looked on their groups as elective associations much like the Palestinian parties after whom they often modeled themselves.

Being based on the common interests typical of collectives selves, the elec-tive association would be established for the good of some other larger group (for example, one's family or household) in order thereby to promote the common collective interest of the membership. Affiliation would be under social pressure. Such elective association members would form fictive kin in that they presumed mutual loyalty and solidarity among persons presumed to be what they had been labeled. Accepting a person simply on the basis of who they are is a function of the commitment or solidarity proper to kinship; but accepting persons on the basis of their rank in some hierarchy is a function of power. Given the kinship labels used by Paul (for example, his letters address "brothers" and "sisters"), his would clearly be fictive kin groups. On the other hand, the social movement organization set up by Jesus was based on loyalty and solidarity toward Jesus himself and his cause rather than among the recruits. Thus while the Jesus faction was elective in its recruitment, it did not have the qualities typical of the fictive kin groups of the post-Jesus movement organization.

Perhaps it would help to note some of the distinctive features of this sort of "elective" association. In the first place, people joined only under pressure, largely in search of benefits for their primary kin group (not in search of benefits for themselves alone). Further, people joined associations because the larger society did not allow their kin group space or voice (not because society did not give them as individuals space or voice). Consider how lepers or other stigmatized persons "voluntarily" joined together. They did so because they were not allowed in society and needed social support. Once people "voluntarily" joined a group, interpersonal ties with central personages and the prestige afforded their kin group made it morally impossible for people to leave without great dishonor (witness Judas). While U.S. persons can leave a team and join another with ease, in the Mediterranean once one joins, it is rather difficult to leave since the unit is the collective self, not the individualistic self, and groups cannot see themselves dissolve without dishonor.

Post-Jesus associations formed expressive groups. They existed primarily to serve the needs of members: social, informational, support. As expressive groups they were not concerned with issues of the larger society and its social and political problems. They were not concerned at all to reform society, and this lack of concern was not because they awaited the coming of Jesus with power. As expressive groups with intragroup focus, they were apolitical, choosing to foster any of various methods of evading group stigma. Thus they would eject deviants, help individuals to correct their faults or defects, adopt socially acceptable life styles, and the like.

So long as post-Jesus associations had an intragroup focus, they formed a "church" only when its members gathered. There were, indeed, extragroup interludes, notably during the rare and sporadic conflicts with more powerful outsiders. Such infrequent conflicts with well-situated outsiders are often called "persecutions." Extragroup interaction produces a more abiding sense of "church" largely because of the boundaries extragroup persons draw. In this sense, the church owes its existence to opposition, much like Pauline morality owes its norms to outsider expectations. Paul wished his groups to win honor acclamations from outsiders, hence to behave at least as well as outsiders did. So too those who believed in Jesus were to hold fast to their movement groups even if faced with extragroup opposition.

By way of conclusion, I should like to mention that from the viewpoint of time or longevity, groups may be enduring or ephemeral. An enduring group has structural features that assure continuance, such as membership requirements, a name, a charter, officers. An ephemeral group lacks these structural features (e.g., coalitions such as factions, gangs, action sets, task forces, crowds, discussion meetings, picnics, and the like). The Jesus movement group was a faction, personally recruited by Jesus for his purposes for a given time. In terms of the famous nineteenth-century apologetic question, "Did Jesus intend to found a 'church'?" if his organization was a faction, then the answer can only be "No!" In the book of Acts, post-Jesus groups take on the qualities of enduring fictive kin groups, much like the groups described by Paul. It is there that one ought to look for the founding of a "church." And in the description of Acts and Paul, since it was God who calls individuals to these post-Jesus groups, it was God who founded the church, not Jesus!

The Jesus group was an ephemeral social movement group. Subsequent post-Jesus groups were not social movement groups at all, but rather Mediterranean elective associations. The Jesus movement group was well into the stage of performing and adjourned rather abruptly. The sporadic but enduring post-Jesus associations (composed of Judeans, Judean creoles, and a sprinkling of foreigners) was largely at the forming, storming, and incipient norming stages. Since post-Jesus associations as described in the New Testament never got to the performing stage, it would be quite anachronistic to describe them as sects. Further, to explain any first-century A.D. embedded religion in terms of church and sect typology is like explaining first-century carts in terms of internal combustion vehicles or automobile typologies. It was at the incipient norming stages that persons in several of these associations, labeled Matthew, Mark, Luke and John, drew up their stories of Jesus with their descriptions of the formation of the Jesus movement group.

Summary

This chapter began by describing the quality of the New Testament documents that tell the story of Jesus. These documents evidence three perspectives: they describe what a final author said (level 3 of the tradition) about what people before him/her said (level 2 of the tradition) that Jesus said and did (level 1: the career of Jesus). In these documents we learn that Jesus formed a group, a faction. The story then tells of the development of that group in a period marking Jesus' movement from Galilee to Jerusalem, where he was apprehended, crucified, and raised by God. To understand what was going on during this period, we first asked, Why did a small group emerge around Jesus? Small groups emerge because some person becomes aware of a need for change, a desire for social satisfaction. That person shares this vision with others who mutually nurture a hope of success in implementing the change in a cultural context in which group formation is expected. Second, we noted how groups develop according to five distinctive and predictable stages: forming, storming, norming, performing, and adjourning. During forming, storming, and adjourning, all group members are in the same phase of group socialization, while such is not the case for the norming and performing stages. Finally, we looked at some of the focuses of small groups as they can be seen in Jesus' group and in post-Jesus groups. The chart that follows summarizes the features of both types of groups as considered in this chapter.

Table 4: Jesus' Group and Post-Jesus Groups Compared

The Jesus Faction or Jesus' Group	Post-Jesus Groups
The Jesus faction was a political action group intent on change in Israel's political institution—a new theocracy.	Post-Jesus groups emerged from a political action group looking to the coming of Jesus as Israel's Messiah with power. These groups quickly developed into fictive kinship groups intent on the mutual support and nurture of group members.
The written Gospels presume to tell the story of Jesus and his group.	The written Gospels tell the story of Jesus and his group as appropriated and applied by post-Jesus groups.
Jesus was holy man (healer, exorcist) and prophet.	Jesus is Lord (and Messiah to come).
Jesus recruits followers to assist him in his task of proclaiming theocracy.	God "calls" individuals to post-Jesus groups to follow Jesus by living a new way of life.
Jesus' group was a task-oriented, political action group.	Post-Jesus groups were socially oriented, fictive kinship groups.
A disciple is one who assists Jesus in his task of proclaiming theocracy.	A disciple is one who lives the way of life taught by Jesus.
Apart from family, "brother" and "sister" refer to fellow Israelites.	Apart from family, "brother" and "sister" refer to fellow Jesus group members.
Jesus, as prophet, proclaims theocracy and clarifies the significance of the kingdom of God in parables.	Jesus, as teacher, teaches a way of living for fictive kin.
Forming involved an extragroup activity.	Forming focuses on intragroup support.
Storming: conflict among faction members.	Storming: conflict among groups and criticism of leaders with emphasis on conflict resolution and greater group cohesion (i.e., "love").
Norming: conflict resolution and agreement on tasks to be performed.	Norming: attempts at clear social-role formation with structures that make group belonging satisfying for all.
Performing: accomplishment of the task of proclaiming theocracy and healing in Israel.	Performing: this phase is barely attested to in the New Testament.

The Jesus Faction or Jesus' Group	Post-Jesus Groups
Adjourning: with Jesus' crucifixion, group members disengage from task activity.	Adjourning: not attested to in post-Jesus groups.
Jesus' faction was an instrumental group with extragroup objectives.	Post-Jesus groups were supportive groups with intrapersonal and intragroup objectives.
Jesus, with his faction, launched a social movement meant to change "elements of the social structure or reward distribution, or both, of a society."	Post-Jesus groups were not social movements since their interests were not focused on change in social structure or societal change.
The Jesus movement group was a type of political action group, looking to societal change by God's intervention.	Post-Jesus groups, on the other hand, were a type of fictive kin group shaped by norms of the prevailing kinship institution.
As a political action group, Jesus' group met in public, in quasi-public places and buildings (on the road, amid crowds, in open courtyards and houses, in the Temple).	As fictive kin groups, post-Jesus groups met in private, in houses of group patrons.
Jesus' political action group was a faction: a group recruited by a specific person for a specific purpose for a specific time.	Post-Jesus groups were elective associations: groups seeking to promote the common interest of the membership, affiliation being based on social compulsion and necessity.

References and Suggested Readings

Anderson, Benedict. *Imagined Communities: Reflections on the Origin and Spread of Nationalism*. London: Verso, 1983.

Barton, Stephen C., and Gregory H. R. Horsley. "A Hellenistic Cult Group and the New Testament Churches." *Jahrbuch für Antike und Christentum* 24 (1981):7–41.

Duling, Dennis C. "The Jesus Movement and Social Network Analysis (Part I: The Spatial Network)." *Biblical Theology Bulletin* 29 (1999):156–175.

_____. "The Jesus Movement and Social Network Analysis (Part II: The Social Network)." *Biblical Theology Bulletin* 30 (2000):3–14.

Esler, Philip F. *Community and Gospel in Luke-Acts: The Social and Political Motivations of Lucan Theology* (SNTSMS 57). New York: Cambridge University Press., 1987.

James, Paul. "Forms of Abstract 'Community': From Tribe and Kingdom to Nation and State," *Philosophy of the Social Sciences* 22 (1992):313–336.

Kleijwegt, Marc. "'Voluntarily, But under Pressure': Voluntary and Constraint in Greek Municipal Politics." *Mnemosyne* 47 (1994):64–78.

Malina, Bruce J. "Religion in the Imagined New Testament World: More Social Science Lenses." *Scriptura* 51 (1994):1–26.

_____. "Early Christian Groups: Using Small Group Formation Theory to Explain Christian Organizations." In *Modelling Early Christianity: Social-Scientific Studies of the New Testament in its Context*, ed. Philip F. Esler, 96–113. London and New York: Routledge & Kegan Paul, 1995.

McCarthy, John D., and Mayer N. Zald. "Resource Mobilization and Social Movements: A Partial Theory." In *Social Movements in an Organizational Society*, ed. Mayer N. Zald and John D. McCarthy, 15–42. New Brunswick, N.J.: Transactions Books, 1987.

Messick, David M. and Diane M. Mackie. "Intergroup Relations." *Annual Review of Psychology* 40 (1989):45–81.

Moreland, Richard L., and John M. Levine. "Group Dynamics over Time: Development and Socialization in Small Groups." In *The Social Psychology of Time: New Perspectives*, ed. Joseph E. McGrath, 151–181. Newbury Park, Calif.: Sage Publications, 1988.

Ross, Robert, and Graham L. Staines. "The Politics of Analyzing Social Problems." *Social Problems* 20 (1972):18–40.

Tuckman, B. W. "Developmental Sequence in Small Groups." *Psychological Bulletin* 63 (1965):384–399.

Wilken, Robert L. "Collegia, Philosophical Schools, and Theology." In *The Catacombs and the Colosseum: The Roman Empire as the Setting of Primitive Christianity*, ed. Stephen Benko and John J. O'Rourke, 268–291. Valley Forge, Pa.: Judson Press, 1971.

Zald, Mayer N., and John D. McCarthy. "Religious Groups as Crucibles of Social Movements." In *Social Movements in an Organizational Society*, ed. Mayer N. Zald and John D. McCarthy, 67–95. New Brunswick, N.J.: Transactions Books, 1987.

Zander, Alvin. *The Purposes of Groups and Organizations*. San Francisco: Jossey-Bass, 1985.

A Theological Conclusion

The careful study of the preceding chapters may leave you surprised and wondering. Now, as you listen to the New Testament authors and imagine the people presented in their documents, you will probably find their concerns about honor and shame, collectivistic personality, limited good, envy and the evil eye, defensive marriage, and purity rules quite irrelevant to your everyday American experiences. As you might well know, Americans, for the most part, are achievement-oriented, individualistic, keenly aware of limitless good, anxiety-prone and guilt-directed, as well as competitive and individualistic in marriage strategies. They also follow purity rules focused pragmatically on individual relations and individual economic success.

The foregoing introductory anthropological models are intended primarily and precisely to help you differentiate your cultural experiences and perceptions from those described and assumed in the New Testament. After all, today's Christianity traces back through Constantine to an original Middle-Eastern, Mediterranean movement. If the earliest Mediterranean accounts of that original movement made immediate and direct sense within our American social system, you might rightly suspect the New Testament writings of being twentieth-first-century forgeries. However, they are not forgeries but documents from the first-century Mediterranean world.

You might now better appreciate the theological problem that has faced Christianity over the past two millennia. That theological problem has been and continues to be how to make known the Good News of Jesus in terms of the ever-kaleidoscoping cultural scripts that cover the world like a crazy quilt. It is all too easy to read into the New Testament and make do with a Jesus in our own image and likeness. The New Testament thus serves as a veritable Rorschach inkblot, with Jesus coming across as a universal polymorph, a chameleon figure standing for and legitimating whatever individuals and groups choose to do "in his name," from a local fundamentalist commune to a worldwide church.

In traditional Christian belief, Jesus of Nazareth, God's Messiah, is the concrete historical instance of the union of the divine and the human. This historical union, called the Incarnation, took place in time and space, within a particular set of cultural norms and presuppositions. The problem with a fundamentalism that is interested only in what the Bible says—and not in what it means in terms of the social context in which it emerged—is that it implicitly denies the Incarnation. It denies the humanity of the God-man, Jesus. It implicitly denies that Jesus was like us in all things save sin. You might reread the introductory chapter with its presuppositions and check out what it means to be "like us" in terms of our cultural makeup.

This book is meant to help in understanding the New Testament writings. If those writings are to resonate in our different cultural contexts, if faith is to be held responsibly, then theology will have to carry out its work of articulating the culture-bound, original symbols of the primordial Jesus movement group and its ancient Mediterranean successors in terms of the clearest language and most adequate models that it can find in the cultures in which it is to be expressed, understood, and lived.

Study Questions for Testing the Hypotheses

This section has been designed to help you test the various models and hypotheses presented throughout this book. It is up to you to validate or disprove them. The subsections that follow provide relevant scripture references for each chapter along with guidelines and questions to aid your analyses.

Study Questions for Chapter One

1. *Like all models, the picture of the workings of honor and shame, along with the challenge-response interaction typical of that picture, has to be tested. If the model covers all instances of honor and shame behavior in the New Testament, then it will have been validated and proven to be an adequate model. It is now up to you to test the model, and disprove it if you like. But if it works, then what sort of meaning behind the behavior in the documents would you say it yields?*

2. *To test the model, you might begin by looking up the vocabulary of honor and shame in a concordance to the New Testament. I am using the Revised Standard Version for what follows, although any version can be used. A perusal of almost any concordance will offer the following:*

    Honor: *equivalents include glory, blamelessness, repute, fame (and verbs like to honor, glorify, spread the fame, etc.)*
    Shame: *disgrace, dishonor (and the verbs to shame, be ashamed, feel ashamed)*
    Dishonor: *scorn, despise, revile, reproach, rebuke, insult, blaspheme, deride, mock (and actions like striking the head, spitting on, etc.)*
    Intention to challenge: *test, entrap, entangle (and questions indirectly addressed to Jesus by being addressed to his disciples; questions that are obviously mocking, normally those of the Sadducees in the Gospels)*
    Perceptions of being challenged or shamed: *vengeance, wrath, anger, the vocabulary of sin (transgression, offense, sin, wrong) with a person as object.*

    The concordance enables you to find where such words are used; now you would have to look up the entire passage to see what sort of behavior is described, then check this behavior against the model. Does the model help you flesh out what is only implicit in the passage?

3. *Perhaps an easier way to test the model is to stick to one New Testament writing. For example, take the Gospel of Mark with the purpose of picking out and explaining the honor and shame interactions explicit and implicit in the document:*

    (a) *As you read the whole of Mark, note how Jesus' fame spreads, how public approval of him mounts from the outset of his ministry up to the passion, for example, Mark 1:28; 6:33; 6:54.*

    (b) *Why do people come up to Jesus and kneel (Mark 1:40; 10:17; 15:19) or worship (= kneel) him (Mark 5:6)?*

    (c) *In the episode of Herod, Herodias, and the daughter, what sort of honor-shame interaction goes on? What is the meaning of his oaths? Is the daughter like her mother (Mark 6:14–29)?*

(d) Why does the interaction of Jesus and the Syrophoenician woman take the turn that it does in the dialogue (Mark 7:25 ff.)?

(e) Note the arguments on who is greater (more honorable) in Mark 9:33 ff. and 10:36 ff. Why this concern among the disciples?

(f) Consider some of Jesus' debates with his opponents. What do they indicate about Jesus' honor (e.g., Mark 2–3:15; 7:1–13; 11:27–33; 12:13–17; 12:18–27; 12:38–40)?

(g) Take the parable in Mark 12:1–9: how does it follow honor-shame rules, with increasing outrage and predictable outcome?

(h) In terms of honor-shame interactions, what is the meaning of the fact that Jesus' enemies take him to trial? How does the trial prove Jesus to be honorable? What is the meaning of Mark 14:65; 15:17–20? What do Peter's denial and oath mean in terms of honor-shame in Mark 14:66–72?

4. Does the model make sense of all the data?

Study Questions for Chapter Two

1. *To test the group-embedded, collectivistic personality model, you might begin by looking up reasons or motivations for behavior presented in the New Testament. An easy way to do this is to look up the conjunctions "for" and "because" in a concordance, then look up the passages and collect those that provide explanation for some line of behavior. For example, here is a sampling of statements containing the Greek conjunction* gar, *meaning "for, because"; it normally sets out a reason for the previous statement. This conjunction is found in all of the following passages, even though your Bible translation might have left it out at times:*

   Matthew 1:20, 21; 2:2, 5, 6, 13, 20; 3:2, 3, 9, 15; 4:6, 10, 17, 18; 5:12, 18, 20, 29, 30, 46; 6:7, 8, 16, 21 24, 32, 34; 7:2, 8, 12, 25, 29; 8:9; 9:5, 13, 16, 21, 24; 10:10, 17, 19, 20, 23, 26, 35; 11:13, 18, 30; 12:8, 33, 34, 37, 40, 50; 13:12, 15; 14:3, 4, 24; 15:2, 4, 19, 27; 16:2, 3, 25, 26, 27; 17:15, 20; 18:7, 10, 20; 19:12, 14, 22; 20:1; 21:26, 32; 22:14, 16, 28, 30; 23:3, 5, 8, 9, 13, 17, 19, 39; 24:5, 6, 7, 21, 24, 27, 37, 38; 25:3, 14, 29, 35, 42; 26:9, 10, 11, 12, 28, 31, 43, 52, 73; 27:18, 19, 23, 43; 28:2, 5, 6.

   1 Corinthians 1:11, 17, 18, 19, 21, 26; 2:2, 8, 10, 11, 14, 16; 3:2, 3, 4, 9, 11, 13, 17, 19, 21; 4:4, 7, 9, 15, 20; 5:3, 7, 12; 6:16, 20; 7:7, 9, 14, 16, 22, 31; 8:5, 10, 11; 9:2, 9, 10, 15, 16, 17, 19; 10:1, 4, 5, 17, 26, 29; 11:5, 6, 7, 8, 9, 12, 18, 19, 21, 22, 23, 26, 29; 12:8, 12, 13, 14; 13:9, 12; 14:2, 8, 9, 14, 17, 31, 33, 34, 35; 15:3, 9, 16, 21, 22, 25, 27, 32, 34, 41, 52, 53; 16:5, 7, 9, 10, 11, 18.

   What did the sampling indicate? Are all the reasons stereotypical, like proverbs, shared maxims, and/or external, outward, and culturally expected? Or did you find some reasons that are introspective, psychologically unique, extremely personal, and unrepeatable in terms of the culture?

2. *Another useful word to look up in a concordance is the word "know" or "recognize" as applied to persons. On what basis do people get to know one another? How many times are persons said to "know" something about others even though they have never met them?*

3. *To test the three-zone model, look up the main words of the model in a concordance (i.e., eyes, heart, mouth, ears, hands, feet, or any of the other words listed in the document). Then check out how the words are used, singly or in conjunction with others, in the passages you found. Does the model make sense of the passages?*

4. *Another way to test both models is to stick to one New Testament writing. This time, take the Gospel of Matthew with the purpose of picking out and explaining*

collectivistic personality and three-zone human makeup. Answer the following questions to help you in your analysis:

(a) *Matthew has a large number of Old Testament passages applied to explain behavior, (e.g., 1:22; 2:5, 15, 17, 23; 3:3; 4:14; 8:17; 11:10; 12:17, 39; 13:35; 15:7–9; 21:4, 16, 42; 26:56). How would the collectivistic personality model explain the use of these passages? Are they stereotypical, unchanging statements from a collection of unchanging words (the Old Testament) applied externally and outwardly to explain a situation, thus indicating it was expected anyway?*

(b) *In the temptation story of Matthew 4:1–11, which zones enter the interaction? What sorts of motives are adduced?*

(c) *In the call of the apostles in Matthew 4:18–22, is there any "psychology" of vocation? By what social roles or ranks are those called described? Why—in terms of collectivistic personality?*

(d) *Note the structure of the final section of the Sermon on the Mount in Matthew 6:19–7:27. Does the first part (6:19–7:10) deal with eyes-heart; the second (7:7–11) with mouth-ears; and the third (7:13–27) with hands-feet?*

(e) *Following the Sermon on the Mount, there are ten healings in Matthew 8–9:32. What is said of the psychological state of the sick? Of Jesus? Is each of the sick persons described in terms of personal, unique name and qualities, or in terms of stereotypical, external, outward social categories?*

(f) *In terms of collectivistic personality, a person's ego-image is shaped by members of his or her significant group. Who is to shape one's ego image according to Matthew 10:34–39? What of Matthew 12:48–50?*

(g) *"For out of the abundance of the heart the mouth speaks" (Matt. 12:34). What does this statement say of the relationship of the three zones? How is this culturally obvious principle applied in Matthew 12:35–37?*

(h) *What does Matthew 13:16–17 mean in terms of the three zones?*

(i) *In the interpretation of the parable of the sower in Matthew 13:18–23, what is the interaction of the three zones?*

(j) *How do people attempt to situate Jesus in Matthew 13:53–57?*

(k) *How do the three zones figure in the discussion of clean and unclean in Matthew 15:1–20?*

(l) *The "evil eye" in Matthew 20:15 refers to envy. Why?*

(m) *In terms of collectivistic personality, what is the meaning of the mother asking for her sons and the others becoming indignant in Matthew 20:20–28?*

(n) *According to Matthew 21:28–32, what is more important, mouth-ears or hands-feet? Why?*

5. *Let us turn to Paul. Briefly, what is the meaning of "conscience" in the following passages: Romans 2:15; 9:1; 13:5; 1 Corinthians 8:7, 10, 12; 10:25, 27, 28, 29; 2 Corinthians 1:12; 4:2; 5:11 (you might also consider 1 Tim. 1:5, 19; 3:9; 4:2; 2 Tim. 1:3; Titus 1:15; Heb. 9:9, 14; 10:22; 13:18; 1 Pet. 3:16,21). Does conscience mean the pain one feels within oneself over some past specific action the individual judges to be bad because it was wrong (this is our use of the term)? Or does it mean sensitivity to what others think about and expect of the individual, pain one feels because others consider one's actions inappropriate and dishonorable (this is the collectivistic personality use of the term)? Is there sufficient information in these passages to distinguish? Can the model fill in the gaps?*

6. *Finally, in 1 Corinthians 4:11–13; 2 Corinthians 6:4–10; 11:23–29, Paul presents the culturally well-known "catalog of difficulties"; in terms of collectivistic personality, he would be looking for the approval or commendation of his significant others. Is this what is going on in these passages?*

Study Questions for Chapter Three

We shall use the Gospel of Luke as a quarry for the data that might validate or invalidate the models presented in chapter 3. However, I would like to begin with a caution. It seems that the author of the Gospel of Luke did not know Palestine very well in the sense that he ranks as cities (Greek: polis) *places that certainly were no more than villages, even large villages, such as Nazareth and Bethlehem. The main preindustrial cities in Palestine during the period of the New Testament were Jerusalem, Caesarea (where the Roman prefect lived), Tiberias (where Herod Antipas lived), Sepphoris, Sebaste and Neapolis in Samaria, and the ten-city league known as the Decapolis (Greek for "ten cities"). And there were some other cities along the Mediterranean shore as well. Perhaps Luke calls certain places "cities" to intimate to his readers that the persons coming from those places were elites of sorts, not just low-ranking peasants. You might test out this idea by looking up the word "city" in an* RSV *concordance, taking out the listing for Luke, and checking on who comes from those places and what roles they have in the Gospel story.*

Use the following questions to help you test the models:

1. *Based on the hierarchy of statuses mentioned throughout chapter 3 rank the following in terms of status as presented in the first three chapters of Luke:*

Luke 1:5:	*Herod, king of Judea (37–4 B.C.); Zechariah, a priest; Elizabeth, an Aaronite, of priestly family*
Luke 1:19, 26:	*Gabriel (the name of "God's power"), angel of the presence (of God)*
Luke 1:27:	*Mary and Joseph of Nazareth, a Galilean village, of low estate (1:48; 2:46)*
Luke 2:1–2:	*Caesar Augustus (27 B.C.–A.D. 14), Quirinius, governor of Syria*
Luke 2:8 ff.:	*shepherds*
Luke 2:25:	*Simeon the Jerusalemite*
Luke 2:36:	*Anna, the Jerusalemite, a widow*
Luke 2:46:	*teachers in the Jerusalem Temple*
Luke 3:1:	*Tiberius Caesar (A.D. 14–37); Pontius Pilate, governor of Judea (A.D. 25–36); Herod Antipas (4 B.C.–A.D. 39); Philip (4 B.C.–A.D. 34 (these last two were children of Herod the Great, mentioned in 1:5); Annas and Caiaphas, high priests.*

If you have the patience, you might try to rank all the persons mentioned in Luke. From the ranking what can you deduce about social interactions?

2. *In the preaching of John the Baptist (Luke 3:10–14), what sort of social reform is involved: a social revolution, sharing the wealth with all, or simply helping people maintain their original status? Who are the greedy, evil ones mentioned here? Why would their calling put them on dubious footing in a limited-good society?*

3. *In terms of limited good, why did Jesus' fellow townspeople reject him in Luke 4:14–30? Note that in 4:15, Jesus' reputation has already grown to such an extent that he was "glorified" (i.e., held in high, publicly acknowledged honor) by all except the folks of Nazareth.*

4. *Jesus heals Simon's mother-in-law in Luke 4:38–39. Does this explain why Jesus could use Simon's boat in Luke 5:3? Notice that Simon has a colleague contract with James and John in Luke 5:10. According to this passage, what sort of debt do Simon, James, and John owe Jesus for the catch of fish? Is Jesus much like a patron soliciting clients in a dyadic way?*

5. *Jesus forms a dyadic tie with Levi in Luke 5:27–30. What is Levi's response? Why a meal with his friends? Does the dyadic contract indicate why?*

6. *The passage at Luke 6:1–5 will make more sense if you read the law behind it, namely Deuteronomy 23:24–25. What does this imply about limited good? To whom does the land, the Holy Land, ultimately belong? To whom are people indebted for the fruit of the land?*

7. *Note the implied cultural rules in Luke 6:32–36: "love those who love you"; "do good to those who do good to you"; "lend to those from whom you hope to receive." To carry on a dyadic contract with another is a sign of mutual gratefulness, honor, and friendship. But what is God like, according to Jesus in this passage?*

8. *In Luke 7:1–10, how does the alien centurion get Jesus to come? Note the role of the village elders who act as "levers," gaining a foothold with the wandering teacher (v. 3); then some friends (v. 6) who attest to the fact that the centurion plays a duly humble role, even though he is a higher status foreigner (vv. 6–8).*

9. *If Jesus controlled evil spirits (Luke 7:18–23, especially v. 21, and throughout the Gospel), where would you be likely to rank him on the hierarchy or ladder of "persons" listed at the end of this chapter? Who would oppose situating him above the category of men? Or might you list the evil spirits on the human or subhuman level?*

10. *In the parable of the creditor (Luke 7:40–42), note the asymmetrical relationship and the degree of debt implied in the patron-client contract. What is the usual behavior toward a guest in one's house in Luke 7:44–46? In the light of the model of patron-client contract, what does it mean to "love much" (v. 47)?*

11. *Why do the wealthy women listed in Luke 8:1–3 provide for Jesus from their means? Does dyadic contract explain why?*

12. *In terms of dyadic contract and honor in limited-good society, how were Jesus' disciples to be supported in Luke 9:1–6; 10:1–12? Why do they have to be sent?*

13. *In the parable of the good Samaritan (Luke 10:29–37), what obligation does the man who was helped owe to the Samaritan? In the light of dyadic contract, why would the priest and Levite pass up the injured man?*

14. *How does dyadic contract clarify the parable of the importunate friend in Luke 11:5–8?*

15. *In terms of limited good, what does the parable in Luke 12:16–21 present as typical of a rich man's behavior?*

16. *How does a rich householder deal with his slaves in the light of the parable in Luke 12:42–48? Why?*

17. *In Luke 14:12–14, we have the same cultural rules as those in 6:32–36, and both sets imply dyadic contract. In this context, who is a poor person? Would it be one who cannot carry on a dyadic contract, who is unable to repay or help out another, e.g., the maimed, lame, blind?*

18. *How does the dishonest steward of Luke 16:1–8 firm up dyadic contracts to ensure him his future salvation?*

19. *The story of Zacchaeus the tax (or toll) collector (Luke 19:1–8) says he was rich. How did he get rich (v. 8)? What is wrong with getting rich this way in terms of limited good?*

20. *According to Luke 19:12–27, how does the elite nobleman get richer in limited-good culture?*

21. *What is implied in Jesus' certainty that the owner would let him borrow a colt in Luke 19:30–34? Similarly, what of the place for Passover in 22:7–13, and*

of Joseph of Arimathea, a member of the Jerusalem Sanhedrin (national council) in 23:50–53? In the light of the models of this chapter, what meaning can you find in Paul's statements about Jesus becoming poor for us, like 2 Corinthians 8:9 and the hymn in Philippians 2:6–11?

Study Questions for Chapter Four

To prove or disprove the models presented in chapter 4, we shall use the New Testament passages that explicitly underscore envy and the evil eye as a quarry for the data that might validate or invalidate the models. As noted at the beginning of the chapter, the Gospel story tells that Jesus is handed over to Pilate to be crucified because of envy. Both Matthew and Mark assert that Pilate was fully aware of this motive: "For he knew that it was out of envy that they had delivered him up" (Matt. 27:18; cf. Mark 15:10). After considering what envy meant in the first-century Mediterranean, we may conclude that there surely was something singular about Jesus that his enemies perceived as threatening to their social well-being. Furthermore, while the mention of the evil eye in the New Testament plays a minor role, it did play a role that should be acknowledged.

Use the following questions to help you analyze the suggested New Testament passages:

1. *In the epistolary admonitions against factionalism and divisions in the Christian community, envy is an undesirable quality (Rom. 1:29, 13:13; Gal. 5:21, 26; Phil. 1:15; 1 Tim. 6:4; Tit. 3:3; 1 Pet. 2:1). Why?*

2. *The New Testament has its share of evil-eye accusations. Four such accusations are attributed to Jesus in the Gospel story (Matt. 6:22–23//Luke 11:33–34; Matt. 20:15; Mark 7:22). What is the significance of these accusations?*

3. *Paul sees the opposition he finds in the groups to which his Galatian letter is directed as rooted in the evil eye: "O foolish Galatians, who has afflicted you with the evil eye?" (Gal. 3:1). Why would Paul think they were struck by the evil eye? What would be the point of his argument, then?*

4. *Finally, the association of eyes-heart with desire or envy likewise reflects the influence of the evil-eye considerations (1 John 2:16; James 4:1–10). How does information about the evil eye assist in interpreting these passages?*

Study Questions for Chapter Five

1. *Throughout chapter 5 I made reference to a large number of biblical passages that are not cited in the text. Consequently, the first step toward validating or invalidating the models presented there is for you to read all the passages previously cited. As you read these passages, judge whether they fit the model or not. Can you think of some other model in which the passages might make better sense? What happens when the passages are interpreted in the light of the American kinship system?*

2. *A second aspect of testing the models is to see whether they help in your interpreting Jesus' parable on divorce: "Everyone who divorces his wife and marries another commits adultery." I call it a parable for two reasons:*

   (a) *When taken literally, it makes as little sense as "You are the salt of the earth" or "You are the light of the world." Obviously, Jesus' followers are not physically and literally salt or light. A parable is a literary form of expression in which the parable's author intends something else and something more than what he or she says, and the hearer has to supply that something else and more. The hearer does this by first imagining what the picture or scenario described by the parable might actually look like. Then the hearer must ask how that picture or scenario fits his or her concrete situation. For example, the parable on the salt of the earth in Matthew 5:13 takes off from the concrete picture of the outdoor Palestinian earth-oven or kiln, called "earth" (see Ps. 12:6; Job 28:5). Fire in such an earth-oven was produced by burning dung. To make the dried dung burn, the bottom of the kiln was faced with flat plates of salt, and the dung itself was sprinkled with salt; the salt served as a chemical agent that helped the dung to burn. However, over time, the heat of the oven caused the salt plates to undergo a chemical reaction that made the plates impede and stifle the burning of the dung. It is when the salt crystals thus chemically change that they must be thrown out—the salt has lost its saltiness. Note that in Luke's version (Luke 14:34–35), the parable concludes, "It [the salt] is fit neither for the land [i.e., the kiln] nor for the dunghill [i.e., to prepare the fuel]; men throw it away." With this parable, then, the hearer has to imagine the concrete situation of salt being used to make fuel burn and sustain the fire. The something else and something more in the picture is that the person following Jesus is to be like salt, causing fire to flame. What is the fire that a Jesus follower is to facilitate? How, when, and where? It is up to the hearer to decide, pass judgment, and act accordingly. This is what a parable is and how it works. When taken literally, it makes no sense. I believe, as we shall see, that Jesus' statement on divorce is such a parable.*

(b) Another reason that I believe it is a parable is that in the Gospels of Matthew and Mark (Luke has it as a one-liner only), this teaching requires further, private explanation, a procedure these authors use for parables. For example, read Mark 4:2–20, with private explanation in verses 10 ff.; Mark 7:14–23, with private explanation in verses 17 ff. (See also Matt. 13:3–23; 15:10–20.) The literary form of public teaching in parable and private explanation is the same for the divorce statements in Mark 10:2–12 and Matthew 19:3–12. Along with these two passages from Mark and Matthew, there are three others that contain the tradition of Jesus' teaching of divorce: Matthew 5:31–32; Luke 16:18; and Paul in 1 Corinthians 7:10–11.

3. *Of the previously cited five passages, which represents as closely as possible what Jesus said? New Testament scholars, following Luke 1:1–4, know that the Gospels present us with what the authors say that the tradition before them said that Jesus said and did (see chapter 7). Between the writing of the traditions and Jesus' ministry stand some forty years. Over those years, Jesus' teaching was remembered and applied and reapplied in diverse situations, in circumstances that differed from what Jesus experienced in Galilee and Judea before the Roman destruction of Jerusalem in A.D. 70. This means that the traditions about divorce presented in the Gospels are undoubtedly shaped in such a way that they might be useful to the communities of Matthew, Mark, and Luke, while Paul hands on Jesus' teaching on divorce in a way applicable to the people at Corinth.*

4. *Relative to this divorce tradition, scholars believe that the original teaching of Jesus is to be found in the first part of Luke 16:18: "Every one who divorces his wife and marries another commits adultery." Now if this is what Jesus said, it has to be a parable. But what does it mean? In line with the kinship norms we have considered, adultery means to trespass on the honor of another male by having sexual intercourse with his wife, who is embedded in the husband. It is something like theft, which is trespassing on the honor of another male by taking some goods that are embedded in that male, the owner. The question that Jesus' statement, in the form above, would raise for a first-century person is, How can I, if I divorce my wife, commit adultery, which only some other male can commit against me or I against him, but never against myself? The statement on divorce cited above has the same semantic quality as the statement "Everyone who sells his TV set and buys another is guilty of theft"; or "Everyone who gives his child*

up for adoption and adopts another is guilty of kidnaping." Literally, such state-
ments would make no sense, because in the ancient Mediterranean, buying and
selling are not theft, and giving up for adoption and adopting are not kidnap-
ing. Similarly, divorcing one's wife and marrying another is not adultery. How-
ever, it is important to note that since the time of Hosea (2:18 ff.), the relation
of God and God's people is depicted in terms of a marriage metaphor. And in
terms of this metaphor, adultery is equivalent to idolatry (see Hos. 2:2 ff.; 3:1
ff.; 4:12 ff.; compare also Jer. 2:2; 5:7; 9:2; 13:22–27; Ezek. 16:32–37; 23:37,
43, 45. In terms of which marriage strategies do these prophets speak?). Pas-
sages in the New Testament such as Matthew 12:39; 16:4; Mark 8:38; James
4:4; and Revelation 2:20 carry the same metaphoric quality.

5. *It is because the statement on divorce makes no sense literally that the post-Jesus*
   group tradition in the Pauline and post-Pauline periods (and perhaps earlier)
   had to interpret the statement to make sense of it and apply it to the social needs
   of the community. To begin with, Luke's addition, "and he who marries a
   woman divorced from her husband commits adultery" (Luke 16:18), points to
   one line of interpretation. For how could one who marries a divorced woman
   commit adultery? Only if in some way she were still embedded in her husband,
   regardless of the divorce procedure. What would such a long-lasting embedding
   point to? Would marriage be a legal relationship or a blood relationship? In this
   chapter, we have already seen some indications that marriage was to some extent
   and in some social contexts considered a blood relationship. With this in mind,
   consider the following questions:

   (a) *Note that it is the statement "What therefore God has joined together,*
       let not man put asunder" in Mark 10:9 that is clarified by the parable
       on divorce in Mark 10:11–12. On the other hand, in Matthew, it is the
       parable on divorce (Matt. 19:9) that is clarified by the parable on the
       eunuchs (castrated males—a dishonor in Mediterranean culture) in
       Matthew 19:11–12. Now, what in the previous models might make
       people believe that in marriage God joins two people together? Collec-
       tivistic, group-oriented personality? Arranged marriages? Marriage as
       blood relationship? Why is it difficult in our culture to perceive God put-
       ting people together in marriage?

   (b) *The statement "And the two shall become one. So they are no longer two*
       but one" (Mark 10:8; Matt. 19:5–6) implies what sort of perception of
       marriage: a legal relationship or a blood relationship? If marriage is a
       sort of blood relationship, when does the relationship end?

(c) *Paul's statement in Romans 7:2 ff., "Thus a married woman is bound by law to her husband as long as he lives," implies what sort of perception of marriage: just a legal relationship, or a blood relationship?*

(d) *Does Paul's interpretation of the teaching of Jesus on divorce in 1 Corinthians 7:10–11 prohibit divorce or remarriage after divorce? Again, what sort of relationship would envision remarriage after divorce as impossible: a legal relationship or a blood relationship?*

(e) *Note that Mark's statement of Jesus' teaching on divorce differs from both Matthew and Luke in that he envisions women initiating divorce (Mark 10:12, compare Matt. 5:32; 19:9; Luke 16:18). What sort of cultural situation would Mark have in mind?*

(f) *Matthew differs from Mark, Luke, and Paul in that he injects an exceptive clause—except for unchastity (Matt. 5:32;19:9). In the light of the kinship norms and defensive marriage strategy outlined in this chapter, what would unchastity be for a married woman? Would it be a marriage situation that somehow permanently dishonors the male?*

(g) *Finally, after you have considered all the passages containing Jesus' teaching on divorce presented in the New Testament and listed in this chapter, would you say that these passages prohibit divorce or simply remarriage after divorce? Given the defensive marriage strategy of the period and the line of argument in Matthew 19:4–8 and Mark 10:3–9, would the logical outcome be no divorce (period) or no remarriage after divorce? What does divorce mean in the culture—even with no remarriage? Do the passages look to individuals or to collectivistic personalities and their families?*

Study Questions for Chapter Six

1. *The first step toward validating or invalidating the models presented in chapter 6 is for you to read all the passages cited in the chapter. As you read the passages, judge whether they fit the models or not. Can you think of some other models by means of which the passages might make better sense? What happens when the passages are interpreted in terms of American purity rules or in terms of our Western traditional understanding of the sacred?*

2. *For the Old Testament, a way to test the model is to read carefully through Leviticus 1–4 to determine the meaning of the various sacrifices:*

   (a) What sort of sacrifices does each of these chapters deal with?

   (b) Note the types of animals involved as well as their ranking. Who could afford the highest ranking animals; who the lowest?

   (c) Note that in each animal sacrifice, the blood is first poured out and sprinkled around the altar and at the door of the Tent of Meeting (in the first century, the sanctuary building or the porch of the Holy Place). Why? What does blood mean (see Lev. 7:26; 17:11–12)? Why does blood have this meaning?

   (d) Note that the carcass is then divided into two: one portion consisting of the fat and some attached organs, the other consisting of whatever is left. The fat (and attached organs) is always part of the offering, to be burned on the altar. It symbols power, vigor, vitality, hence prosperity, and it too is prohibited to humans (see Lev. 7:22–23). Why? Whatever is left is the residue; how is that treated?

   (e) Cereal offerings are not to contain leaven or honey (Lev. 2:11) because they would cause the cereal to ferment. Fermenting, among other things, is clearly a process of oozing or spreading beyond given boundaries. Why would this be forbidden in the Temple sacrifice?

3. *In the New Testament, the following passages speak of holy, hallowed, saint, and the like; they all contain the Greek word* hagios *and might be translated variously. Look up the passages and, on the basis of the models, determine why the person or object is considered holy:*

   Matthew 4:5; 7:6; 24:15; 27:52, 53

    Mark 1:24; 6:20; 8:38
    Luke 1:35, 49, 70, 72; 2:23; 4:34; 9:26
    John 6:69
    Acts 3:14, 21; 4:27, 30; 6:13; 7:33; 9:13, 32, 41; 10:22; 26:10
    Romans 1:2, 7; 7:12; 8:27; 11:16; 12:1, 13; 15:25, 26, 31; 16:2, 15, 16
    1 Corinthians 1:2; 3:17; 6:1, 2, 19; 7:14, 34; 14:33; 16:1, 15, 20
    2 Corinthians 1:1; 8:4; 9:1, 12; 13:12
    Ephesians 1:1, 4, 15, 18; 2:19, 21; 3:5, 8, 18; 4:12; 5:3, 27; 6:18
    Philippians 1:1; 4:21, 22
    Colossians 1:2, 4, 12, 22, 26; 3;12
    1 Thessalonians 3;13; 5;26, 27
    2 Thessalonians 1:10
    1 Timothy 5:10
    2 Timothy 1:9
    Philemon 5,7
    1 Peter 1:15, 16; 2:5, 9; 3:5
    2 Peter 1:18; 2:21; 3:2, 11

4. *In the foregoing passages, I omitted all mention of the Holy Spirit. Given the model of the holy, what would Holy Spirit mean?*

5. *The following passages deal with the process of making holy, that is, sanctification or sanctifying. Do the models in the text help explain what such passages might mean?*

    Sanctification: *Rom. 6:19, 22; 1 Cor. 1:30; 1 Thess. 4:3, 7, 9; 2 Thess. 2:13; 1 Tim. 2:15; 1 Pet. 1:2*
    To sanctify: *Matt. 6:9; 23:17, 19; Luke 11:2; John 10:36; 17:17, 19; Acts 20:32; 26:18; Rom. 15:16; 1 Cor. 1:2; 6:11; 7:14; Eph. 5:26; 1 Thess. 5:23; 1 Tim. 4:5; 2 Tim. 2:21; 1 Pet. 3:15.*

Study Questions for Chapter Seven

1. *For a simple, opening exercise to help you prove or disprove the model presented in chapter 7 consider the steps you and your friends go through in getting up a game. Let's say that on a weekend or after a day of classes, you decide to play basketball or volleyball. What stages do you go through to get prospective players together and to actually play the game? If you think it is a good idea to have a game, what are the aware, share, compare, and declare steps? Then what is involved in forming, storming, norming, performing, and adjourning (home, to the showers)?*

2. *Another exercise more relevant to the theme of this book is to look up the passages listed in chapter 7 for the stages of group development in the story of Jesus. Put these passages in order, using the stages of group development as chapter headings, then preface these passages with the information about John provided in the Gospels (Matt. 3:1–17; Mark 1:1–15; Luke 3:1–22). What sort of story of Jesus do you get? What about the leftovers in the Gospel documents that you have not used? Where would you put those passages? Do you obtain a coherent picture of Jesus' life? For your convenience, I list the relevant passages here:*

    (a) forming: *call of the disciples (Mark 1:16–20; Matt. 4:18–22; Luke 5:1–11; John 1:35–51).*

    (b) storming: *the dispute about who is greatest (Mark 9:33–37; 18:1–5; Luke 9:46–48); a general argument about precedence (Mark 10:41–44; Matt. 20:24–27; Luke 22:24–27); concern for sitting next to Jesus in the kingdom (Matt. 20:20–23—mother; Mark 10:35–40; not in Luke); the general concern about rewards (Mark 10:28–31; Matt. 19:27–30; Luke 18:28–30—appropriated); Peter's rebuking Jesus after talk about suffering and death is an attempt to persuade Jesus to change goals to fit what the group is concern about (Mark 8:32–33; Matt. 16:22–23; not in Luke).*

    (c) norming: *the so-called "mission" discourse (Matt. 10:5–16 and expanded with vv. 17–25; Mark 6:7–11; see 3:13–15; Luke 9:1–5) provide the task norms for Jesus' group. Motivation is also provided (Matt. 10:40–42; Mark 9:41; Luke10:16).*

    (d) performing: *reports of return from successful task performance (Mark 6:12–13; Luke 9:6; no report in Matthew); the Luke report of the sending of the seventy (-two) and their success (Luke 10:1–20) points to enlarged activity; at times without success (Matt. 17:14–21, Mark*

9:14–29; Luke 9:37–43). Disciples have altered-state-of-consciousness experiences as Jesus does: (Matt. 9:2–10; 14:22–23; 17:1–9; Mark 6:45–52; Luke 9:28–36; John 6:16–21).

(e) adjourning: *Jesus' final prediction, "You will all fall away" (Mark 14:27; Matt. 26:31), notably Peter (Luke 22:31–34), indicates how his disciples abandoned him at the end. The only ones present at Jesus's death, and this "at a distance," were a group of supporting women (Matt. 27:55–56; Mark 15:40–41; Luke 23:49). The definitive indication of the adjournment of the Jesus movement group is, of course, the death of Jesus (Matt. 26:36–27:61; Mark 14:32–15:47; Luke 22:39–23:56).*

Indexes

Index of Scriptural References

Index of Ancient Authors

Index of Subjects and Names

defensive marriage, 151, 153, 154, 157–159, 173, 174, 176, 188, 221, 240
defilement, 165, 184
Derrett, J. Duncan M., 144, 159
desecration, 39, 184
deviance, 20, 21, 57, 65, 66, 80, 118, 185
deviant, 121, 194
devil, 104, 110
dirt, 28, 165
dishonor, 31, 35, 39, 40, 42–48, 53, 56, 109, 128, 146, 149, 150, 172, 188, 216, 225, 239
divorce, 11, 48, 137, 145, 149–151, 153, 154, 157–160, 202, 237–240
divorcée, 48, 159
Douglas, Mary T. 25, 106, 178, 179, 197
dyadic contract, 94, 96, 104, 141, 232, 233
dyadic personality, vii, 141; see collectivistic personality

ears–mouth, 68, 71, 74–76, 228, 229
elective grouping, 45, 214–217
elites, 23, 83, 84, 86–88, 98, 100, 103, 104, 109, 110, 119, 151, 152, 167, 174, 175, 187, 189–191, 213, 231
Elliott, John H., 124
empathy, 19
enculturation, 14, 16, 24, 28, 38, 59, 164
endogamy, 136, 138, 146, 158, 159
envy, viii, ix, xii, 65, 93, 108–133, 189, 210, 221, 229, 235
equality and challenge, 33–36
ethnocentrism, 10, 13
eunuchs, 2, 6, 160, 174, 175, 239
evil eye, viii, xii, 118, 120–125, 129–133, 221, 229, 235
exogamy, 135
exorcism, 102, 166
eyes–heart, 68, 71, 73, 75, 76, 228

face, xiii, 37–39, 47, 59, 70, 71, 84, 93, 109, 121, 122, 147, 166, 167, 180, 184, 195, 201, 203, 204
family, xiii, 4, 10, 12, 16, 20, 21, 27, 29–33, 36, 37, 42–49, 51–53, 55, 56, 58, 59, 62–64, 66, 70, 75, 77, 78, 80,

82–84, 89–92, 94, 98, 100, 109, 111, 113, 121, 123, 132, 134–144, 146–148, 155, 158–160, 163, 172, 204, 213, 215, 218, 231
family of orientation, 47, 135, 141
family of procreation, 47, 51, 135, 138
feeling, xii, 9, 11, 12, 15, 16, 24, 39, 48, 62, 108, 109, 127, 132, 141, 162, 164, 186
feet–hands, 68, 71, 74–76, 228, 229
food, 4, 17, 86, 98, 122, 123, 161, 168, 186, 195, 197
fool, 32, 38, 49, 122

Geertz, Clifford, 22, 61, 62
gender division, 47, 78, 90
genealogy, 32, 131, 160
God, vii, xi–xiii, 1, 3, 4, 13, 16, 22, 27, 30–33, 36, 38, 41, 42, 59, 60, 67, 71–76, 82, 93–96, 98, 100–106, 110, 111, 115–117, 121, 125–127, 129–131, 146, 147, 149–151, 155, 156, 161, 163, 164, 167, 169–175, 177, 180, 182–196, 202, 203, 206, 211, 214, 217, 218, 222, 231, 232, 239
gratitude, 2, 93, 95, 122
Great Tradition, 87, 88
greed, 97, 98, 122
groupings, 44–46, 49, 50, 53, 214, 215
guilt, 52, 55, 59, 60, 62, 114, 152, 221

hands–feet, 68, 71, 74–76, 228, 229
head, as honor symbol,
healing, 79, 80, 93, 94, 102, 168, 187, 188, 204, 208, 210, 219
health, 55, 56, 80, 82, 89, 93, 103, 113, 120, 122, 128, 169, 170
Holiness Code, 151
honor, vii–ix, xii, xiii, 27–33, 35–53, 56–59, 62, 66, 67, 75, 79, 81, 84, 89–92, 94, 96, 99, 100, 103, 108–114, 119, 120, 125, 127, 130–134, 139, 142–149, 151–153, 158, 164, 168, 169, 172, 185, 186, 190, 196, 197, 202, 203, 206, 210, 216, 221, 225, 226, 232, 233, 238
  acquired honor, 32, 33, 52, 53
  ascribed honor, 32, 33, 52, 53, 168